D0948247

BELO

BELO

FROM NEWSPAPERS TO NEW MEDIA

Judith Garrett Segura

University of Texas Press
Austin

Printed in the United States of America
First edition, 2008

Requests for permission to reproduce material from this work should be sent to:
Permissions
University of Texas Press
P.O. Box 7819
Austin, TX 78713-7819
www.utexas.edu/utpress/about/bpermission.html

∞ The paper used in this book meets the minimum requirements of ANSI/NISO Z39.48-1992 (R1997) (Permanence of Paper).

LIBRARY OF CONGRESS CATALOGING-IN-PUBLICATION DATA

Segura, Judith Garrett, 1944–
Belo : from newspapers to new media / Judith Garrett Segura.
p. cm.
Includes bibliographical references and index.
ISBN 978-0-292-71845-6 (cloth : alk. paper)—ISBN 978-0-292-71846-3 (pbk. : alk. paper)
1. Belo (Firm)—History. 2. Mass media—United States—History. 3. Mass media—United States—Biography. I. Title.
P92.U5S37 2008
338.7'61302230973—dc22

2008005504

In memory of my great-grandmother Maggie Pevoto Bland,
who indulged my every request to tell me a story about her childhood;
her daughter and my grandmother Winnie Bland Toal, who was my
model of personal strength and independence; her daughter and my
mother, Peggy Toal Garrett, who raised me to believe that I could do
anything; and specially dedicated to my father, Julian W. Garrett,
and my husband, Avelino F. Segura.

CONTENTS

Acknowledgments ix
Prologue 1
Chapter 1. Leaders of Legend: A. H. Belo & G. B. Dealey 7
Chapter 2. The Children Confront the Legacy (1912–1945) 42
Chapter 3. The Grandsons Return from War (1946–1955) 68
Chapter 4. The Dark Days of Dallas (1956–1964) 97
Chapter 5. A New Era Dawns (1965–1972) 125
Chapter 6. Enter the Fourth Generation (1973–1976) 150
Chapter 7. Competitive Gains and Rapid Change (1977–1981) 170
Chapter 8. The Modern Belo Emerges (1982–1986) 197
Chapter 9. The World Takes Note (1987–2000) 231
Chapter 10. New Century, New Media 263
Epilogue 273

Appendixes
A. G. B. and Olivia Allen Dealey Family Tree 277
B. Chairmen and Directors of Belo Corp., 1926–2007 279
C. Time Line of Significant Events in Company History 282
D. Text of the Black-bordered Advertisement Run on November 22, 1963, in the *Dallas Morning News* 284

Notes 288
Bibliography 296
Index 307

ACKNOWLEDGMENTS

This book is full of the names of those who helped me collect the stories and materials that formed the basis for my writing, the most important of whom are Robert Decherd and the late James M. Moroney, Jr. Their support and encouragement over more than twenty years resulted in the archives from which this history was drawn.

I must also acknowledge the contributions of many others, too numerous to list, whose interest in preserving the history of the institution added enormously to the archives of stories, memorabilia, and artifacts over the years. In particular, I want to thank Joe Dealey, Jr., for holding on to the extensive collection of personal business files and mementos belonging to his father and grandfather, and for donating them to the Belo Archives.

During my writing, my husband, Avelino Segura, and my dear friend Murray Smither were most helpful with their insightful comments following readings and re-readings of the manuscript. Several others spent countless hours reading sections and providing me with helpful comments and suggestions. In alphabetical order, they are Dr. Richard Halsey, Dr. Ann Die Hasselmo, Dr. Nils Hasselmo, Dr. Michael V. Hazel, Rice R. Jackson III, and Michael J. McCarthy.

Alisha Brown of Belo Corp. was especially helpful to me throughout the process as I worked in the Belo Archives, and many others at Belo were always available when I needed to verify a fact or date or other detail. They include Joe Daume, Carey Hendrickson, Jake Martinez, Judy Sall, Jerome Sims, and Marian Spitzberg, among others.

Another whose passion for the history of Belo Corp. provided invaluable insights to me over more than twenty years is retired Belo director Bill Smellage. WFAA retiree Clarence Bruyere helped me understand the era of transition from radio to television. And a retired director of the Times Herald Printing Company, Robert Solendar, provided not only important archival material, but also his memories and observations of the era during which he was active in that newspaper's management.

In addition, I want to recognize media historian Dr. Patrick Cox for his encouragement and advice along the way, and my sponsoring editor, William Bishel, for his kind encouragement throughout the process.

BELO

PROLOGUE

An institution is the lengthened shadow of one man; . . . and all history resolves itself very easily into the biography of a few stout and earnest persons.

RALPH WALDO EMERSON

That well-known passage from one of Emerson's most widely quoted works, from 1841, could have been written about Belo Corp., which got underway only a year after Emerson wrote his essay. In today's volatile media world, with announcements almost weekly about one or another of the media giants selling off properties or splitting into several companies, or even selling out completely, the timing is good to examine the history of a company that has endured for more than 160 years.

Even as this book goes to press, the description of that company must be revised to acknowledge a transition that was announced at 7:00 a.m. on Monday, October 1, 2007. In a story published on the front of the Business section of the *Dallas Morning News* on October 2, the staff writer Terry Maxon reports that "Belo Corp. officials surprised Wall Street Monday with a bold strategy aimed at bolstering the company's lagging stock price by splitting the company." The large headline proclaims, "Wall Street applauds Belo's split." The headline in the *New York Times* the same day read "Belo Corp. to split its newspapers off from its TV business."

Addressing the turmoil in the media business in 2006, Belo's chairman, chief executive officer, and president, Robert W. Decherd, had told Wall Street analysts, "We are in the midst of transforming Belo's businesses to compete effectively in what is becoming an increasingly Internet-centric marketplace. . . . We are determined to remain the content provider of choice in our local markets and are confident that we have the assets and management talent to succeed."[1]

Even as Belo Corp. continues what he described as an "enterprise-wide transformation process," both of the new entities still bear the name of one of its earliest leaders, Alfred H. Belo, who died more than a hundred years ago, in 1901. His successor in ownership and in leading the company, George Bannerman Dealey, built on Belo's solid foundations, adding his own considerable strengths, as well as a succession of descendants who still lead the company today.

This book is about the vital institutions that bear the Belo name and the culture and leadership over time, so it is also about G. B. Dealey and his descendants. The story unfolds through the consistency of purpose of all of the company's leaders who have sustained the institution, which of necessity evolves and continues to invent itself every day, in step with the fierce rhythm of events, technological advances, and the interests of its audiences and shareholders.

The main body of this manuscript was declared complete on an auspicious day in 2006, in order not to have to continue updating on a near daily basis, as the entire media industry grapples with its transformation. That special day was October 1, the 122nd anniversary of the first day of publication of the *Dallas Morning News*. Then one year later, of course, the change in the structure of the institution required some revision.

The new structure encompasses two individual publicly owned companies: Belo Corp., which owns twenty television stations and seven cable channels, and A. H. Belo Corporation, which owns four metropolitan daily newspapers. Altogether, the television and cable properties, along with the newspapers, own and operate more than thirty Web sites.

Belo Corp. is listed on the New York Stock Exchange, and its influence is felt in cities across the breadth of the United States. When the division is complete, A. H. Belo Corporation will also be a public company, with approximately one-half the annual revenue and half of the employees, but with no debt. But the combined companies are also the modern manifestation of a Texas legend: they are the oldest business institutions in Texas, and among only a few companies in the United States to have the fourth generation of the same family working in the business.

In some ways Belo has continued to operate like a private company serving its readers and advertisers; however, it has had to deal with the intense pressures of the public marketplace in terms of Wall Street's and shareholders' expectations for revenue growth and price per share.

The four daily papers have received a combined thirteen Pulitzer

Prizes, the most recent one awarded to the *Dallas Morning News* in 2006 for its photographic coverage of Hurricane Katrina in New Orleans. In 2005, the *News*'s Web site DallasNews.com was awarded the Scripps Howard Foundation National Award for Web Reporting. And the television stations have twenty-one Alfred I. DuPont-Columbia University Silver Baton Awards, including one given to WWL-TV in New Orleans in 2006 for its incomparable coverage of the 2005 hurricane and the aftermath. In the 2006 national Edward R. Murrow Awards competition, Belo stations won five awards, more than any other station group in the country. And even more awards have been announced since I concluded this study.

Writing a book on the history of Belo Corp. was the natural culmination of my twenty-six years of gathering information about the company, interviewing countless former and current employees and former and current competitors, and organizing the company history materials into what came to be called the Belo Archives.

I have used the primary sources in the archives and various other libraries, conducted more interviews with more key individuals, and tracked the outside perceptions of the corporation over its history through reports in other publications.

I have attempted to write the true story of the company's development over time in a straightforward way, addressing a reader who is curious about the company and its mystique and not interested in company hyperbole or revisionist history. However, I readily admit that *attempting* to tell the true story is the best I can do, because the real stories behind the stories are rarely recorded, even if all those involved could agree on a single version; and even then, what is recorded is often told aslant, as Emily Dickinson poetically advised those attempting truth.[2]

My first few years at Belo were spent at the *Dallas Morning News*, which began a major modernizing process about the time I arrived, in early 1980. Executive leadership changes on January 1, 1980, were followed by new, and in many cases, much younger department heads taking over from longtime managers. Retirements were announced every day, it seemed. The combination of excitement and fear that always accompanies change led to managers scrambling to clean out the accumulated clutter, dusting off the filing cabinets, and generally updating operations throughout the newspaper.

I had been hired as a consultant to the *Dallas Morning News* to assist in its early efforts to develop young readers by introducing newspapers into the classrooms of area schools. My first few months were spent trying to learn everything there was to know about the company, its history, and how the newspaper was put together every day, so that I could be a credible representative. With the support of management, I set about talking to people throughout the company—from the pressroom to the executive suite and every place in between.

Loving a good story, and hearing plenty of them in my visits around the building, I soon discovered that not only is a newspaper a daily miracle, but the operation of a media company is a microcosm of the human experience. From the lofty heights of the editorial suite where the philosophers argue daily, to the glamorous trappings of a television news studio, and the deafening noise of the manufacturing plant known as the pressroom, I found the most interesting mix of people that anyone could hope to meet.

Everyone I met, from the writers and producers to the salespeople to the cleanup crews, seemed to feel that their jobs held special meaning, that they were serving a useful purpose in society and generally serving the public good. Many of them had been at the company for years and never considered working anywhere else.

I was hired as a full-time employee of the *News* in January 1981 and continued to document and write about the history of the company, along with other responsibilities. I moved to the corporate ranks in 1986, as Belo's first public affairs manager. Throughout my tenure, the company's executives supported my efforts to assemble an archive, including the minutes of stockholder and director meetings from the days of private ownership, almost eighty years of internal departmental reports, and the private papers of a succession of leaders. I have cleaned out the closets, quite literally, and collected information about the company and its leadership from countless sources, internal and external.

I retired from my full-time duties at Belo at the end of 2004, in order to focus on writing the history I have come to know through the people of Belo. The story of Belo is a great and complex one, and I have tried to do justice to it and to the people who have lived it.

Belo began operations as the *Daily News* in 1842 in Galveston, Texas. The origins and early days were documented in two authoritative books by authors who knew many of the company's early leaders. The more comprehensive of the two books was written by Sam Acheson, who was a Texas historian and editorial writer for the *Dallas Morning News*. It was published in 1938. The other, a biography of George Bannerman Dealey, who established the *Dallas Morning News* in 1885 at the behest of Alfred Horatio Belo, was written by Ernest Sharpe, a professor at the University of Texas at Austin, and it was published in 1955. While much has changed over the years, some things have remained constant.

This book will recount the main story from its beginnings and then bring the story up to date, connecting the dots that form the big picture of a company formed in the Republic of Texas that survived both the industrial revolution of the nineteenth century and the first technology revolution of the twentieth century. Like every other media company in the twenty-first century, Belo continues its transformation within the electronic revolution, and, as with all revolutions, the outcome is far from clear.

Chapter 1

LEADERS OF LEGEND

A. H. BELO & G. B. DEALEY

Belo is one of the nation's most familiar names among professional journalists, journalism professors and students, and those who follow the media industry for investment opportunities. However, the name "Belo" is not so well known to everyone else, including the many millions of viewers and readers spread across the country who regularly turn to Belo's television stations, daily newspapers, and Web sites. Until recently, that unfamiliarity of the Belo name has been quite deliberate, and the company has been consistent, even obstinate, about not calling attention to itself.

The philosophy of the company's owners through six generations of leadership has been to focus public attention on its newspapers, such as the *Dallas Morning News*, and on its television stations, the first of which was WFAA-TV in Dallas. In keeping the name of the parent company in the background, the executives aimed to build loyalty to the local sources of news and information, rather than to the parent company and its brand.

However, as a twenty-first-century-style brand, the simple name Belo, with its two-syllable punch and long vowels, is about as distinct as any marketing genius could invent. In fact, the marketing genius who came up with the Belo "brand" was a pre–Civil War businessman by the name of Edward Böhlo or Boehlo, Alfred H. Belo's father. Edward Boehlo's parents had emigrated from Germany in the late 1700s to join an orderly

Moravian community in North Carolina. The village they helped establish was named Salem, from the Hebrew word *shalom*, meaning peace.

By 1849, Edward Boehlo, a highly skilled cabinetmaker, also owned a foundry, a linseed oil mill, and a large general merchandise store. To house his store, as well as his family of nine children, the servants, and shopkeepers, he built a large Greek Revival building and painted it stark white, in the middle of the otherwise modest red brick and wood buildings of Old Salem. By the time his stately, whitewashed building was complete, Boehlo had grown impatient with the mispronunciation and misspelling of his German name, so he changed it to the phonetic spelling B-e-l-o, matching the pronunciation by then in general use. To enact the change, he placed twelve-inch-high gilt metal letters spelling B E L O over the entrance to his mercantile business on Main Street.[1]

Meanwhile, out beyond the western frontier of the United States, Galveston was the largest and most vibrant town in the independent Republic of Texas in 1842. It had sprung up on a small island in the Gulf of Mexico, just southwest of the Louisiana state border. It had a natural port on the bay side, which accommodated commerce and immigration. A copy of the *Daily News*, Galveston, Vol. 1, No. 8, Tuesday, April 19, 1842, which is held in the Belo Archives, is said to be the earliest extant issue of the newspaper that began the long history of Belo. The fragile, single-fold sheet printed as a four-page newspaper seems to have been handed down publisher to publisher, surviving fire, wartime, hurricanes on Galveston Island, and the company's relocation to Dallas in 1923.

The very existence of this early newspaper in the Belo Archives and the stories passed along with it through the generations have perpetuated the claim that Belo grew from that particular early newspaper. However, over the years, various writers have come up with different interpretations of the early records. In a March 1857 edition, the *News* states, "We today issue the first number of the fourteenth volume of the *News*," which would appear to date the origin to March 1844. But then an 1874 edition, on a line below the masthead on the front page, clearly states, "Established in 1842."

On June 14, 1884, about a year before it launched the *Dallas Morning News*, the *News*, under the direction of A. H. Belo, published a feature story in which it said, "In March, 1842 the French Brothers started a little paper called the *Daily News*, but soon discontinued it, and there was no connection between that paper and the present *Galveston News*."[2]

According to contemporary reports, that newspaper, the *Daily News*, went out of business on June 21, 1842, a mere nine weeks after its launch.

The 1884 feature story continues, "[in] June 1843 Michael Cronican and Wilbur Cherry, both printers, started a semi-weekly called the *News*, which was the real parent of the present publication." However, accurately dating that "real parent" newspaper is difficult too, because other early accounts place it in the fall of 1842.

In the seventy-fifth-anniversary edition of April 11, 1917, the *Galveston Daily News*, still owned by A. H. Belo & Co., printed this history:

> Except for the name, the *News* may trace its existence to March 20, 1841, when Sam Bangs, printer, who first visited Galveston Island with Jean LaFitte, issued the first copy of the *Daily Galvestonian*. George H. French was the editor. French had edited the *Houston Mosquito* even earlier. The *Daily Galvestonian* suspended publication early in 1842. Before its suspension the *Daily Galvestonian* had become the property of George H. and Henry R. French. . . . When French determined to renew his publication he leased the equipment from Sam Bangs and in the same building that had housed the *Daily Galvestonian* launched the *Daily News*.

The one thing no one disputes about those earliest days is that the well-known printer Samuel Bangs owned the press that was used to produce both of George French's short-lived publications, the *Daily Galvestonian* and the *Daily News*, as well as the *News* published by Michael Cronican and Wilbur Cherry. In fact, the Bangs press was used to print a great many other newspapers in Galveston both before and after those three early papers. Some records show that at that particular time as many as eighteen newspapers were being published in Galveston, feeding the immigrants' hunger for news of the countries left behind. Numerous entrepreneurial frontiersmen, experienced in journalism or not, took it upon themselves to meet the needs as best they could. The only one of those early island publications to survive became the *Galveston Daily News*.

Sam Acheson, in his widely cited 1938 book about the company, titled *35,000 Days in Texas: A History of the* Dallas News *and Its Forbears*, gives Samuel Bangs and his brother-in-law George H. French the distinction of creating the original publication that grew into the *Galveston Daily News*. But Acheson, who worked closely with G. B. Dealey and his son

E. M. (Ted) Dealey, admits to speculation about the matter. He seems to have reconciled the early confusion for himself by stating that "Bangs and French tired of the *News* and transferred it within a few months to Michael Cronican and Wilbur F. Cherry." With those few words of conjecture, Acheson closed the gap between the two early newspapers.

Using any of the various stories of the company's origins recited over the years, Belo Corp. remains the oldest continuously operating business institution in Texas. However, it is important to remember that today's *Galveston County Daily News*, as it is called now, rightfully makes a parallel claim, as the oldest continuously published newspaper in Texas.

That paradox was established in 1923 when A. H. Belo & Co. sold the Galveston newspaper to W. L. Moody and Co. in Galveston. The sale of the company's first newspaper was precipitated by the company's long and ultimately successful battle to defeat the growing political power of the Ku Klux Klan in Texas. Both of the company's newspapers had reported almost daily on the Klan's lawless activities, without regard for what their reporting might cost the company. In fact, the Klan called for a boycott of both the Galveston and Dallas newspapers and of the businesses that advertised in them. By 1923, the *Dallas Morning News* was the larger of the two Belo newspapers, but it had lost so many advertisers and subscribers that the company's management decided to sell the Galveston paper to sustain the Dallas operations through the financial crisis.

G. B. Dealey, who was by then president of A. H. Belo & Co., signed a gentleman's agreement with W. L. Moody, Jr., representing W. L. Moody and Co., in which the two institutions divided the "oldest" claim between them. They agreed that both institutions rightfully would claim the same origins, but thereafter A. H. Belo & Co. would call itself the "oldest business institution" in Texas, and the *Galveston Daily News* would call itself the "oldest newspaper" in Texas. Their agreement was forgotten a time or two over the years, and accusations flew back and forth. However, G. B. Dealey was always cordial in his correspondence with Galveston officials on the matter, reminding them of the parallel histories and the agreement, as necessary.[3]

From its beginning, the *Dallas Morning News* has numbered its issues from October 1, 1885, rather than incorporating the span of the Galveston paper into its own history. But over time, company leaders have celebrated milestones in some confusing ways. For example, in 1942 the *Dal-*

las Morning News published its first "Centennial Edition," and in 1985 it published another one.

In spite of uncertainty about the exact date or name of the paper that became the *News*, the paper began to thrive in 1844 when Willard Richardson was invited to become editor. Then-publisher Wilbur Cherry had noticed Richardson's work as editor of the *Houston Telegraph* beginning in 1841, and he invited him to join the Galveston newspaper. In the April 11, 1917, issue of the *Galveston Daily News*, recounting its own history on its seventy-fifth anniversary, the following paragraph paints the scene:

> Without the telegraph, without railroads, with only the most primitive methods of communication, publishing a newspaper in Texas in 1840–1850 was decidedly precarious. . . . It might even have been so with the offspring of the *Daily Galvestonian* and the refreshed *Daily News* but for the chance that brought Willard Richardson to Galveston.

It was Richardson's successor, however, who had joined him in 1865, who had the vision and the means to make the *News* the state's most influential voice. That was the company's namesake, Alfred Horatio Belo. Belo lived until 1901, and on his death *Harper's Weekly* published an extensive obituary beneath a five-and-a-half-inch portrait of Colonel Alfred H. Belo. The following tribute is taken from that obituary, which was written by John A. Wyeth:

> No one has done more for the material development and moral upbuilding of Texas, and of the entire South, than this man, for his papers were widely circulated throughout the entire Southern section. He always stood unflinchingly and unselfishly for what he believed was highest and best in morals and in politics, for his courage was of that sterling quality that could not be intimidated by threat or influenced by gain.

At the time of his death, Belo was president of A. H. Belo & Co., publisher of both the *Galveston Daily News* and the *Dallas Morning News*, and he had recently worked with a few others to reorganize and fund the

Associated Press. However, after all these years, A. H. Belo's identity as an individual has faded into the company that bears his name.

The modern Belo Corp. was formed by Belo's protégé, George Bannerman Dealey, in 1926, when Dealey and a few partners acquired the company from A. H. Belo's heirs and changed the name from A. H. Belo & Co. to A. H. Belo Corporation. It is no coincidence, though, that the Texas-based media company still bears his name, because the principles upon which A. H. Belo established the *Dallas Morning News* are still in play. To fully understand today's Belo Corp., it helps to understand the background, character, and accomplishments of A. H. Belo, the man.

Even his beginnings were auspicious. He was born into a large, well-established, and prosperous family in the Moravian community of Salem, North Carolina, in 1839. He lived sixty-two years, dying in 1901, in Asheville, North Carolina, in the family's summer home, and he was buried within a few minutes' walk of his childhood home in Salem, near his parents' graves in the family plot. In 2004, the only identification of his resting place was a small footstone with the initials AHB. The large white marble cross at the other end had long since toppled on its face, spanning the length of the grave. A. H. Belo's legacy in his home village is simply that he was the son of one of Old Salem's most distinguished brethren.

However, A. H. Belo's life was one of superlatives: great intelligence, curiosity, courage, and daring, all of which combined in his many accomplishments. His upbringing included a private classical education; his youth brought gallantry in service of the Confederacy during the Civil War; and his daring led to the creation of one of the most influential daily newspapers in Texas, the *Dallas Morning News*.

In addition to being Salem's leading merchant before the Civil War, A. H. Belo's father, Edward Belo, was a founder and president of the North Western North Carolina Railroad during the time of its construction, and it is likely that he knew Cornelius Ennis, the Texas railroad tycoon whose daughter A. H. Belo later would marry.

Toward the end of his life, A. H. Belo dictated a memoir to his son-in-law, Charles Peabody, great-nephew of George Peabody, founder of the Peabody Museums at Harvard and Yale. Charles was the son of Robert Singleton Peabody, founder of the Department of Archaeology at Phillips Academy at Andover, Massachusetts, and he was a recent graduate of Harvard with a Ph.D. in archaeology.[4]

Dr. Peabody was conducting postgraduate studies in anthropology through the Peabody Museum at Harvard when he invited Belo to tell of his life experiences, and the resulting memoir covers mainly Belo's youth and his days as a soldier during the Civil War. Belo died soon after telling of those years, and the story of his later years was left to others to tell. By Belo's own account, he was very well educated from an early age. He attended school through the sixth grade in Salem, following which he was sent away to two different boarding schools for another four years. His father had intended that Alfred attend college, but he was summoned home to assist in the businesses before the start of the Civil War. Of his education, A. H. Belo said, "Greek was my favorite study and I kept it up simply for the love of it. I was far enough advanced to read and enjoy Homer and even Herodotus; it was hard to give up, but other events crowded it out."[5]

When the war commenced, although he stated that he was personally opposed to secession, he followed the course of his native state and was among the first to volunteer. In his memoirs, he recalled, "In about a week's time we had sufficient men enrolled to form a company and I was unanimously elected captain." He was twenty-one years old, and the company was called the Forsythe Riflemen.

Belo served the Confederacy throughout the "Great War," 1861–1865, fighting in the 55th Regiment of the North Carolina Troops. After the battle of Bull Run he was promoted to major, and in 1862 he won further respect and admiration from his regiment by fighting a duel (with Mississippi rifles) against an officer of another regiment who had allegedly questioned the courage of the 55th North Carolina Regiment. Neither of the participants was badly injured, and they later became affectionate friends. Belo soon was made lieutenant colonel, and by the time he was twenty-five he was colonel of his regiment. Although his military career was brief, he was known throughout the rest of his life as Colonel Belo, sometimes simply as the Colonel.

He was severely wounded twice. At Gettysburg on July 2, 1863, he received a terrible injury to one leg from an exploding bomb. Then, almost a year later, in the battle of Cold Harbor on June 2, 1864, his left upper arm was shattered, and although his arm was saved, he lost the use of it. He suffered for the rest of his life from the complications of both wounds, which rendered him vulnerable to other ailments. Ultimately those complications were named as the cause of his death.

Before the Civil War, Alfred had begun to assist his father in the mercantile business, traveling to New York to buy goods. He could have returned after the war to resume that work and take over the business, but instead he chose to make his own way in the world. After the surrender of his command at Appomattox in 1865, Belo, along with a friend from school days who was a fellow officer, left North Carolina with their horses and their two servants and made their way to Texas. The two young officers sought and were given permission by Union officials to travel in uniform, and they set off first by train to Mobile, then by steamer to New Orleans, and finally by means of a government transport ship from New Orleans to Galveston. But they didn't stay in Galveston long.

Belo was twenty-six years old, and his aim was to reach San Antonio, where he felt he could make a prosperous life for himself in the developing frontier. On his way, he stopped off in Richmond, just outside Houston, to visit another old friend from boarding school and to gather supplies. On the way by train, he met a Richmond doctor who, upon learning of the young men's ambitious plans, urged them not to proceed west. The doctor pointed out that if they continued, they would likely be killed for their horses before many miles. Seeing the good sense in that advice, Belo and his friend decided to stay in Richmond, each to establish a school where he would teach for a while as they determined what to do next. Here is what he said about that in his unflinching memoir:

> On the first day my scholars reported, I found about 25 or 30, all the way from 5 or 6 years of age up to 20 years. I should have had to read Latin with some and teach others their ABCs. . . . The problem proved too much for me, and I decided not to teach school.

His friend, Capt. Lillington, stayed on in the Richmond area teaching for the full school term, but then he returned to North Carolina. Belo, on the other hand, was determined to find something more satisfying to do in Texas, and he began making inquiries of friends and acquaintances about opportunities in Houston. Houston had grown rapidly because of the Union blockade and occupation of Galveston, and Belo was recommended to Willard Richardson, the publisher of the *Galveston News* and the *Texas Almanac*. Richardson had established the *Texas Almanac* in 1857 as a means of attracting settlers to Texas and informing recent immigrants of all things Texan. Richardson's publishing company was in some disarray, having moved its mechanical operations from Galveston to Houston during the blockade, and it had many uncollected accounts for both advertising and subscriptions.

On August 31, 1865, Belo agreed to a six-month assignment as bookkeeper for the newspaper, signing on for the sum of $500 in gold for that service. But, even before the six months were up, the bright young Belo had so transformed the business operations that Richardson invited him to buy an interest in the paper and become his partner. With financial assistance from his father, Belo bought half of the company on March 1, 1866, and the partners renamed the company Richardson, Belo & Co. By then, the printing operation had been moved back to Galveston, and Belo had persuaded Richardson to invest in a new small-cylinder Taylor press to replace the old press, which was powered by a horse walking on a treadmill.

Shortly after Belo became a partner in the business, he was called on to handle a controversial matter for the company, which he managed with great integrity, establishing himself for all time as a man of fairness and upright dealings. The matter concerned a threatened strike by the local chapter of the National Typographical Union. In his memoirs, Belo told of this early experience:

> In 1866, before the new press was put in, we had an expert pressman who came to me one day and said he had been invited to join the Typographical Union. This he did, and after application he was black-balled. After this I was notified by the Union that unless this man was discharged within thirty days the Union would strike.
>
> The foreman in our office, J. Storner, was opposed to this movement and told me that the majority of printers of the office were not in favor of it and that it was outside persons who were moving in the matter. There were then two other newspapers established in Galveston: *Flake's Bulletin* and the *Civilian*. These were members of the Union. I authorized Mr. Storner to submit the case in writing to the Executive Committee of the National Typographical Union, of which this was a division. The point at issue was, on the part of the *News*, that the Typographical Union

had nothing to do with the employment of pressmen. They claimed that the Union had arbitrary control over all printers and pressmen.

The conservative members of the Galveston Union were disposed to take our view, but were overruled. At about the expiration of the thirty days, finding the strike movement on and no chance of compromise, I took the steamer for New Orleans, arriving there the next afternoon in time for a conference with Colonel Smith, foreman of the *Picayune* and resident member of the Executive Committee of the National Union. . . . On learning the facts of the case he telegraphed to Galveston that unless the Union accepted my plan of arbitration by the National Executive Committee, Union printers would be sent over from New Orleans. A reply came from Galveston offering to leave the matter to the New Orleans Typographical Union instead of the National Committee. Accepting this proposition, a meeting was called for the next Sunday, the Galveston Union sending over J. Conrad, an old printer.

The meeting was largely attended and the hall was full, as at that time there were a large number of printers in New Orleans. Mr. Conrad made a strong appeal and presented his case very ably. Upon his sitting down I was invited to state my case, which I did in about fifteen minutes. There being no further diversions, a series of resolutions were introduced and recorded.

One man rose and asked for information from the president whether the resolutions were intended to justify the actions of the Galveston Union or those of the proprietors of the *News*. He was told that they unquestionably supported the *News*, namely that the Union had nothing to do with the employment of pressmen. He said he would vote No. Another rose and said he would vote No, because he believed the Galveston Union had done right and he would sustain their action. The president asked for further remarks, but receiving no reply, a vote was taken. There being only two Noes, the matter was disposed of.

Mr. Conrad came to me and said, "Well, young man, you have downed us this time." I told him I only wanted justice and fairness and that in all my dealings with the Union in future I should be actuated by the same motives. In all the succeeding

> years, when questions have arisen, I have made it a point to meet the men fairly and squarely upon an amicable basis.

Two years later, in 1868, Belo married Nettie Ennis, whose father, Cornelius Ennis, was a prominent and wealthy Texas businessman who had helped form the Houston & Texas Central Railroad, and for whom the town of Ennis was named. The couple began their married life in Galveston, where, after Willard Richardson's death in 1875, Belo bought the remainder of the company, renaming it A. H. Belo & Co.

Ten years later, when his young protégé, George Bannerman Dealey, started up the *Dallas Morning News* at his behest, Belo relocated his wife and their two children to Dallas. By then he had a daughter, Jeannette, and a son, Alfred Jr. The family was accustomed to living part of the year in a home in the gentler climate of Asheville, North Carolina, and spending their summers at a resort in the Adirondacks in New York. When they moved to Dallas from Galveston, they appear to have lived in rented quarters for a brief time until 1889, when they acquired the property at the corner of Ross Avenue and Pearl Street. That corner was one of the most prominent residential addresses in the city at the time, and they moved into an existing house while planning for the mansion, which was to be built after the Greek Revival manner of the Belo home in North Carolina.

The exact date of the home's completion was not recorded, but it was likely in late 1899 or very early 1900. A wedding announcement in the June 13, 1900, issue of the *Dallas Morning News* stated that Alfred H. Belo, Jr., and his new bride, Helen Ponder Belo, would return from their honeymoon to live in the Belo home on Ross Avenue. Following his graduation from Yale, Alfred Jr. had joined his father in the company, and after his marriage they jointly attended to business. Years later Helen Ponder Belo, in a letter to G. B. Dealey, recalled her earliest married days:

> I soon learned there was no conversation at the breakfast table. There were several copies of the *News* and the day's work had begun. Col. Belo and my husband read their papers with intense interest. No detail escaped them. All communication was brief and confined only to comments on the *News*. All criticism was constructive and the blue pencil marked places where praise was to be given as well as criticism.[6]

Helen Ponder's family also was prominent in North Texas. The wedding announcement reported that the wedding was held in the Ponder family's home, described as one of the finest in Denton. The Denton County town of Ponder was named for her family.

In spite of the grand home that A. H. Belo built for his family on Ross Avenue in Dallas, he and Mrs. Belo were often away, seeking more agreeable climates than that of Texas, usually at the recommendations of Belo's doctors. Belo was never healthy after his war injuries and a subsequent bout with yellow fever in Galveston. For the remainder of his life he spent much of his time away from the operations of his newspapers in Texas. Even before moving to Dallas from Galveston, Belo had been ordered by his doctors to spend six months of 1880 in Europe, resting at sanitariums in Germany and Austria.

In the spring of 1885, as his company worked on establishing the *Dallas Morning News*, Belo's doctors recommended a stay of several months in Mexico, taking cures at various health resorts following a bout of pneumonia. Then, from Mexico, they returned to their favorite summer retreat in New York.

In the late winter and early spring of 1901, Col. Belo was particularly low, and the family decided to go east earlier than usual. On April 19, 1901, one week after arriving at their home in Asheville, Alfred Horatio Belo died, just before reaching his sixty-second birthday. He was buried in the Moravian cemetery in Salem, which borders on the property of his childhood home. When Belo died, his old friend President Grover Cleveland, with whom he had spent summer evenings playing cards on his New York retreats, wrote his condolences to the family, saying that Col. Belo's passing was "a loss to the entire country." Adolph S. Ochs, publisher of the *New York Times*, wrote to "the *News* family": "The country loses a foremost citizen, journalism one of its most useful and honorable workers. The high ideals he successfully maintained in his profession for years have been the admiration of every self-respecting newspaperman."[7]

At a citizens' meeting at Dallas City Hall, those assembled drafted a resolution recognizing Belo's contributions: "In his life work he illustrated the power of a private citizen by use of an independent press to promote the best interests of the whole country."[8]

Belo's widow, along with Alfred Jr. and his young wife, Helen, returned to Dallas and continued to live in the Belo Mansion. Alfred Jr. followed in his father's footsteps in operating A. H. Belo & Co., and he and his wife had two daughters. But with his having no sons, the Belo surname was not to be carried by any other descendants of Col. Alfred Horatio Belo. Belo's daughter Jeannette had earlier graduated from Radcliffe College, and soon thereafter married Charles Peabody, a professor of archaeology at Harvard. After their honeymoon, which was a field expedition on horseback in the western United States, they continued to live in Cambridge, where their home was known as a center of social and intellectual activity. Jeannette and Charles Peabody had four children, three of whom had several children.[9]

After his father's death in 1901, Alfred Jr. was named president of the company. G. B. Dealey, who had joined the *Galveston News* in 1874 and had been general manager of the *Dallas Morning News* since its founding, added the title vice president at that time. Then only five years later, at age thirty-three, Alfred Jr. succumbed to meningitis in early 1906. He was buried in Oakland Cemetery south of downtown Dallas, rather than being taken to Salem. Later his wife and members of her family were buried near him. In fact, G. B. Dealey's parents and several of his brothers and sisters are also buried at Oakland Cemetery, very near the Belo gravesite. Alfred Jr.'s grave is marked like his father's, with a tall, white stone cross. The impressive monument has the large letters BELO at the crossing point.

When Alfred Jr. died, his mother, Nettie Ennis Belo, asked G. B. Dealey to become president of the company. But in his customary humility, G. B. declined the honor, insisting that Mrs. Belo herself should hold the title of president, which she did until her death in 1913. Following Mrs. Belo's death, G. B. continued to insist that a Belo family member should hold the title. Mrs. Belo's brother-in-law, Cesar Lombardi, who had been a vice president since 1906, was named president.

By the time of Cesar Lombardi's death in late 1919, G. B. Dealey had long been handling the business matters of the company for "the ladies," as everyone called Mrs. A. H. Belo and Mrs. Jeannette Belo Peabody. He corresponded regularly with them regarding operations of the company, and they met in person at annual meetings of shareholders or as business matters required in Dallas, Galveston, or Boston. In 1920, following the deaths of Mrs. Belo and Cesar Lombardi, Jeannette Belo Peabody asked G. B. Dealey to become president of the company, and he accepted. He maintained his regular correspondence with Jeannette regarding business operations, reporting to her on a weekly basis at first. Over time, she requested that the reports be reduced in frequency, but she did not lose her keen interest in the management of the company.

Jeannette's sister-in-law, Helen Ponder Belo, Alfred Jr.'s widow, inherited the family's Dallas home, but she was not involved in company management. She maintained the Dallas home for her sometime use, and she also maintained an apartment in New York and traveled widely, particularly in Europe. Her two daughters eventually inherited the home on Ross Avenue.[10]

Although A. H. Belo lived in Dallas only sporadically after 1885, and he survived only fifteen years after establishing the newspaper there, he made many notable contributions to the early development of Dallas. He was a founder of the Dallas Public Library and gave the first donation toward the purchase of books. He is credited with giving the first donation toward purchasing artwork for what became the Dallas Museum of Art, as well. His widow, Nettie Ennis Belo, was also involved in civic improvements, establishing the first Belo Foundation, which was created to present lectures for Dallas residents by learned individuals from throughout the country. The first lecture was delivered by William Allen White in McFarlin Auditorium.

In 1876, A. H. Belo had visited the Centennial Exposition in Philadelphia, and he was so intrigued by the invention of the telephone, which he saw there, that he acquired the first two telephones in Texas. In 1878, he installed one in the *Galveston Daily News* and the other in his home. It was another year before the first commercial telephone exchange was installed. That first commercial telephone was given the number 1, and it was listed in the name of George Dealey, an immigrant tea and coffee merchant, whose sons Thomas W. and George Bannerman already worked for Belo at the newspaper.

George Bannerman Dealey lived an unusually long life for his time. He was born in Manchester, England, on September 18, 1859. His father, also George Dealey, was English, and his mother, Mary Ann Nellins Dealey, was Irish. The family, including their five sons and four daughters, immigrated to Texas in the summer of 1870 onboard a sailing ship called the *Herbert*, which set sail from Liverpool and landed in Galveston. The trip took six weeks, and the large family, with its many children, made the crossing in a makeshift shelter built on the deck. Throughout his life, G. B. retold the story of his first impression of Texas. It had been a sweet one, because it was established by his first bite of watermelon, which he and his brother Thomas spied on the docks and soon sampled.

Three of the five Dealey sons who arrived on the docks that day, Thomas, G. B., and James Quayle, were to play significant parts in the development of Belo Corp., beginning with the *Galveston Daily News*. The eldest, Thomas, got a job as office boy at the *Galveston Daily News* soon after the family's arrival in 1870. Younger brothers G. B. and James attended school, as did the other children, and G. B. began working after school at various jobs, such as pumping the organ and ringing the bell at Trinity Episcopal Church.

A few years later, Thomas came home from work at the paper one evening with the news that he had been promoted to mailing clerk. Thomas had recommended G. B. as a replacement in his former job as office boy, and he invited G. B. to accompany him to work for an interview the following day. G. B. was fifteen, and he left his schooling behind to begin a seventy-two-year career with the institution then known as Richardson, Belo & Co.

G. B. worked essentially every day from the age of fifteen until he died at age eighty-six. His grandsons, three of whom succeeded him one after the other at the helm of the company, remembered him as kindly and dignified, but remote to their childhood experiences. To a large extent, their lives within the company had been foreseen and the way prepared for them by their grandfather, who is widely acknowledged as one of the most visionary leaders in Dallas history.

When G. B. Dealey began working at the *Galveston Daily News* in 1874, it was owned jointly by Willard Richardson, seventy-two, who had been publisher for thirty years, and Alfred H. Belo, thirty-five, who had been with him for nine years. Ulysses S. Grant was president of the United States. By the end of G. B. Dealey's life, he owned the company, and he had directed operations through fifteen more presidencies and two world wars. Harry Truman was president when G. B. died in 1946.

By the time the Dealey brothers joined the *News* in Galveston, it was the most influential newspaper in Texas. Richardson had established the paper as politically "independent but not neutral," and Belo had added his lasting imprint of what he called "impersonal journalism."[11] He believed that a great newspaper must act with a distinct personality of its own, separate from that of its editors or owners. In 1881, several years after

Richardson's death, Belo restructured the company as a joint stock corporation, calling it A. H. Belo & Co. The articles of incorporation stated that the restructuring was "for the purpose of printing and publishing one or more newspapers in the City of Galveston and at other points in the State of Texas."[12]

On the day the restructuring was announced, the following editorial appeared in the *Galveston Daily News*, setting the tone that would be maintained thereafter:

> A great newspaper conducted in the spirit of the *News* must absorb or eliminate individualities, because it must itself be a distinct personality, a moral and responsible person. A great newspaper must be serenely indifferent to personal likes and dislikes, personal opinions or prejudices inside or outside of its organization which would interfere with its functions as a faithful collector and disseminator of news; as a voice, an intelligence and a reasoning conscience, to interpret for the reading public the ripest thought and best judgment of the time, touching all questions of public concern. A great and rightly inspired newspaper must sink all personality but its own.[13]

Brothers Thomas and G. B. were joined at the *Galveston Daily News* for a time by their younger brother James, and all three were on the payroll at the time Belo reorganized the company in 1881. All three were promoted at the time, with Thomas becoming an officer of A. H. Belo & Co., taking on the responsibilities of secretary and treasurer. His elevation in rank recognized his role as one of Belo's most trusted colleagues in the company, along with Belo's father-in-law, Cornelius Ennis, who was an investor and a member of the board of directors.

With his older brother taking an important role in running the company, and his younger brother James preparing to leave Galveston to pursue studies at Brown University in Providence, Rhode Island, G. B. focused on his own self-improvement. He began a course of studies at the Island City Business College, attending night classes, and he established for himself a scholarly reading program that was to last throughout his life. Then, in May 1882, he met the young woman who would become his wife. Olivia Allen arrived in Galveston by train with her father, a well-known newspaper publisher from Lexington, Missouri, who was part of a publishers' delegation visiting Texas.

G. B. assisted his brother Thomas and A. H. Belo in hosting the group, and he and Olivia got acquainted well enough to promise to write each other. By 1884 they were married and setting up their first home in Houston, where G. B. had been posted as a traveling agent for the *Galveston Daily News*. At the time the *News* was the chief rival of the *Houston Post*, and his assignment included seeking ways to overtake the *Post*'s circulation lead.

His Houston assignment was the third in as many years, the first having been Waco, then Dallas. Part of his responsibilities during those years was to evaluate the various small towns in the northern part of the state and to report where he saw the most promise for future business development. Dallas's population in the 1880 census was listed at 10,358, and G. B. concurred with others in the company that it was the place.

In the summer of 1885, Belo sent G. B. to Dallas as business manager of a new operation created to publish a sister newspaper to what everyone referred to simply as the *News* in Galveston. It was called the *Dallas Morning News*, rather than simply the *Dallas News*, because a couple of speculators had gotten wind of the new enterprise and started a publication with that title during the summer. Hoping to make a quick buck, they offered to surrender the title to A. H. Belo & Co. for a price, but their gamble did not pay off. The company simply inserted "Morning" in the name of the new newspaper and went on its way.

G. B. Dealey's sixty-year career at the *Dallas Morning News* began when he negotiated with a downtown Dallas property owner to erect a building suitable for publishing a newspaper, which the company would lease until the Dallas paper was on its feet and could build a permanent home. G. B. supervised construction of the first Dallas Morning News Building on Commerce Street, in the middle of the block between Austin and Lamar, and publication began on October 1, 1885.

On the front page of Vol. 1, No. 1, directly under the name of the newspaper, the address was given: "OFFICE OF PUBLICATION: Nos. 500 and 511 COMMERCE STREET, DALLAS." The new building was state of the art for newspaper publishing, and it was the first building in the South to be equipped with Edison's new lightbulbs. That innovation attracted crowds at night just to see the building glow from a distance. The company ultimately bought out the owner of that early building and expanded in either direction, taking up the whole block bounded by Commerce, Lamar, Main, and Austin streets. The *Dallas Morning News* stayed at that location for sixty-four years.

The company's early interest in adopting new technologies was a preview of things to come. The foray into North Texas was the first known example of leased, dedicated telegraph wires between two distant cities to transmit content of one newspaper for reproduction simultaneously in a sister newspaper. Each paper had its own local staff and editorial writers, but the two papers were to be duplicates in large part. Jointly the two papers were called the *News*, and both A. H. Belo and G. B. Dealey knew that what they were doing was significant and would affect the future of newspaper publishing. They were confident that it would enable the *News*, in its dual form, to maintain dominance as the state's most influential newspaper.

The sister newspapers were linked across 315 miles by telegraph, and they shared a network of correspondents around the state. The *Dallas Morning News*, like its sister newspaper, was intended to be a statewide publication, and it was immediately successful, beginning with a circulation of 5,000.

The Dallas assignment established the direction for the rest of G. B. Dealey's life. His young wife remained in Galveston briefly, because their first child had been born in early 1885. Olivia and their daughter Annie joined him in Dallas soon after the newspaper was launched, and they spent the rest of their lives there. They ultimately had five children, three daughters and two sons, each of whom was to play a part, one way or another, in establishing the modern Belo Corp.

In late 1885, Belo and his family also moved to Dallas in order to focus on getting the paper off to the right start. However, as he spent much of the time seeking medical treatments or a better climate elsewhere, Belo continued to entrust the business operations of the *Dallas Morning News* to G. B. Dealey and the editorial management to senior editors who relocated from Galveston. The executives of A. H. Belo & Co., including Thomas W. Dealey, remained in Galveston, managing the dual operations from their offices at the *Galveston Daily News* for the next thirty-eight years. Not until the Galveston paper was sold in 1923 did A. H. Belo & Co. move to Dallas.

Belo showed his great appreciation of G. B. Dealey's leadership on many occasions, but in 1895, he gave a special tribute in recognition of G. B.'s twenty-first anniversary. It was already the custom at the company that employees were considered to have "come of age" after twenty-one years on board. On that anniversary date, October 12, 1895, G. B. arrived at his desk in the business office of the *Dallas Morning News* to find a gift accompanied by a letter from Belo. The letter was dated October 2, 1895, and it was written in Belo's own hand on the letterhead of the Saranac Inn, "In the Adirondacks," Franklin Co., New York, where Belo was staying at the time:

> Mr. G. B. Dealey
> Dear Sir:
> On the 12th inst. you will complete your 21st year with the "News," & accompanying testimonial is intended to commemorate the event. It affords me great pleasure to assure you that all of our relations have been of the most satisfactory character. I have watched your career with much interest and you have won your place by your own merit. Your close identification with the "Dallas News," as business manager, from its beginning to its present very prosperous condition, is the best tribute to your ability.
>
> It is very gratifying to me to testify to your unswerving loyalty and devotion to the "News."
>
> With assurances of highest regard, I remain,
> Yours truly,
> A. H. Belo
> Pres.[14]

The letter accompanied a silver tea set consisting of "three pieces, a tea pot, sugar dish and spoon-holder, all of the latest and most elegant design," according to a news report in the October 13, 1895, issue of the *Dallas Morning News*. The tea pot was inscribed "George B. Dealey, from A. H. Belo & Co, 1874–1895." The *Dallas Morning News* report of the event said that the tea set "was christened in the *News* business office yesterday by the *News* employees."

In responding to Belo's recognition of his achievement, G. B. wrote to him, opening his handwritten letter with, "My dear Colonel,"

> The gift is a handsome and a lasting one, but I value the letter much more. Words can never express the satisfaction that it has afforded me to know you hold me in such high esteem and I shall always preserve the letter as faithfully as I shall the gift.

Later in the letter he said,

> I have done my best and since I reached manhood and learned the meaning of responsibility, it has been my aim always to do the work assigned me with as much fidelity as if I owned the property. My success, though, has been due in no small degree to the uniform kindness and encouragement received at your hands.[15]

The day after the gift was announced in the *News*, the *Dallas Times Herald*, the largest of several afternoon dailies at the time and the *News*'s chief rival, published the *News*'s report of the tribute and followed it with an effusive statement of its own:

> The *Times Herald* extends hearty greeting to the recipient of the testimonials. Almost a quarter of a century continuous service with one establishment is unusual in this newer country, and of itself speaks a volume of eulogium. But when that service is so emphatically testified to as having been pre-eminent, as in this case, it is worthy of more than passing comment. . . . On this, his silver anniversary, the *Times Herald* sincerely wishes for him at least a half century more of favored life "on golden hinges turning."[16]

As it turned out, G. B. did live, as the *Times Herald* wished for him, "another half century," or fifty-one years to be exact, and, by all accounts, every one of them turned "on golden hinges," as he continued to apply all of his business sagacity and courage to his newspaper and his city. He continued the tradition of recognizing the achievements of employees reaching their twenty-first anniversaries with the company, a practice continued by Belo Corp. to this day.

Later in the year 1895, Belo elevated G. B.'s position to general manager, as Belo's own health grew worse and he spent even less time in Dallas. Although there was some pushback from longtime editors, who resented having a business-side manager elevated beyond the news management, G. B. prevailed with his quiet manner and innate humility. Ultimately his authority was respected throughout all departments.

When A. H. Belo died in early 1901, and his son Alfred Jr. took over as president of the company, the directors of the company elected G. B. Dealey to the board, where he joined his brother Thomas, who had been secretary and treasurer since the 1881 reincorporation, and Colonel R. G. Lowe, who had been vice president for the same duration. G. B. had by then acquired a small number of shares in A. H. Belo & Co., which was a requirement of board membership.

For five years, that team of seasoned executives served their young president, Alfred Jr., bringing him along to take the full responsibility for running the company. The correspondence between Galveston and Dallas during those years focused on which of the operations would contribute what amount toward the payment of the dividends to shareholders. Then, on January 15, 1906, R. G. Lowe died suddenly of a heart attack in Galveston. Alfred Jr., who had depended heavily on Lowe for guidance as he took over running the company, left his sickbed in Dallas, where he was recovering from influenza, to call a meeting of the directors in Galveston. The meeting was not only for the purpose of electing a new vice president to replace Lowe, but also to elect a new secretary/treasurer to replace Thomas Dealey, whose health was failing as well, and who had expressed his wish to retire. At the meeting, G. B. was elected vice president, to replace Lowe; and John Lubben, in Galveston, was elected secretary/treasurer to replace Thomas. G. B. and John Lubben had known each other since childhood, and they were personal friends as well as business colleagues.

Returning to Dallas after the meeting, Alfred Jr. became seriously ill in a relapse of the influenza, which developed into cerebral meningitis. Less than a month after the meeting, on February 15, 1906, Thomas Dealey died, but the news of his death was kept from Alfred Jr. because of Alfred's own weak condition. In a letter to G. B. on February 23, Jeannette Belo Peabody wrote:

> My mother and I look to you for help in our great trouble—the greatest that could come upon us. . . . All our lives are wrapt up in Alfred and if anything should happen to him I do not know what would become of us. We have perfect confidence in you and you

> have been a great comfort and help to Alfred always and I know will continue to be to him and to us.[17]

Jeannette ended her letter, "With regards to Mrs. Dealey and prayers that when this reaches you my brother may be out of danger." But that was not to be. Four days after the date of her letter, on February 27, 1906, Alfred Jr. died. A. H. Belo & Co. had lost its top three executives within a six-week period, and the new principal owners, Mrs. A. H. (Nettie Ennis) Belo, Mrs. Jeannette Belo Peabody, and Mrs. Alfred H. (Helen Ponder) Belo, Jr., called upon their trusted next-in-command, George Bannerman Dealey, to take over.

The elder Mrs. Belo asked G. B. to become president of the company. However, he deferred to her, insisting that Mrs. Belo herself hold the title, assuring her that he would run it on her behalf. She agreed to that arrangement, and she held the title of president until she died in 1913. When she took the title of president, Mrs. Belo persuaded her brother-in-law, Cesar Lombardi, husband of her younger sister, to move to Dallas from San Francisco, where he had recently retired. Lombardi was elected a vice president to look out for the interests of the family, and G. B. continued in his role as vice president and general manager. The letterhead of the company, however, for many years thereafter continued to show "A. H. Belo, President," which could not have been an oversight.

Mrs. Belo regularly corresponded with G. B. during those years, using notepaper with bold black edges until as late as 1910 in expression of her ongoing mourning for her husband and son. In a letter dated January 15, 1912, sent from Paris, she wrote, "I want to express to you my appreciation of your management of the *News*, and I want you to know that I feel deeply the efforts you are making to keep the *News* a power for good and progress." When she died in 1913, her daughter and daughter-in-law turned to G. B. Dealey once again, asking him to assume the title of president in recognition of his ongoing leadership of the company.

G. B. declined, suggesting that a Belo family member should rightfully continue to head up the company, so the title and the responsibilities of president were given to Cesar Lombardi, who had become an important part of the company's stability during his seven years as vice president alongside G. B. However, G. B. continued to lead the company, as he had since 1901, retaining his modest titles of vice president and general manager. Jeannette Belo Peabody also became a vice president at that time, reflecting her position as one of the two principal owners, but her sister-in-law did not become involved in management.[18]

In 1912, G. B.'s older son, Walter Allen Dealey, had joined his father in the company and spent a year moving through various departments, learning all aspects of the business. In 1915, his younger son, Edward Musgrove Dealey, who was always known as Ted, also joined the company, focusing his considerable energy on reporting and editorial writing. Then, following Cesar Lombardi's death in 1919, the sisters-in-law named G. B. president of A. H. Belo & Co., which position he assumed, at last, on January 27, 1920. The employees threw a surprise party for him to congratulate him on the elevation to president. He told them, "My attainment to my present place is not so much due to any perfection in me as to the fact that I stuck to the job. That is the advice that I would give to others. Always stick to the job."[19]

He continued to manage the business in both Dallas and Galveston, but it would become clear that the Belo sisters-in-law sorely missed having one of their own relatives in the company and newspaper management. They both read the Dallas and Galveston newspapers every day, receiving them by mail a few days after publication. Correspondence regarding cost-cutting measures and payment of dividends increased between the women and G. B. They became more open in expressing concerns whenever dividends were affected by the business operations.

Dividends were deeply affected before very long. The company experienced extreme financial difficulties when G. B. Dealey, through the *Dallas Morning News* and the *Galveston Daily News*, mounted an unrelenting campaign to expose the atrocities and lawless tactics of the Ku Klux Klan, to which many of the leading business and government leaders, as well as Protestant clergymen, had attached themselves. By then, the *Dallas Morning News* was the larger and more prosperous of the company's two newspapers.

From the first emergence of the Ku Klux Klan in Dallas in 1921, the *Dallas Morning News* vigorously opposed it—almost daily—in both news coverage of its illegal activities and editorials decrying its existence. On May 24, 1921, the day after the first formal march in Dallas, the *News* published an editorial titled "Dallas Slandered," which said in part:

> The spectacle of 800 masked and white-gowned men parading the streets of Dallas under banners proclaiming them Knights of

> the Ku Klux Klan and self-appointed guardians of the community's political, social and moral welfare . . . has a serious significance which will not be lost on the minds of men who cherish the community's good name and have the intelligence to understand how well designed that exhibition was to bring it under reproach.

As Klan activity sprang up around the state, the *News* covered every rally, every march, and every speech to which it could get its reporters and correspondents. Many of the reports were made from the field by G. B.'s son Ted, who tracked the rallies and reported on who attended. The paper's news stories reported illegal actions and quoted the hate-filled speeches, and editorials denounced the Klan-backed political candidates. The Klan retaliated against the *Dallas Morning News* with a boycott of the paper and its advertisers, which caused the paper great economic hardship as readers canceled subscriptions and advertisers dropped out, fearful of Klan retributions.

There were four daily newspapers in Dallas at the time, three of which opposed the Klan and suffered for it.[20] The *Dallas Morning News* was the largest and the most powerful of the local papers to fight against the Klan through its pages, and one of the others was A. H. Belo & Co.'s own afternoon paper, the *Dallas Journal*, which it published from 1914 until 1938. The *Dallas Dispatch*, a smaller daily that was part of the Scripps chain, was the third of the local newspapers that opposed the Klan. However, the other large daily, the afternoon *Dallas Times Herald*, did not report Klan incidents and gave the Klan sympathetic treatment when pressed to take a stand. Edwin J. Kiest, publisher of the *Dallas Times Herald*, maintained a middle-of-the-road stance because many "solid citizens," he said, were recognized members of the Klan. In addition, that newspaper's managing editor and one of its foremost reporters were known to be Klan members.[21]

On March 2, 1922, the *Dallas Morning News* ran an editorial titled "Bed Sheets in the Meeting-House," in which it criticized the growing support of the Klan by the Protestant clergy in Dallas. Then in April, in an editorial critical of the Dallas Police Department, the *News* stated:

> The *News* is but stating an indisputable fact in saying that the community has lost faith in the integrity of its police department,

> . . . due to the feeling that many members of the department are under a secret constraint which deprives them of their freedom in developing clews [*sic*] which may lead to the exposure of members of the Ku Klux Klan.[22]

The *News* interviewed the two announced contenders in the 1922 U.S. Senate election and found them both to be backers of the Klan. In an August editorial, the newspaper explained to citizens how to write in another candidate, whom the paper knew to be anti-Klan. The anti-Klan candidate did not win the election, but the write-in campaign drew many supporters statewide to the cause of Klan opposition.

Meanwhile, the Belo sisters-in-law were alarmed by the financial crisis brought on by their newspapers' position, as Jeannette Belo Peabody wrote in a letter of July 30, 1922. However, G. B. stood firm, and in her next letter of August 31, Jeannette wrote the following from her summer residence in Chocorua, New Hampshire:

> I certainly think you should be most heartily congratulated on the fine work done in this most trying campaign. It seems to be the policy of the papers was just right and the expression dignified and sound. I am sorry that we are located in the very centre of the K.K.K. activities and suppose they will continue to harass us, but we now have the State at large with us and it is most remarkable to read every day in the Eastern papers of the Texas situation.[23]

By the end of 1922, the *Dallas Morning News* had lost considerable circulation and advertising revenue, and dividends were threatened. Although G. B. had maintained a steady course as president, the sisters-in-law revealed a distinct uneasiness about not having a Belo family member in the executive ranks of the company. They were concerned that G. B. had not acted quickly enough to find "a strong man of ripe judgment and broad point of view to take the place Mr. Lombardi so nobly occupied."[24]

Jeannette wrote to G. B. in 1922 to ask that her first cousin, businessman Ennis Cargill of Houston, become a director of the company. While G. B. welcomed Cargill as a director, he responded that he would also like to add his son Walter to the board. Walter had been made assistant to the president in 1920, when his father became president. However, Jeannette responded for herself and her sister-in-law, "It seems to us that Walter is too young to be a director at present. As your assistant, he has power under you."[25] As the company's financial strains of those years continued to affect their incomes, the sisters-in-law increasingly pressed G. B. to reduce expenses and to build stronger management with younger leaders to follow in his footsteps.

Earlier in 1922, during its campaign to defeat the Klan, the *Dallas Morning News* had continued its practice of leading the way in adopting new technologies for journalistic purposes. On June 26, 1922, the company launched WFAA Radio, which it called "A Radio Service of the *Dallas Morning News*," detailing the call letters to mean Working For All Alike. WFAA Radio was the first newspaper-owned clear-channel radio station in America. The radio station was the brainchild of G. B.'s older son, Walter, of whom it was said later that he "was so fully convinced and so convincing, he soon brought all others with voice in the management to a willingness to follow his recommendations. . . ." Of course, that meant winning over "the ladies" as well, which he was able to accomplish.

G. B. must surely have been gratified shortly thereafter by a letter from Jeannette following her attendance at the annual meeting in Dallas in January 1923. In that letter she apologized for the several months of letters criticizing G. B.'s actions, and she expressed her sincere appreciation for Walter's abilities, which she said she had fully recognized only upon meeting him. In that letter, she went on to say, "My one thought is to express to you my gratitude for holding the property together and my profound belief that we should have sold out long ago had you not wished to continue to manage the property."[26]

In spite of those words of trust and praise, the early 1920s were trying times for G. B. Dealey in many ways. As the *News* battled the Klan and revenue dropped, many felt that launching the radio station was a waste of money, and the sisters-in-law wrote regularly, fretting about cost controls even as they praised him. During those trying times, W. L. Moody, Jr., of Galveston had quietly made an offer to buy the *Galveston Daily News* from A. H. Belo & Co. G. B. presented the offer to Jeannette and Helen, making the case that most of the revenue of the company was generated in Dallas, rather than in Galveston, anyway.

The sale of the *Galveston Daily News*, the company's former flagship newspaper, was finalized on March 22, 1923, and the company was able to pay debts that otherwise would not have been paid on schedule, and to pay Jeannette Belo Peabody and Helen Ponder Belo their full dividends.[27] However, when it was made known that A. H. Belo & Co. had sold the Galveston newspaper, the Klan boasted publicly that it was running A. H. Belo & Co. out of business.

In the 1924 governor's race, the powerful but controversial former governor James E. Ferguson, who had been impeached and barred by the Texas Senate from holding state office again, took a firm stand against the Klan and fielded a candidate in his place, his own wife, Miriam "Ma" Ferguson. She became the Democratic nominee selected to face the Klan's handpicked candidate running on the Republican ticket. The Klan's candidate was Felix Robertson, a Dallas district judge.

It was an awkward move for the *Dallas Morning News*, which had supported barring Governor Ferguson from further elected office, but the newspaper forcefully backed Mrs. Ferguson and her anti-Klan message, and she won. Following their loss to the surrogate candidate, who had never before run for office, the Klan began to recede in prominence in Texas. By 1926, the membership of Klan No. 66, the Dallas chapter, had dropped from 13,000 members to only 1,200. A. H. Belo & Co.'s strong leadership through its newspaper editorials and news coverage was credited nationwide with defeating the Klan's hold on Texas politics.

In 1924, shaken by the threat to the Belo family's livelihood, Jeannette began an exchange of letters with G. B. in which they explored means by which to safeguard the "future of the property." Over twelve to eighteen months, they came to an agreement that G. B. would buy the company, with a few partners from within the executive ranks of the company. By that point, G. B. had worked for the Belo family for fifty-two years and essentially had run the entire operation for more than twenty years. Yet he was not a wealthy man and certainly could not buy the company on his own.

In his letters, G. B. made it clear to Jeannette that if she were inclined to sell, he wanted to be the one to buy, even though he did not have the money. In search of a way to buy the company without putting his own personal financial well-being at risk, he consulted his friend, former Belo colleague-turned-banker George Waverley Briggs, who knew the situation very well. Briggs explained to him that "the paper itself is in position to finance the purchase."[28]

G. B. asked Dallas attorney Eugene P. Locke, of the firm Locke & Locke, to represent him in the matter; and the sisters-in-law engaged the

Houston firm of Baker, Botts, Parker & Garwood to represent them. In an arrangement that included securities, such as bonds, common stock, and preferred stock, and a fair price of $2,725,000, G. B. Dealey and a few partners bought A. H. Belo & Co. from the Belo heirs and the other holders of small numbers of shares.

The transaction was completed at a meeting on July 15, 1926, transferring all of the assets of A. H. Belo & Co. to a newly formed A. H. Belo Corporation, of which G. B. Dealey was elected president.

In buying A. H. Belo & Co., it would have been unthinkable for G. B. Dealey to change the company's name to his own or to anything other than Belo. It was the very institution known as A. H. Belo & Co. that he was acquiring with both pride and humility. The minutes book from the reorganization meeting includes a transcript of comments made by several of those present at the time, including the following from G. B. Dealey:

> I think I should say that I and my associates are under obligations to Mrs. Peabody [Jeannette Belo Peabody] and her children and to Mrs. Belo [Helen Ponder Belo] and her children for the confidence which they have exhibited in turning this property over to us.

And he continued to express his sense of responsibility:

> I think that our large duty and the important thing for us to think about is, how much good can we do [for] the people and the State of Texas, and how can we continue, even more than in the past, to add laurels to the record of this institution during its past eighty-four years of existence.

G. B. held 52 percent of the stock of the newly formed A. H. Belo Corporation. Five others held 8 percent each, and two held 4 percent each. After G. B., the partners were listed in the documents in the following order: Walter A. Dealey; John F. Lubben; Tom Finty, Jr.; E. M. (Ted) Dealey; E. B. Doran; Ennis Cargill; and George Waverley Briggs.

G. B.'s closest ally in the buyout, other than his son Walter, was John Lubben, who had been with the company since the reorganization in 1881 and was serving as a director and officer of the company at the time.

At the meeting, Walter was elected vice president, John was elected secretary-treasurer, and the other directors elected were Tom Finty, Jr.; E. B. Doran; Ted Dealey; and Ennis Cargill, who was the cousin of the Belo sisters-in-law. All the directors of the new company already were thoroughly familiar with the company and its history.

G. B. spoke further to his new board following the reincorporation:

> We have a wonderful property here—but, more than that, we have a marvelous responsibility. Let us realize that responsibility. Let us bear with one another; and, when our end comes, as praising the Lord, it will come, it will be said of us: "Well done, thou good and faithful servant. . . ."

In that same meeting, Eugene C. Locke said this about those with whom he had worked to arrange the purchase:

> I have been a reader of the *Dallas News* from my earliest years. It has been helpful in forming my ideals and in forming the ideals of all of the younger generation here. This is [my] first employment by the owners of the *News*. It gave to me the first insight that I have had in the inner workings of this institution.
>
> In no institution with which I have been familiar has there been discovered by me such manifestations of unselfishness, of such idealism on the part of the management and of the personnel of the employees of the *News*.[29]

In 1928, G. B. Dealey's younger brother James returned to the company and joined the editorial staff. In 1929 he was named editor of the newspaper. James had retired from Brown University after a distinguished thirty-five-year career as an author, professor, and head of the department of political and social science. During his career at Brown, James had written eleven books and traveled widely as a speaker and authority on his subjects. Following the death of company director Tom Finty, Jr., the directors of A. H. Belo Corporation elected James to the board. His election to the seven-member board brought the number of directors with the name Dealey to four, including G. B., president; James, editor; Walter, vice president; and Ted. The other three directors were John Lubben, Ennis Cargill, and E. B. Doran.

James became a crucial part of the newspaper, directing editorial operations with his substantial intellect during the difficult 1930s, the period that came to be known as the Great Depression. When James died at age seventy-six in early 1937, G. B. suffered the loss immeasurably. Not only did he lose the trusted and dependable editorial voice, he also lost the second of his brothers who had helped forge the institution. Then in January 1938, G. B. lost his chief partner in the purchase of the company, and his longtime friend, John Lubben, who died at age seventy-two after fifty-seven years with the company.

In his private life, G. B. and his beloved Olivia Allen Dealey had five children, including three daughters in addition to their two sons. Their first child, and the only one born in Galveston, was daughter Annie; the second child was Fannie; the third was Walter; the fourth was Ted; and the fifth was Maidie, a golden-haired child ten years younger than her sister Annie. Throughout his career G. B. worked long hours, six days a week, and half a day on Sundays. He left most of the responsibilities of rearing the children to Olivia and her household staff. His son Ted wrote in an essay about life with his father, "When I was growing up and even in my elementary school days, my father was to me and to the other children in the family a rather shadowy figure."[30] In later years he developed close relationships with his children, often traveling with one or more of them on annual vacations away from Dallas. He brought both of his sons into the company as very young men, grooming them to be newspapermen.

Over the course of his life, G. B. helped influence the development of Dallas as few others have. Today it is hard to imagine that such basic services as sewers and a safe water supply should need the promotional efforts of the newspaper. However, when the *Dallas Morning News* began publication, Dallas was a fairly rough-and-tumble place with few paved streets, sanitary sewers a rarity, and civic order periodically threatened by lawlessness unthinkable in more mature communities, such as in Belo's hometown of Salem, North Carolina, or even Galveston, where G. B. grew into maturity. Calling for a reduction in vice, particularly in gambling houses, the newspaper declared the problem to be caused by a city "teeming with speculative and adventurous people."[31]

In 1885 there were already several newspapers in publication in Dallas at various levels of profitability and dependability. The town had grown rapidly with the railroads, and by 1885, five railroads connected Dallas with the rest of the world. The population explosion created by the greater accessibility had outstripped the rudimentary civic structure. The editorial campaigns launched by the *Dallas Morning News* in its first few years set the pace for city leaders to follow, when it tackled such issues as safe water supply, trash receptacles on street corners, land reserved for parks, and so on. These campaigns reflect publisher Belo's sophisticated sensibilities, as well as the passion and vision of business manager G. B. Dealey for the betterment of his new home city.

G. B. believed that it was the responsibility of the newspaper to improve the civic and social order by leading citizens first to awareness of problems, then to their solution. Throughout his years as business manager, then general manager, vice president, president, and publisher, he used the newspaper's pages to propose, promote, and accomplish countless civic programs and projects that are still serving the city of Dallas and its citizens today.

In 1893, the *Dallas Morning News* hired the first woman on its editorial staff, Isadora Miner, who used the pen name Pauline Periwinkle. The paper supported her twenty-year career of promoting women's rights and writing about issues of importance to women beyond the traditional society reports of tea parties and club meetings, and publishing recipes. Pauline Periwinkle implored women to become active in the betterment of their city, state, and country. In 1897, the *News* launched a campaign to improve farming techniques and the well-being of farmers; in 1900, the *News* began consistently to write about the fine arts, including books, music, art, and cultural development in general, providing critical essays, news reports, and promotional announcements. In fact, the *News* consistently supported all movements for cultural institutions, including the establishment of a library. In 1902, a local branch of the American League for Civic Improvement was organized under the *News*'s leadership, and the *News* consistently advocated improvement in the parks programs of Dallas and the state of Texas.

In 1906, the *News* began its efforts to have all city government and civic improvements be made in accordance with a long-range plan, urging city leaders to hire a professional city planner to make a plan for Dallas. The urging culminated in the city's engagement of the country's leading planner, German immigrant George Kessler. In writing about the growing city, the editors began in 1907 to campaign for a more stable banking system for Texas, publishing more than fifty editorials and news articles. In 1908, the *News* began its ongoing promotion of Trinity River reclamation and improvement, beginning with the building of levees to control flooding. The Kessler Plan, the first city plan created for Dallas, was adopted in 1910, and the newspaper has promoted following its recommendations ever since. Also in 1910, the *News* began a campaign for bringing all of the railroads into a single Union Terminal and did not stop until it was accomplished.

G. B. Dealey's progressive ideas were presented daily to citizens through the newspaper's editorial positions on important issues of the day. Additionally, he worked throughout his life behind the scenes with other civic leaders to organize institutions he believed would benefit the rapidly growing city. Because of his editorial efforts, the city of Dallas created the Park and Recreation Department with its own Park Board in 1905 to oversee the development of parks and green spaces in Dallas. He was instrumental in the 1911 establishment of Southern Methodist University, which was the first four-year college in Dallas. He led the effort to persuade the Federal Reserve to establish a regional bank in Dallas in 1914. He led the movement to create the Dallas Foundation, a community charitable organization, which was established in 1920 and continues to serve Dallas County today.

In 1922, G. B. Dealey founded the Dallas Historical Society after the newspaper received a letter to the editor from a man who had visited the city and been unable to find any information about the history of Dallas anywhere in town. The Old Red Museum of Dallas County History and Culture, completed only in 2007, uses many of those documents and artifacts from the earliest days of Dallas that were donated to the Dallas Historical Society soon after its establishment and held ever since.

G. B. also led the establishment of a children's hospital in 1924, which has become today's Children's Medical Center, and when the city's leaders formed an association to make a bid to host the celebrations of the centennial of Texas's independence, G. B. Dealey was a director of its board and Belo Corp. bought bonds in support of the fund-raising effort. The bid was successful and resulted in the Texas Centennial Exposition at Fair Park in 1936.

On August 29, 1935, as a result of G. B. Dealey's tireless efforts to improve the quality of life in Dallas, Jim Dan Sullivan, president of the Dallas Park Board, announced to the Park Board that a newly created park on the west side of downtown that had been developed in conjunction with the new triple underpass leading into the city would be named

Dealey Plaza. In a story appearing in the August 30, 1935, edition of the *Dallas Morning News*, Sullivan is quoted as saying, "In that way the city can have Dealey Plaza constantly as a reminder of the good Mr. Dealey is doing and has done in the years he has lived and worked among us."

G. B. was out of town when the announcement appeared, staying at his summer cottage in the cooler climate of Winslow, Arkansas. His son Ted sent him a telegram with the news, and G. B. responded to Ted with his usual modesty and put-things-in-order manner: "Very fine indeed & makes my head swell. But the attached represents my honest conviction. Please print it." And on the next page was written,

> The suggestion of President Sullivan of the Park Board is most generous and complimentary and I sincerely appreciate it. But it will not do at all. In my judgment it should not be named after any living person. Since it will be completed next year, why not call it Centennial Plaza, or since it is a triple underpass, would not Trinity Plaza be appropriate?[32]

Ted, however, withheld G. B.'s response from publication, and instead persuaded his father it was better to accept the great honor graciously than to risk offending the leaders who had chosen to honor him. In September, after the Park Board made the name official, G. B. wrote to Jim Dan Sullivan:

> In the office yesterday you informed me that the Park Board had unanimously named the park at the entrance to the triple underpass, Dealey Plaza. I consider this a great honor, one that is very much appreciated, and I want to express sincere thanks to you and all members of the Park Board.[33]

On May 1, 1936, the Triple Underpass was officially dedicated and opened for the first cars to pass under the railroad tracks. G. B. Dealey was a passenger in the first car to pass through the underpass and drive up the hill through Dealey Plaza into downtown Dallas.

Following G. B.'s death in 1946, the Dallas Park Board passed a resolution citing many examples of his support for public parks, beginning with efforts in 1907, as well as his leadership in founding the Marsalis Park Zoo in 1912. The resolution said in part, "In modest recognition of these and his many other contributions to the benefit of the city park system, Dealey Plaza, acquired by the city in 1936 and which has been called the 'Front Door of Dallas,' was named in his honor."[34]

Later on, in 1949, a larger-than-life-size bronze sculpture of G. B. Dealey was added to Dealey Plaza, facing the city he loved and served for his whole life. It was created by the nationally recognized artist Felix deWeldon and dedicated on November 14, 1949. His great-granddaughter Dealey Decherd Herndon, who was not quite three years old, was the "designated unveiler." She clearly recalls the ceremony, with its large crowd, many speeches, even what she wore, because her parents had told her, "This is who you were named for."[35]

G. B. Dealey continued to work six-and-a-half days a week until he died in 1946, after seventy-two years with the company. By then, his son Walter had died, and his son Ted had taken over the day-to-day running of the company along with son-in-law Jim Moroney. But "The Boss," as Ted called him, continued to call the shots until the end, including how his son was to dress for work. According to several who were interviewed, an elderly G. B. Dealey was known to send his son Ted, the president, home if he showed up without tie or jacket.

Shortly before his death, G. B. was filmed for a promotional movie about the *Dallas Morning News* called *Textbook of Democracy*. Sitting at his desk in the newspaper offices, looking straight at the camera, he states his policy for publishing the *News*: "Do the job well today. Do it faster and better tomorrow." He then waves his hand in a gesture that almost seems to say, "Now get back to work."

He was wise beyond his years as a young man, and energetic for change and growth throughout his long life. He lived to be eighty-six years old, and he never lost interest in his newspaper or his city.

Following the lead of his predecessors, Willard Richardson and A. H. Belo, G. B. posted various signs around the newspaper offices encouraging his colleagues to "Be Gentle and Keep Your Voice Low," "Do Your Work as Well as You Can, and Be Kind," and reminding them to "Keep Everlastingly at It and You Will Succeed." Another of his signs was posted along with a portrait of Davy Crockett, from whom it was quoted: "I leave this rule for others when I'm dead, Be always sure you're right—then go ahead!"

Perhaps the most intriguing of the signs read: "Responsibilities gravitate to the person who can shoulder them; power flows to the person who knows how." Some of those signs are still in existence in the Belo Archives, but others were recorded in photographs taken around the old building, which are themselves in the archives.

George Bannerman Dealey was a kindhearted man whose sincerity and tenacity permeated the company during his tenure at the helm. In a resolution passed after he died, the board of directors of the Dallas Historical Society gave this tribute:

> To his native temperament—predominantly blended of fortitude, tolerance, courtesy, imperturbable poise, affability, and gentle and engaging humor—his long, active, full, useful and godly life added the supreme achievements of spiritual loveliness and grace which the perfecting processes of time bestow only to mark and glorify the best of mankind.[36]

Chapter 2

THE CHILDREN CONFRONT THE LEGACY

1912–1945

A straightforward time line of significant events in a company, while essential in evaluating its history and future prospects, leaves out the interesting details of how things happened, who made them happen, and especially why they happened as they did. For 120 years, G. B. Dealey and his descendants who followed after him in the leadership of Belo Corp. have wielded a powerful influence in Texas and, ultimately, in the many other states nationwide where the company's voice is heard. It is impossible to understand today's Belo Corp.—its business philosophy, its corporate culture, and its power as a media company—without knowing something about the individuals who have enabled it to succeed through four generations.

G. B. Dealey entered civic life on October 1, 1885, when he supervised the publication of the first issue of the *Dallas Morning News*. As a young, idealistic newspaperman, he established the voice of the fledgling newspaper as an outspoken advocate for civic improvement; for honesty in business practices; for clean, well-run government at all levels; and for fairness, tolerance, and compassion in human affairs. The moderate and steady institutional voice of A. H. Belo & Co. rang clear under G. B.'s management. He was lionized during his lifetime, and he has been revered by Dallas civic leaders and journalists throughout the country ever since.

His successors at Belo Corp. have been challenged to hold on to his idealism about the news media's responsibility to serve the public. Their interpretations of the precept varied from man to man among his descendants who have led Belo over all these years, and those variations have affected the company profoundly over time. All of the successors have been reminded of G. B.'s legacy every day that they came to work for the last fifty-five years, at least, as they drove past the monumental bronze statue of him standing on a pedestal in the plaza that bears his name on Houston Street in downtown Dallas.

G. B. Dealey had been employed by A. H. Belo & Co. for fifty-two years when he finally acquired it from the heirs of Alfred H. Belo in 1926. By then he had already brought two of his five children into the company's management. His son Walter came into the company in 1912, and Walter's early business acumen changed the company with the establishment of WFAA Radio in 1922. His son Ted joined the *Dallas Morning News* in 1915 as a reporter. Ted wrote many of the stories that exposed the atrocities of the Ku Klux Klan during the early 1920s, and the *News*'s extensive coverage of Klan lawlessness was credited nationally with defeating the Klan's power in Texas.

When their father acquired the company, both Walter, with fourteen years' tenure, and Ted, with eleven, were brought in as equity partners at 8 percent each, and both were elected to the first board of directors. But G. B. Dealey also had three daughters, Annie, Fannie, and Maidie. Although all three were college educated, none of the daughters was invited to become an equity partner or to join the newly reincorporated company's board of directors, much less to work at the newspaper. In those days it was not the custom to include daughters in the family business, especially since, in this case, all three had married well. However, in the long run, all three of the daughters were to have powerful, if indirect, roles to play in the future of the company.

The first two children born to young Olivia Allen and G. B. Dealey were daughters. Their first child was Annie, who was born on February 6, 1885, in Houston, where G. B. was assigned as agent for the *Galveston Daily News*. Annie was born shortly before G. B. was given responsibility for starting up the new Belo newspaper in Dallas. Annie was followed by a sister, Fannie, only eighteen months later, on October 14, 1886. The family had moved to Dallas by then, but Olivia traveled to her own family's home in Lexington, Missouri, to give birth in order to have her mother's help with the eighteen-month-old Annie, who had been seriously ill.

Throughout childhood the two young sisters, Annie and Fannie, were actively engaged in the same music classes and social clubs. They finished high school in the same graduating class in 1904, and attended the same prestigious school in the East, Lasell College in Auburndale, Massachusetts. Both married socially prominent physicians, who were themselves friends, and who were about ten years older than their brides. The sisters remained close throughout their lives, and their children grew up together.

While Annie pursued art studies in Dallas and Europe, Fannie was married first, on April 12, 1911, to Dr. Henry Benjamin Decherd. Annie returned to Dallas in time to help Fannie with her wedding plans and soon met one of Dr. Decherd's friends, a fellow physician, Rice Robinson Jackson, who like Dr. Decherd was tall and slender and already established in his medical practice. Annie and Dr. Jackson married about a year later.

The third of the Dealey daughters, Maidie, was born almost exactly ten years after Annie. She was the baby of the family, remaining close to her parents throughout their lives, and ultimately she was the one who would host the large family gatherings in later years, along with her husband, James M. Moroney.

Texas historian Ernest Sharpe, in his biography of G. B. Dealey, described the young family in 1895, right after Maidie was born, when G. B. was attempting to read fifty selected classic texts in one year to enhance his modest formal education:

> Somehow work and children conspired to reduce his spare time to almost nothing. . . . Although Ollie managed the children entirely, still when he came home a little early in the evenings, the children contrived to prevent his reading until they were sent to bed, and then there were calls for glasses of water, coughing spells to stop, and occasional crying or fighting to be quieted.[1]

The firstborn child, Annie, was a lively, creative spirit after overcoming a lingering illness during her first two years of life. The illness was diagnosed as *cholera infantum*, which was usually fatal, but somehow the baby survived. From early childhood, Annie had piano lessons, and in addition, she took art classes from one of Texas's foremost artists, Frank Reaugh, who lived in Dallas. Reaugh specialized in the use of pastels to depict the frontier landscapes of Texas and the Southwest. Annie later formed the

Frank Reaugh Art Club in 1922, and the club sponsored annual juried exhibitions of artwork created by Reaugh's pupils, who by then were numerous. The Reaugh Art Club remained active long after both Annie's and the artist's lifetimes.

For many years, Reaugh took a select group of his advanced students on summer sketching trips to West Texas and New Mexico, and Annie made several of those trips. Among Reaugh's other students who became well-known artists were Alexandre Hogue, E. G. Eisenlohr, Reveau Bassett, and Florence McClung, all of whom Annie knew and whose work she collected. She later gave many of her collected paintings by these preeminent artists to her children and grandchildren. Annie's own work was shown on many occasions in the Reaugh Art Club exhibitions, and her grandchildren have retained many of her pastel paintings from those days.

Annie's independent spirit was shown in 1910 and 1911, when she pursued her art studies in Dresden, Germany. She and Fannie had traveled in Europe before that, and she had learned of the opportunities in Germany while visiting her uncle, Dr. James Q. Dealey, and his family, who were spending a year in Leipzig while Dr. Dealey was on sabbatical from Brown University. For many years, Annie maintained a lively correspondence with Dr. Dealey, as well as with his son William.

As a young woman, Annie showed her father's ability to organize significant and lasting civic institutions. Maintaining her interest in art throughout her life, Annie was one of the founders of the Creative Arts Center, which was originally housed in Frank Reaugh's former home and studio called El Sibil, near Lake Cliff Park in Oak Cliff. Her name appeared frequently in the society columns throughout her youth, as she attended parties and traveled with friends, and she was active in several service organizations. Among her strongest interests as a young woman was the formation in 1908 of the Young Women's Christian Association of Dallas, of which she was a founder and an original board member. Annie seems to have been inspired by her father's progressive ideas about the rights of women in the workplace. She served as recording secretary of the first board of the YWCA, and in 1909, when the organization had acquired its first permanent home, the accomplishments of the YWCA's first year were described in an article in the newspaper:

> You will like to know that we learned there were 114 places in our city employing young women; within a year at different times

> all of these places were visited. . . . It has been a year of hard work, but the loyalty, hopefulness and willingness of all members, as well as many who are not members, has been the answer of prayer and has linked us together.[2]

The report goes on to recount their efforts to improve working conditions for the women, as well as to find more companies that would hire women.

In June 1912, her sister Fannie hosted an afternoon party in her honor that was described in a newspaper column called "Dallas Social Affairs," and which was the formal occasion for announcing her engagement to Dr. Rice R. Jackson and their upcoming wedding date of July 25.

Dr. Jackson was born in Mexia, Texas, on June 7, 1877, and he attended medical school in Pennsylvania at Jefferson Medical College in Philadelphia. He moved to Dallas after graduation and set up his practice in East Dallas, where he was a resident of the Lakewood neighborhood throughout his life. He practiced medicine for forty years, until shortly before he died at age seventy-three on December 7, 1950.

The Jacksons returned from their wedding trip to his East Dallas home in the 3700 block of Swiss Avenue. After her marriage to Dr. Jackson, Annie became active in organizations in support of her husband's medical career, and she continued her participation in art and civic organizations. Annie was a director of the Dallas Art Association, president of the Dallas County Medical Society Auxiliary, and, in her own words, a "constant worker for Community Chest." She was also an active member of the Marianne Scruggs Garden Club and a devoted gardener. Her grandson Walt Jackson recalls his childhood walks with her along paths through her Gaston Avenue garden, which he describes as "somewhere between a jungle and a botanical garden." She knew the names of every plant in the garden and pointed them out enthusiastically to him and his sister Julie. Walt recalls that she would encourage him to pick flowers, exclaiming, "There's one that wants to be picked!"

More than anything else, Annie was a devoted mother of four tall, handsome, and much beloved sons, "all mine own," she wrote in 1939 when she filled out a biographical survey form for the reference library of the *Dallas Morning News*. It was on the line specified for "Business, profession, or occupation" that she wrote in a beautiful cursive hand "Raising four boys." The Jackson's first son, Henry Allen, was born in November 1913. Next was Rice Robinson, Jr., who was born in March 1915. And then on June 22, 1919, Annie gave birth to twin boys, Gordon Dealey and Gilbert Stuart Jackson. The four sons, none of whom ever worked at Belo Corp., ultimately played a part in the modernizing of Belo as beneficiaries of the G. B. Dealey Trust.

Annie was remembered with fondness by her nephew James M. (Jimmy) Moroney, Jr. In interviews he recalled that she was a pleasure to be around because she had a lively personality and enjoyed children. Jimmy said that after G. B. Dealey's death in 1946, when he and his three cousins first went to work at the *Dallas Morning News* after World War II, Annie regularly brought bouquets of flowers from her garden to the newspaper offices and placed them on the table below the Douglas Chandor portrait of her father. He said that whenever he noticed flowers on the table, he thought to himself, "Annie's been here!"

Other company executives from the 1950s recall that Annie's visits were not always so warmly considered, noting particularly that her brother Ted, who had succeeded their father as president, viewed her visits as an intrusion on the business operations. Former Belo vice president and director William C. Smellage, who worked for Belo from the early 1950s, recalls that when Annie would arrive at the office unannounced, she and her brother Ted could become quite combative. In Bill Smellage's accounts, Annie was a good match for her brother, both in the bluntness of her language and in her willfulness. Although no formal evidence exists of friction between the two, stories of it abound, including reports of shouting matches over stock dividend issues and her not having a say in the company's governance. Another story claims that because of their sibling friction, Ted refused to allow Annie's son Gordon to work at the company following his graduation from the University of Texas in 1941. When the young Gordon showed up at the newspaper to protest being excluded from employment alongside his cousins, his clashes with his uncle only increased Ted's resolve.

Another story, which was not recorded except in oral history interviews many years later, holds that a rift occurred in the close-knit family when Annie's physician husband borrowed money from his father-in-law, G. B. Dealey, for some purpose, and did not repay it. G. B. was known for his generosity and willingness to help all those who came to him, family members and employees alike. And it is known that Annie and Dr. Jackson divorced, but none of her grandchildren knows the story of the family's relationship with G. B. Dealey or Ted Dealey.

The Dealey's second daughter and next-born child arrived on October 14, 1886. Like Annie, the young Fannie Dealey studied piano and participated in recitals throughout her childhood. Her name appeared frequently in the society columns during her youth, as she, too, traveled, attended parties, and participated in social and civic organizations. All who remember her recall her reserved, gracious, and dignified manner. Fannie, like Annie, attended Lasell College in Auburndale, Massachusetts, for her first two years, after which she attended the University of Texas at Austin. There she became a member of the Kappa Kappa Gamma sorority, in which she remained active throughout her life.

On April 12, 1911, Fannie married Dr. Henry Benjamin Decherd, who was a prominent eye, ear, nose, and throat physician. Dr. Decherd, who was exactly ten years older than Fannie, attended the University of Texas at Austin and, following that, the University of Texas Medical School at Galveston. He then completed graduate studies at Harvard Medical School and served briefly in the New York Eye and Ear Infirmary, before setting up a practice in Dallas in 1905. The Decherds' first child, daughter Ruth, was born April 28, 1912, and in June the baby was on hand to help her mother announce Annie's engagement at the afternoon party in the Decherds' new home. The news account of the engagement party described the decorations, the tea cakes, and the celebration, and it noted that the announcement was written on a card carried into the party in the tiny hand of the new baby. The Decherds' son, Henry Benjamin Decherd, Jr., was born three years later, on March 14, 1915, and he grew up close friends with the Jackson brothers, especially Rice Jr., who was born within a few days of Ben.

After her marriage, Fannie became active in the wives' auxiliary of the Dallas County Medical Society, and in addition to rearing her children, she was active in the Dallas Woman's Club and other service organizations. She and Dr. Decherd suffered a terrible loss in 1936, however, when their daughter Ruth contracted tuberculosis and died at age twenty-four. Records of Fannie's participation in civic life dwindle after that loss, when she appears to have retreated to a quiet life focused on her family.

The third daughter and fifth child of Olivia and G. B. Dealey, Maidie, was born on March 15, 1895. Maidie appears in family photos as a cherubic blonde child, and her son Jimmy Moroney, Jr., remembers her as a warm and joyful person, very attentive to her parents as well as to her own three children. She followed her sisters' path to Lasell College in Auburndale, Massachusetts, and then, following Fannie's lead, she attended the University of Texas at Austin, where she too became a member of Kappa Kappa Gamma. Maidie was sociable and outgoing, and like her two sisters was often mentioned in the society columns of the *Dallas Morning News*.

On April 10, 1917, Maidie married James M. Moroney, whose father, also named James, had emigrated as a child from County Clare, Ireland, and moved to Dallas in 1875 to open a hardware store with his brother and brother-in-law. At the time of his marriage to Maidie Dealey, young Jim was employed at the family business known as Moroney Hardware Company. It was located at the corner of Market and Pacific streets, not far from the Dallas Morning News Building on Commerce Street at Lamar.

The elder James Moroney was a prominent business and civic leader in Dallas, one of the organizers of the original American National Bank, and an early president of the State Fair of Texas. He was also one of the original stockholders of the *Dallas Morning News* when it began publication in 1885. A. H. Belo & Co. advertised for investors in Dallas, "with the idea of enlisting their aid and interest in the enterprise."[3] Among the seventy-three businessmen or companies that invested, in addition to James Moroney, were some of the more prominent of that early time in Dallas: J. S. Armstrong; S. H. Cockrell & Co.; Flippen, Adoue & Lobit; Royal A. Ferris; W. H. Gaston; Thomas Fields; Gano Brothers; E. M. Kahn; T. L. Marsalis; Murphy & Bolanz; Padgitt Brothers; W. H. Prather; and Sanger Brothers. In marrying Maidie Dealey, Jim Moroney moved quite naturally into a family role that eventually led to his joining Belo Corp.

Maidie, who was reared a Protestant, converted to Catholicism when she married, and she was an active member of Holy Trinity Catholic Church throughout her life. She and Jim had three children altogether, two daughters and one son. The first to arrive was Mary Elizabeth (Betty), who was born on February 11, 1918. Two years later, on March 29, 1920, daughter Jean was born; then, fourteen months later, James M. (Jimmy) Moroney, Jr., was born on July 10, 1921. In a photograph of eleven of the twelve grandchildren of Olivia and G. B. Dealey, Jimmy has taken his mother's place as the cherubic toddler among his older cousins.

Like her sister Annie, Maidie was a gardener and active in the Dallas

Garden Club as well as the Dallas Woman's Club. Maidie had many nicknames, according to Jimmy. He recalls that his grandfather called her Pud'n, and he and his sisters called her Muddy, a sort of child's combination of Mother and Maidie. She loved the outdoors and later owned two different farms near Dallas, on which she kept livestock.

She also showed her father's commitment to community service, working tirelessly for years in the Junior League of Dallas, serving as president and initiating numerous service projects. Maidie was the last of the Dealey children to be born, and ultimately she was the last to die, on August 25, 1971. Her death triggered the five-year countdown specified in G. B. Dealey's will, at the end of which the G. B. Dealey Trust would expire and the ownership of Belo would go from the trust to the beneficiaries.

G. B. Dealey's will specified that all of his company shares, 68 percent of the outstanding capital stock, would be held in a trust that would expire exactly five years after the death of his last surviving child. His will specified that his four surviving children and his one grandson, whose father had died, would receive only the dividend income from their portions of his stock. They were not to have ownership of the stock, which would be voted on their behalf by three trustees designated in the will. As it turned out, the G. B. Dealey Trust lasted until even the ten surviving grandchildren were nearing retirement age, without their having access to their inheritance.

While it is impossible to know specifically what G. B. Dealey had in mind when he and the other stockholders established the company's bylaws in 1926, or when he created the Trust in his will in 1936, it is easy to see the outcome. It meant that G. B. Dealey and his own children never had direct access to the wealth that was locked up in the company, and that ultimately G. B. himself managed to hold Belo Corp. together for thirty years after his death.

Only two of his five children benefited directly from ownership of the company, each having been given 8 percent of the shares at reorganization. And only those two benefited from the operations, in the form of salaries and bonuses paid to them as officers of the company. Those two were the boys, Walter and Ted.

The first-born of G. B. Dealey's sons, Walter Allen Dealey, arrived on September 11, 1890. He was a reserved child and a good student, and from an early age he was fascinated by inventions having to do with communications. Like his sisters, he went to college at the University of Texas, where he graduated with a Bachelor of Arts degree in 1912. He joined his father at the *Dallas Morning News* immediately upon his graduation and was married a year later, in April 1913. His bride was Willie Pearl Gardner, whose family was prominent in Palestine in East Texas. Their only child, Walter Allen Dealey, Jr., who was known as Al, was born on December 24, 1915.

Walter was an astute businessman from the beginning. He first worked in the business offices and right away showed an aptitude for finance and planning. When his father was named president by the Belo heirs in 1920, Walter was already familiar with the operations of the business, and he became his father's second in command.

When Walter learned of the invention called radio, he became fascinated with the possibilities for expanding the newspaper's reach and community service with the transmission of information over the airwaves. G. B. rebuffed Walter's first recommendations that the newspaper should start a radio station, reflecting the attitudes of most of his colleagues in the newspaper business nationwide. Undaunted in his interest, though, Walter volunteered his efforts to the Dallas Police and Fire Department, where his friend Henry Garrett was chief electrician. The two of them rigged up a system that enabled the city of Dallas to establish WRR Radio as a means of notifying the police and firemen when their services were needed. WRR was licensed on August 4, 1921, the first broadcasting station in Texas, and the first municipal broadcasting station in the world. The call letters were said to mean "Where Radio Radiates," although some joked that it meant "We Reach Rockwall."[4]

With that success, Walter was able to persuade his father that it was in the best interest of the *Dallas Morning News* to establish its own station, and WFAA went on the air on June 26, 1922. At the time, other newspapers around the country were refusing even to print the schedules for radio, fearing that the new medium would put them out of business. At the *News*, however, the new medium was embraced, although it wasn't expected to be a money-making enterprise. It was promoted instead as a public service of the newspaper, and the early programming consisted of live readings of stories from the newspaper and other sources, and live performances of music.

Early on, a scheduled pianist failed to show, and one of the newspaper's writers reluctantly admitted that he could play piano. The writer's name was Victor Schoffelmayer, and he was well known to readers of the newspaper as the expert on farming and agriculture issues, which were of great interest to the general public in those days. Schoffelmayer didn't want his readers to know that it was he playing the piano, so he requested a pseudonym, which he heard for the first time as he was introduced for his premiere on the air: ". . . the announcer introduced him as 'Count Rubinoffsky, a refugee from near death at the hands of the Bolsheviks,' and he was described as tall, dark and bearded with long black hair."[5]

Of course, the real pianist, who was in fact a German immigrant, looked nothing like that, and "he was so convulsed at the introduction he sputtered, which sounded a good bit like Russian." The station, which was an immediate hit with those few who had radios, used the call letters WFAA, and it was identified as "A Radio Service of the *Dallas Morning News*." The call letters were said to stand for "Working for All Alike."

The few surviving veterans of those early radio days, who were interviewed in the 1980s for an oral history project, told amusing tales of improvising both the technical aspects of the operation and the content of programs; of staffers writing dialogue and rehearsing in the halls seconds before going live with a performance; and of careers launched when latent talents in engineering or performance were discovered within the newspaper ranks. Those who remembered Walter praised him as a man of vision and persistence—a man with a passion for his calling as a newspaperman that extended to what he saw as the future of communications.

When the radio station was launched, the Belo descendants still owned the company, and until that point Helen Ponder Belo and her children had continued to live in Dallas for parts of every year. However, in 1922 they permanently moved east. Then, after the sale of the *Galveston Daily News* to W. L. Moody, Jr., in 1923, the A. H. Belo & Co. executives who had remained in Galveston moved to Dallas. One of those was John F. Lubben, whose family was invited by Helen Ponder Belo to live in the Belo home on Ross Avenue until the Lubbens could find a suitable home of their own. The Lubbens used the home for a few months, but for the most part, it remained unoccupied most of the time until 1926, when the Belo family agreed to sell A. H. Belo & Co. to G. B. Dealey and his partners.[6]

The legacy of A. H. Belo the man continued to live in people's hearts, though. In 1928, Adolph Ochs, speaking at a luncheon in his honor hosted by *Houston Chronicle* publisher Jesse H. Jones at the Rice Hotel in

Houston, said that when he bought the *New York Times* in 1895, he was determined to keep its columns as free of the "vulgar, the inane, and the sensational" as was humanly possible. Standing next to G. B. Dealey, who was seated with him at the head table, Ochs was reported to have put his hand on G. B.'s shoulder and said: "I received my ideas and ideals for a clean, honest, high-class newspaper from the late Col. A. H. Belo, once publisher of the *Galveston Daily News*. In New York I put into effect those ideas and ideals; therefore the record of the *New York Times*."[7]

Meanwhile, Walter's many business successes with radio and other aspects of the Belo operations were offset by persistent personal failures, which according to his son included years of marital conflicts, the result of an intractable addiction to alcohol. In a 1986 interview, Al Dealey, Jr., said this of his father: "My father, unfortunately, lived in the era before Alcoholics Anonymous, and he was an alcoholic. It gave us a lot of heartache and ultimately cost him his life." In a letter written and delivered to his father on January 20, 1934, just ten days before he was found dead in his home, Walter wrote this:

> Dear Papa:
>
> I have been sticking around waiting for Mr. Lubben to complete his annual statement, in order to help you out with your annual report—but I find today that you have given that job to Donosky, so I am cleaning up and pulling out.
>
> The other day when I told you I was awfully sorry, I didn't mean that I was sorry for myself. I am determined not to be sorry for myself. I tried to tell you that I was very sorry that after so many years I had failed you. You have been awfully good to me, Pops, and while I leave under a cloud and with a feeling of shame, I leave too with the determination to make something of myself and a desire to repay you, somehow, some day, for the many kindnesses you have shown me. I'm a bashful sort, and may sometimes seem unappreciative, but really I'm not and I sure wish I could have delivered—for you. God bless you.[8]

Walter attached letters of resignation as an executive of A. H. Belo Corporation and as a director of the company, both dated January 20, 1934, and they were read into the minutes of the January 26 meetings. The letter to the board read thus: "Gentlemen: My doctor has suggested that I take a complete rest for some months. Consequently, I offer my resignation as Vice-President of A. H. Belo Corporation effective Jan. 26, 1934."

At the same meeting at which Walter's resignation was accepted by the directors, they elected G. B.'s son-in-law James M. Moroney to the Belo board, filling the vacancy. Less than a month later, on February 17, 1934, Jim was invited to join the executive management ranks at the company, taking Walter's place in the supervision of the broadcasting operations, as well as in the financial management.

Jim Moroney was well-prepared for his new role at Belo. His family had already sold Moroney Hardware Co., where he had acquired extensive business experience, and he had established his own investment firm. Marking his anniversary of employment twelve years later, his father-in-law, G. B. Dealey, wrote a note telling him that his joining the company was "a memorable day for the *News* because there came into our organization on that day a gentleman whom we all love and who has proved himself to be a valued, trustworthy and competent person. . . ."

When Walter resigned from Belo, he had completed twenty-one years and seven months with the company. He died four days after the board meeting at which his resignation was read, on January 30, 1934. The news stories of his death at age forty-three attributed it to a heart attack, but the timing and the circumstances seem to suggest that his alcoholism got the best of him. In a brief biographical sketch of his brother, which Ted wrote thirty years later, he said, "My older brother, Walter Dealey, was one of the ablest newspaper men I have ever known in the business sense of the word. . . . Walter Dealey would undoubtedly have become president and probably publisher of the paper in due time except for the fact that he had family problems."[9]

Ted went on to explain how the family problems were the cause of his brother's alcoholism, an explanation that might be typical of one who had his own problems with alcohol and looked for excuses. Walter's son Al came to understand that the "family problems" were the result of his father's alcoholism, and not the other way around. However, the stigma attached to such failings was intense and long-lived.

When Walter died, his unique legacy of business accomplishments was memorialized in several news accounts and obituaries, as well as in Sam Acheson's 1938 book *35,000 Days in Texas* and subsequent histories of the beginnings of radio. But Walter had almost destroyed his financial legacy by the time he died. Upon his death in 1934, Walter held only fifty and one-half of his original eighty-six shares, and he owed A. H. Belo Corporation $29,400, which debt he had contracted to repay by relinquishing a specified number of his shares back to the company in two parcels, one in 1935 and the other in 1936, at a pre-established value. That contract was left unfulfilled when he died.

Walter's decisions regarding his shares in the company over the years affected his son's future profoundly, and not just in terms of money. Years later Al Dealey revealed that he was never entirely comfortable working alongside his three cousins, Ben Decherd, Joe Dealey, and Jimmy Moroney, at the *Dallas Morning News* after World War II, because of a sense of shame he felt for how his father had disappointed everyone. Ultimately, his sense of shame created a lifelong insecurity that took him through multiple marriages and caused him to retreat from at least three promising careers.

Al was a student at the University of Texas when his father died, and he was drawn into a difficult, even humiliating, role when his maternal grandfather, B. H. Gardner, a former judge, wrote the officers, directors, and stockholders of A. H. Belo Corporation on behalf of his daughter Willie Pearl and grandson Al. Judge Gardner was a state legislator at the time, and he protested to the Belo executives that his son-in-law's indebtedness to the company should be forgiven and, further, the proceeds of a company-paid business insurance policy on Walter's life should be given to his daughter and grandson. The letter was curt and included a threat of legislative action that would require Belo's compliance with his demands.

The Belo board, on advice of their attorney, Eugene P. Locke, voted unanimously to ignore the demands, determining that there were neither legal nor moral grounds for the claims against the company. Their decision was communicated to Judge Gardner in a letter. However, young Al suffered the personal indignity of being called, along with his mother, to meet with his grandfather G. B. Dealey, who at the request of his board told them that the company was not in a position to agree to the demands made by Judge Gardner. G. B. reported back to the board that Willie Pearl and Al "positively asserted that neither would ever consent to any action involving the Corporation in a law-suit."[10]

However, subsequent to her meeting with G. B., Willie Pearl Gardner Dealey, whom Ted described as "puritanical," counter-proposed to the shareholders and directors that her husband's contract with the company to repay his indebtedness be rescinded, and instead his indebtedness be discharged by a lesser number of his shares revalued upward after including the proceeds of his life insurance policy in the calculations of the company's worth. The directors voted to accept the compromise. However, the minutes reflect the tone of their discussion, as well as their recognition of the real source of the demand:

> President [G. B.] Dealey stated that he wished it put in the record that he and the other directors (who unanimously concurred) agreed to the demands of Judge B. H. Gardner, as representative of Mrs. Walter A. Dealey, and son, W. A. Dealey, Jr., in this affair, not because we considered the demand and settlement concluded as equitable or fair, but rather because it was deemed expedient so to do, and for once and for all end the dispute.[11]

Throughout these difficult days, Walter's younger brother Ted was in attendance at all meetings as a shareholder and company director, as well as an employee of A. H. Belo Corporation. He was the fourth-born child and second son of Olivia and G. B. Dealey, and he had dutifully accepted his father's call to join him in the company. At the time of Walter's death, Ted was pursuing his own dreams to oversee the editorial side of the business, in partnership with his brother, who was to oversee the business side.

Edward Musgrove (Ted) Dealey was born on October 5, 1892, and he lived until November 26, 1969. He was born seven years after the family moved to Dallas, while they were living in a two-story brick home on Thomas Avenue, near Fairmount Street. The family remained there until after Maidie was born, and then the Dealeys built a large home on Maple between McKinney and Cedar Springs, where the Crescent Court development now stands. They moved into the new home in August 1901, a few months after company owner Alfred H. Belo died.

After Belo died, G. B. was elected a director of the company and his responsibilities grew, which meant that he had even less time to spend with his children. And Ted was a rambunctious child. Here is a description of his early school days written by Frank H. King, longtime Associated Press staffer, taken from the introduction to Ted's 1966 book, *Diaper Days of Dallas*. The quotation marks King used indicate that the words are taken from Ted's own writings in the book.

> After Ted Dealey was "kicked out" of the McKinney Avenue School (now the William B. Travis School) by the principal, he was taken on sufferance at the Cumberland Hill School for a year. Then, with other "more or less renegades and outcasts who had been suspended or expelled" from other schools, he was accepted at Terrill Prep School by a disciplinarian who turned unruly roughs into model students.[12]

The schoolmaster, M. B. Terrill, diagnosed Ted's problem as being "just a little too smart." His cure was to double the amount of work he required of Ted, and to use harsh physical punishment when necessary, as he did with the other boys. Ted wrote of his school days at the Terrill School for Boys:

> I have seen him back a pupil against the blackboard and deliver rights and lefts to him until his head was bouncing off the blackboard like a punching bag. . . . In this way Mr. Terrill sacrificed his own popularity to the advantage of youngsters who might otherwise have gradually grown into juvenile delinquents.[13]

Apparently, the extra work and threat of brutal discipline had a salutary effect on Ted. He was the top-ranked student for three years at Terrill School and graduated in 1910. From there he went to the University of Texas, where he finished a bachelor's degree in three years and played left end on the Longhorn football teams of 1911 and 1912. After graduation from Texas, Ted went to Harvard for graduate work, on his father's recommendation, and in only one year finished a master's degree in philosophy.

His father had intended that Ted pursue studies in business, but Ted later wrote that he found the business courses uninteresting and switched right away to the study of philosophy. Following completion of his master's degree, Ted remained at Harvard and continued to follow his own interests, beginning work on a doctoral degree in philosophy. That course of study was cut short, however, when his father called him home to begin working at the company.

Ted's character as a young man is revealed in an anecdote he later recorded about his days as a graduate student at Harvard. His father was in Boston to pay a visit to Mrs. Belo and her daughter, Jeannette Belo Peabody, with whom she lived. Mrs. Belo still owned the company at the time. Ted accompanied his father to the Peabody home, and when the butler answered the door, the modest and dignified G. B. mistook him for Peabody, extended his hand, and introduced himself. Ted quickly corrected him and later blackmailed his father into buying him a new automobile that he coveted, in exchange for a pledge not to tell anyone back in Dallas what a hayseed his father was in confusing the butler for Professor Peabody. Ultimately, he betrayed that pledge to his father by recounting the details as an amusing story in his own writings.

The job his father arranged for Ted at the *News* was secretary to the publisher, Cesar Lombardi, who was Mrs. Belo's brother-in-law. According to a lengthy news story of Ted's life published in the *News* without attribution on his death, Ted stayed in that lowly position only briefly before moving to the newsroom as a reporter.

> He was by instinct a reporter. In the next 10 years, his bylines appeared above the stories on some of the most important events in that decade of Texas history. As a staff writer, he wrote many of the stories when the *News* was carrying on a fight, often dangerous and now historic, against the Ku Klux Klan in Texas.[14]

In his own unpublished writings, Ted revealed that his effectiveness in exposing the Klan was enhanced by his having been "in the 'big middle' of all the scraps—from 1920 to 1924. . . . In short, I was present at the birth of the Klan in Texas and I was a happy pallbearer at its demise."[15] He attended one of the first organizational meetings held at the Southland Hotel in Dallas at the invitation of a close personal friend, who like him was in his twenties and "not yet completely dry behind the ears." He described the experience:

> It was all very impressive and solemn. Most of us in the room were practically hypnotized by [Bertram G.] Christie's forceful eloquence. Then came the administering of the Klan oath which we all intoned like a bunch of sheep—except for one man whom I did not know nor ever will be able to identify. But for that man I will have an undying admiration for the rest of my life. He had guts! He stood up in the meeting and said: "As an American citizen, I cannot subscribe to such an oath. . . . So, if you gentlemen will excuse me, I'm leaving!"[16]

Ted never officially resigned from the Klan, even though he was quickly disenchanted. He later explained, "I was a newspaper reporter and in that capacity wanted to know all that I could find out about the inner workings of the Klan." He traveled as a political reporter throughout the state during those years, and by infiltrating the Klan meetings he was able to document activities of the Klan that were not otherwise known to the public. In addition to writing news stories that helped discredit the Klan, in 1922 Ted also secretly wrote a passionate campaign speech for the anti-Klan candidate for U.S. senator, the impeached Governor Jim Ferguson, who delivered it almost verbatim.[17] Unfortunately, the speech didn't prevent the Klan candidate, Earl B. Mayfield, from winning that election; however, Ted and the *News* stayed the course until the 1924 Texas gubernatorial election, when the anti-Klan candidate, Ferguson's wife, Miriam "Ma" Ferguson, defeated Klan candidate Felix Robertson.

Ted never told his father that he had written a campaign speech for Governor Ferguson while covering him as a reporter. He surely knew that his father would have considered it a breach of journalistic ethics. In his later writings he admitted that he never told his father of taking the Klan oath, either. He wrote, "You can be darned sure I never told him. If I had, he would have literally scalped me!"

By the time Ted was traveling the state reporting on Klan activities, he was already married and had children. Soon after returning to Dallas from Harvard, on March 3, 1916, Ted had married Clara MacDonald, the daughter of a wealthy and prominent mining executive in the West. They had met when Clara was a student at Lasell College, where Ted's sisters had been students. Their first child, Edward Musgrove Dealey, Jr., was born on January 6, 1917. Two and a half years later, Joseph MacDonald Dealey was born, on July 18, 1919. When the boys were only four and two years old, little Edward was outside playing unsupervised at the family's home when somehow a fire was started and went out of control. Little Edward was badly burned and died soon thereafter. In 1924, their third and last child was born, a baby girl they named Clara Patricia Dealey.

Also in 1924, in his role as writer and editor at the *News*, Ted established a Sunday literary magazine in which he published the early writings of J. Frank Dobie and Walter Prescott Webb. He soon became Sunday editor of the newspaper and joined the editorial page staff of writers. When his father bought A. H. Belo & Co. in 1926, Ted was elected a director of the new company and continued his writing and editing. In 1928, he was named assistant to the publisher, his father, and in 1932 he was named vice president, but he continued his association with the news department.

Following Walter's death in 1934, Ted was compelled by circumstances to follow in his father's footsteps in the business management of Belo, although by all accounts he protested all the way. In his writings, Ted revealed that he pleaded with his father not to make him move to the business side of the company. When his father would not relent, Ted went to his mother for support but was not successful. He left the editorial department and moved into the executive suite in 1934. Thereafter, his strong personality, quirky judgment, and iron will affected the company and everyone involved with it well beyond his own life.

In a 1992 interview, Stanley Marcus, the legendary Dallas retail merchant who knew Ted well, both professionally and personally, said this of him: "Ted was pushed into a role that he actually didn't want and fought and finally succumbed to and never did particularly well at it." Marcus then added, "Ted and I had a mutual fondness for each other, but we disagreed pretty much about everything." The paradox implicit in that statement is a quick portrait of the complicated man who headed the company from the time of G. B. Dealey's death in 1946 until 1964, when he reluctantly agreed to relinquish control to his successors. However, he continued to call himself publisher until his own death in 1969.

Another Dallas businessman and community leader at the time, John Stemmons, recalls Ted in a similarly ambiguous context. Stemmons's father had worked closely with G. B. Dealey in his efforts to defeat the Ku Klux Klan, to create a city plan for Dallas, and to build levees for the Trinity to eliminate the annual flooding. Stemmons recalled that "Ted didn't feel the obligation to the community that Mr. [G. B.] Dealey did. He felt like his job was more or less a reporter's job and that he didn't want to get involved, and he chewed on Joe [Dealey] somewhat when Joe took on [leadership of] the United Way." Stemmons said that Ted made it clear throughout his tenure at Belo that he had no interest in the running of the business or in the company's public service activities.

Thus, moving from the newsroom into the management office suite was simply a physical relocation for Ted. His heart and his energy remained focused on the news and editorial side of the business throughout his life. When G. B. Dealey decided to hand over the reins of active management to Ted, naming him president in 1940, it was a significant turning point for the company. However, even then, Ted took little interest in the business operations, continuing his writing and active participation in the editorial board discussions and decision-making.

It was also in 1940 that A. H. Belo Corporation was sued in U.S. federal court by the Wage and Hour Division of the United States Department of Labor for violating the Fair Labor Standards Act. G. B. Dealey had spent his entire lifetime personally tending to the welfare of the *Dallas Morning News* and its employees—including private, no-interest loans, as well as quiet gifts of cash in times of need. However, the company had not put in place the Fair Labor Standards Act's requirement of a forty-cent minimum wage and forty-hour workweek, with time-and-a-half pay for overtime. Its reasoning was very straightforward: its own policies at the time were more generous and provided more flexibility for employees than those proposed by the Department of Labor. Belo countersued, and the federal court ruled in Belo's favor. In his oral opinion, the presiding judge stated:

> The two suits spark from a clash in systems. . . . One deals only in dollars and cents. The other with happiness of employer and employees. . . . Neither system is fixed by statute. . . . I find the following facts: That there has been no violation of the wage and hour statute by the A. H. Belo Corporation.[18]

The Department of Labor filed an appeal, and the U.S. Circuit Court of Appeals upheld the earlier decision. But that was not the end of it. The Department of Labor took the case to the Supreme Court, and on June 13, 1942, G. B. Dealey's so-called "Belo Plan" finally won the day. The U.S. Supreme Court upheld the original findings of the first trial. The publicity generated nationally for the Belo Plan was overwhelmingly positive, both for G. B. Dealey and for A. H. Belo Corporation. It must have been a career-capping triumph for G. B., proving as it did that fairness wins in the end.

Having come up through the ranks, and with no formal education, G. B. Dealey had always identified with and maintained a keen interest in the welfare of his employees. In 1919, while he was still general manager of the company, working for the Belo heirs who owned the paper, he convinced them that it was in the best interest of the company to provide a paid-up employee insurance program. At a banquet for all employees announcing the new program, he said: "This is the dawn of a new day in the relations between the owners of this concern and those who are making it successful . . . and it is the beginning of some other things that we are going to do."[19]

The "other things" that G. B. announced at the banquet were a retirement program, an employee welfare fund, and annual bonuses for all employees at Christmastime. He also created an employee library for use during breaks, and a cafeteria, to which all ranks retreated for coffee twice a day. Although those benefits later came to be standard practices in most large U.S. companies, they were uncommon at the time, and they were taken into account in the Supreme Court's 1942 ruling in favor of the Belo Plan over the Department of Labor's objections. Ultimately, many other newspaper companies adopted the Belo Plan for use with their employees.

Many years later, speaking of the contrasts between G. B. and Ted, retired executive Bill Smellage recalled that when he first began working at Belo as controller in the early 1950s, Ted indulged the first two or three of his detailed monthly financial reports. Soon thereafter, Ted interrupted Bill as he delivered one of his reports, saying, "Bill, I want to ask you one question. Were the took-ins more than the took-outs?" When Bill told him they were, Ted said, "That's all I ever want to know about the financial affairs of this company from here on out." Bill Smellage delighted in retelling that story every spring at the Belo Corp. annual meetings, until he was asked to desist sometime in the 1990s.

Ted was not interested in the income of A. H. Belo Corporation, beyond knowing that the bills were paid. He was not interested in growing the company. Smellage recalled that Ted "didn't care about the corporate structure or the financial affairs of the business. He was not interested in radio or television. He was a newspaperman." Furthermore, "he didn't like hiring and firing people; he didn't like insurance, the taxes, the plant." Explaining Ted's approach to running the business, Bill added, "He was not a person to expand and broaden the company beyond the realm of workmanship that he could control. I heard him say many times that 'I don't know that we need to get any bigger.'" Ted was an outdoorsman and didn't much like the office environment, so over time he spent less and less time on the job, but he did not relinquish any of his authority and control. He was firm about having his staff carry out his wishes.

In his own financial affairs, as in the company's, Ted had little interest in money, so long as he had enough to live as he pleased. However, his salary and modest dividends were not enough to fund the life he enjoyed. Like his brother Walter, Ted sold many of his own original shares of Belo stock back to the treasury over the years, and he borrowed additional money from the company, both formally and informally, all his life. Another quality that Ted shared with Walter was a drinking problem, of which there are many stories among company lore. One of the more temperate stories was told by a dinner guest at the Dealey home while Joe was still a boy. One evening, as the whole family dined together, the guest accidentally tipped over his wine glass, spilling wine on the formal white-linen tablecloth. Joe spoke up and said, "Oh, that's all right! Daddy does that all the time."

Ted's private interests ranged widely from international travel to big-game hunting, fishing all over the world, and collecting art, particularly Western art and paintings by Dallas painter Reveau Bassett, Annie's friend, who painted game birds and animals in their natural habitats. Ted always wrote about his travels and insisted on having the articles published, which made his travel expenses tax-deductible. However, his stories were usually long, detailed criticisms of the food, the people, and the places he visited, rather than alluring descriptions, as one might find in the travel section of the newspaper.

In a 1986 interview, Tom and Jean Simmons, retired executive editor and travel editor, respectively, who knew Ted well, said that Ted wanted his stories to be run as they were. When in frustration the Simmonses sought advice from the executive editor at the time, Jack B. Krueger, who later was elected a director of Belo, Jack recommended that Ted's accounts be run as news reports, rather than as travel features, to avoid alienating diplomats from those countries or the travel agents who advertised in the travel section. Jack himself edited those stories, removing crude remarks and libelous comments, and he stood up to Ted when he protested. One of the stories opened, "Port Moresby, Territory of Papua, New Guinea, Feb. 26—From the viewpoint of the average tourist, Port Moresby is a dump!" Ted went on to comment, "But the very lousiness of the place makes it rather interesting."[20]

When G. B. died in 1946, resolutions were adopted by countless civic and charitable enterprises that G. B. had founded or furthered in his long career as a champion of civic improvement and responsible citizenship.

One such resolution, passed by the board of directors of a charitable organization he had helped found called Family Services, said that G. B. Dealey was "recognized, loved and acclaimed as the very fountainhead of the blended spirit of sympathy, resourcefulness, resolution and hope. . . ."[21]

Ted basked in the afterglow, and he then recommended that his mother be made chairman of the board, rather than assuming the title himself. Bill Smellage explained that giving Mrs. Dealey that title enabled Ted to put her on the payroll, so that she would continue to have G. B.'s income. Bill recommended discontinuing the setup when he began auditing the company's books around 1950. He told Ted that the Internal Revenue Service might not agree with Ted's thinking on the matter.

Very soon after G. B.'s death, the company lost another key figure in its organization, when Eugene P. Locke died suddenly. The learned and much-loved attorney had been G. B.'s close advisor through the 1926 reorganization of Belo, and his close friend thereafter. Without the restraint of G. B.'s oversight, and without the institutional guidance of Eugene Locke, Ted wasted no time in remolding the *Dallas Morning News* in his own image, even with his mother as chairman. As Tom Simmons pointed out in recalling those days, Ted's nature was completely opposite that of his father, and "there were some aberrations." During the next fifteen years the aberrations and paradoxes of Ted's personality and style profoundly changed his father's newspaper, even though the ownership and stability of Belo was maintained intact with the company's bylaws and the terms of G. B. Dealey's will.

But as in Stanley Marcus's assessment of Ted, most people in the company who knew him expressed affection for him, even while describing him as "different." Felix McKnight, the managing editor of the *News* who went on to become executive editor of the *Dallas Times Herald*, described Ted fondly in a 1992 interview:

> He was big, physically, and sort of lovingly gruff. Very, very knowledgeable. Brilliant educational background. He was a classic writer and a good guy. He was everybody's friend and the first one there for anyone who needed help.[22]

Jack Krueger, executive editor and a director of Belo Corp., said later, "Ted was a very good friend to the news department."[23] He explained that Ted always took the side of the news department over any objections that might come from advertisers because, unlike G. B., Ted ran the paper from the news side, rather than from the business side. Sol Katz, another director and vice president over circulation, commented that Ted was very friendly and down to earth. "And you could get right down with him, and you could talk business with him, and he would listen to you and come up with a decision. . . . He was a great guy—he was different—he wouldn't mince words, but he was great."[24]

Executive vice president and director Richard D. Blum described Ted as a very loyal man. "When we had problems in the labor relations area, Ted would listen to the problems, he would listen to recommended solutions, and he would say 'Okay, do it.' And he would stay with it, regardless of whether or not strikes could result. They didn't, but they could have, and he stayed right with it."[25]

Ted himself eloquently expressed his passion for the newspaper, if not the business, in his first annual report to the directors following G. B. Dealey's death:

> Whatever it takes to produce an outstanding editorial product we must be prepared to pay. For no newspaper, nor any business of any character for that matter, can afford to rest on its laurels. Not to advance is to stagnate. Not to grow better is to grow worse.[26]

But those rousing words were delivered right after he had admonished the board, all but one of whom were company executives, to cut expenses everywhere else: "All unnecessary expense must be done away with. Rigid economy must be practiced in all departments."

G. B. Dealey's hallmark qualities of self-restraint and self-sacrifice were not duplicated in his two sons. Walter, the natural businessman, was stricken with an uncontrollable addiction to alcohol, wasted his equity in the company as he battled his demons, and ultimately was consumed by them. And Ted, completely uninterested in the business operations of the company, paid more attention to his personal interests and cashed out a large part of his own equity to fund a lifestyle that must have been baffling to his father.

Fortunately, G. B. lived long enough to know his grandchildren, the offspring of his daughters as well as of his sons. It must have been satisfying to him as he wrote his will to create a plan that would ensure A. H. Belo Corporation's viability for his grandchildren and great-grandchildren. Tying up his interest in the company in a long-term trust may have inconvenienced his four surviving children and even the grandchildren, but it also stabilized both the company and the family dynamics, both of which had been rocked time and again over the years by Ted's public and private actions.

However, long before the succeeding generations had access to their inheritance, they had to contend with Ted's ironfisted and capricious style. Just as difficult, they had to figure out how to remake the company in spite of him. At the recommendation of WFAA Radio general manager Martin Campbell, Belo launched a frequency-modulated, or FM, station on October 5, 1946, the first one in the Dallas/Fort Worth market and only the second FM station in Texas. The new station was named KERA, and within a few months it had a new antenna on top of the Mercantile Building, which gave the station 1,000 watts of power.

The directors had voted several years earlier to pursue the FM station, rather than to take a chance on the other new medium, television, about which no one in the company had knowledge. A choice had to be made between them because of the substantial investment required; however, because of the focus on establishing the FM radio station, Belo missed out on acquiring the first Dallas television license when the licenses were made available soon thereafter. Executives realized right away the significance of that missed opportunity, and they began trying to rectify the situation. However, they had other pressing matters to contend with as they set about applying for a television license.

Even before World War II, the directors had begun to focus on another problem endemic to the institution. Employees were permitted to stay on the job, like G. B. Dealey, as long as they wished. Like G. B., there were numerous workers past sixty-five; indeed, there were many workers, both men and women, who were older than seventy-five. In late 1942, the directors decided to establish an endowed pension plan, which they hoped would encourage the older workers to retire voluntarily. No one in management wanted to make retirement mandatory, especially considering the advanced ages of the senior executives and directors, but they knew the issue was affecting work productivity.

The G. B. Dealey Retirement Pension Plan was formally adopted on December 31, 1943, but by then the military draft, along with voluntary enlistments, had begun to affect the headcount of younger employees. Little, if anything, was done to encourage retirement, because the older workers were then needed on the job. However, when the war ended and the veterans returned to work, the company was hard pressed to accommodate everyone with desks, not to mention with paychecks.

All of those who had left to serve in the war were guaranteed a job upon their return, and all of those who had been hired in their absence, including many women, were kept on the job, in all fairness to them. At the end of 1946, there were 630 employees at the *News* and 135 at the radio station. Less than a year later, the *News* had ninety more employees on its payroll, a 12-percent increase, as the returning vets resumed work. Those and many other challenges created dramatic change during the next few lean years.

Chapter 3

THE GRANDSONS RETURN FROM WAR

1946–1955

In his president's report for the year 1946, which Ted Dealey delivered to the board of directors on February 12, 1947, he announced the return to the *News* of Ben Decherd, Al Dealey, Joe Dealey, and Jimmy Moroney, following their service in World War II: "Upon this quartette of junior executives great responsibility will be placed within the near future. They are destined to become the future operators of the business after the older generation has retired or passed to its reward."[1]

Everyone at the *News* and WFAA Radio knew these four first cousins and referred to them as "the boys." All four of them had worked at the newspaper or radio station during the summers before graduating from high school, and two of them had begun full-time employment at the company before World War II. Following the war, all four of them returned from the armed services about the same time and were given one cramped office to share and one secretary for the four of them. Helen Roter had been G. B. Dealey's secretary, and following his death in February 1946, she was reassigned to assist in the boys' transition into their full-time careers at Belo. The newspaper and the corporation, which were essentially indistinguishable from each other at the time, were still in their original Dallas location on the northwest corner of Commerce and Lamar streets.

Space was tight in the old building, after more than sixty years and countless expansions and remodeling projects, including the outright collapse of the first building. To accommodate the incoming junior executives, four desks were moved into what had been Ted Dealey's office before his recent move to his father's vacated office. Plans already were underway to build a new headquarters a few blocks away, but meanwhile, the boys officed together in what Ted named the "JAB Room," using the initials of the first names of Joe, Al, and Ben, who were the first to arrive. When Jimmy arrived soon thereafter, the spelling was revised to the "JJAB Room."

At first the two boys who had worked full-time before their military service simply resumed their former roles. Ben Decherd was already recognized for his organizational skills, and he resumed his work in company administration. Al Dealey resumed his work in accounting and finance. The other two, a few years younger, were regarded more as apprentices and were assigned tasks to complete throughout the operation, so that they could learn about various aspects of the business. Gradually, all four found niches where they were most inspired and began to establish themselves.

The boys had been encouraged by their families to come into the company, and all of them seemed eager to accept the opportunities offered them. However, it is unlikely that the young men fully understood just how much was expected of them by their recently deceased grandfather. Three of them, who were interviewed in the 1980s, recalled their grandfather as a kindly, loving, even saintly figure, but someone who was fairly remote to their daily lives. However, C. B. Dealey's unwavering vision for the future of his beloved company clearly anticipated important roles for his grandchildren. The nature and clarity of his vision for Belo's future are integral to the careful way he structured the company in 1926 to begin with, and later to the terms of his Last Will and Testament, which he signed on December 17, 1936, more than ten years before he died.

Two of G. B.'s most trusted employees—Leven T. Deputy, mechanical superintendent, and Myer M. Donosky, assistant secretary, both of whom later became directors of Belo—witnessed his signing of his will that day. The will was written less than three years after Walter's death, and several years before G. B. promoted Ted into the top management position of the company. The terms of the will followed the dictates of a contract signed by all eight holders of the company's Class A common stock on July 29, 1926, two weeks after ownership of Belo had been transferred from the heirs of A. H. Belo to G. B. Dealey, John Lubben, and six others.

In the minutes of the 1926 meeting at which the contract was signed, the purpose of the contract was specified to be "for the stabilization of the control of the corporation." At the same meeting, the eight stockholders and directors also passed a resolution to incorporate the terms of their contract into the bylaws governing the company. The original bylaws adopted on July 15 were amended with bylaw 25 to make the terms of the stockholder contract part of the corporate governance. Bylaw 25 was said to be an expression of trust in the "sense of justice" shared by the original stockholders, and it guaranteed that their collective judgment would prevail in the future, as well.

The stockholder contract and bylaw 25 specified that no shares of Class A common stock of A. H. Belo Corporation could be sold, given, or bequeathed to anyone without the owner having first offered it for sale back to the corporation or to the other holders of Class A common stock. It further allowed for six of the eight directors, with approval of the holders of three-fourths of the Class A common stock, to buy out any stockholder they deemed it necessary to exclude. Those terms automatically guaranteed G. B.'s participation in any such decisions with his 68 percent of the shares, and they protected his company from unwise decisions by any individual stockholder, including his two sons.

The key stipulation of bylaw 25 was that all stockholders were required to pass their stock on to their heirs by means of a trust, with the voting rights given to the trust, rather than to the direct beneficiaries, for at least twenty-one years following the death of the stockholder, unless the stockholder's will specified a longer period. It further declared, ". . . this by-law shall not be amended or repealed, save by the unanimous consent of all holders of Class A common stock of the corporation and all persons owning the equitable title of or beneficial interest in any of such stock."[2]

When G. B. Dealey established the trust in his will to hold all of his shares of Class A common stock in A. H. Belo Corporation, he designated three trustees who were to manage the trust estate, and five beneficiaries, who were to receive twice yearly payments distributing the net income. He further specified the percentage each was to receive of the income: for his surviving children, Annie, Fannie, Ted, and Maidie, all of whom had two or more children at the time, he specified 15/64ths each; and for his grandson Walter Allen Dealey, Jr., who was the only child of the late Walter Dealey, he specified 4/64ths.

As trustees, G. B. designated three men: Ted Dealey, Jim Moroney, and George Waverley Briggs, his longtime friend, banker, and advisor, who was one of the original stockholders. The terms of the trust gave the trustees power to take action only if they obtained the consent of the beneficiaries of half of the shares, and it required that in making any decision their "sole test" would be that they "shall deem the transaction expedient for the purpose of preserving and promoting the business of A. H. Belo Corporation, of stabilizing its management and gradually or ultimately realizing for the beneficiaries of the trust the proper value of the said Class A common stock possessed by the trust estate."[3]

Further clarifying his wishes, G. B. Dealey specified, "The trustees shall keep intact the said shares of Class A common stock of A. H. Belo Corporation, and shall not sell any part thereof unless and until they sell the whole thereof." Later in the document he added, "The trust shall continue so long as either my wife, Olivia Dealey, my daughter Annie Dealey Jackson, my daughter Fannie Dealey Decherd, my son, Edward M. Dealey, or my daughter Maidie Dealey Moroney is living, and for five years after the death of the last to survive of the said five mentioned persons." In those words, G. B. Dealey ensured that his grandchildren, or great-grandchildren, would inherit the company intact.

G. B. Dealey had twelve grandchildren to survive to adulthood: eight grandsons and four granddaughters. Four of the grandsons worked in the company, but the other eight grandchildren did not. Like their parents, none of the grandchildren could access the wealth from their inheritance beyond the income distributions paid twice annually on their fractions of the shares in trust. While Belo was a profitable company, its business plan had always called for substantial reinvestment of income in the betterment of the plant and equipment, so the net income was never substantial, which meant that dividends were usually fairly modest.

There is no doubt that G. B. anticipated that the restrictions put into the 1926 contract and bylaw 25 would be crucial in maintaining the stability of the company over time. His will followed the tenets of bylaw 25 precisely, as had all other distributions of stock owned by other shareholders. As years passed, the beneficiaries of the trust paid more and more attention to the terms and effects of bylaw 25. They knew that if the contract and bylaw 25 were still in effect when the G. B. Dealey Trust expired, they too would be subject to the same restrictions and requirements established in 1926. The matter was discussed off and on, and yet no action was taken because there was never unanimous agreement that dissolving the restrictions would serve the company and the beneficiaries equally well.

Meanwhile, when "the boys" returned from World War II to follow in the footsteps of Ted Dealey and Jim Moroney, the third most influential executive and shareholder was not a Dealey family member. His name was Joe Lubben, and he was as much a part of the *News* family as anyone else at Belo at the time. Joe Lubben was the son of John F. Lubben, who had been one of G. B. Dealey's partners in buying the company from the Belo heirs.

John Lubben owned nearly as many shares of the original A. H. Belo & Co. as G. B. Dealey did in 1926, when all of the outstanding shares were called in to accommodate their purchase of the company from the Belo family. Over the succeeding years, the elder Lubben was one of G. B. Dealey's closest allies in the management of the company following the 1926 reorganization. He was a substantial shareholder, senior executive, and director of Belo. Joe Lubben followed in his father's footsteps and brought along a personal loyalty and love for Belo easily matching that of the descendants of G. B. Dealey.

Joe joined the company in Dallas in 1928 as a reporter, fresh from the University of Texas at Austin. Although his father was a lifelong friend and close associate of G. B. Dealey, Joe was closer in age to the Dealey grandchildren, being just eight years older than the eldest of them. Joe's career with Belo had begun in Galveston, where he was born and grew up working part-time at the Galveston sister newspaper. His father was an officer of A. H. Belo & Co., where he had worked alongside G. B. Dealey throughout their careers. When the Galveston paper was sold in 1923, the corporate officers moved from Galveston to Dallas. The Lubbens moved their family to Dallas at that time in order for both father and son to continue their employment with the company. Ultimately, between the two of them, John Lubben and Joe Lubben completed 101 years of service to Belo.

Joe's career with Belo included nearly every job in the company, from delivering newspapers to reporting and editing, and on to executive vice president and general manager. He was elected to the board of directors in 1948 and served for twenty-eight years. But his passion for reporting never waned, even after he left the news side for the business side. In an interview in 1986, Joe reminisced fondly about his early days at the *News*, chuckling often and fighting back the tears: "In those days, bootleggers were all over the place, and they were fighting each other. And if we didn't have a bootlegger killed every night, well, I had a pretty poor day on the police run."

Joe was a charming individual with a quick wit and a passion for life in general. His good humor, ready smile, and hearty laughter set the tone for the camaraderie that existed in those days after World War II when the grandsons came back into the company. When they arrived, Joe was ready to make them feel at home and to serve as their guide. Indeed, Joe Lubben's brand of good cheer was so distinctive that over the years a term was invented to describe it. After an evening of socializing with Joe and his wife Rene, one was said to have been "Lubbenized."

The eldest of the four incoming junior executives was Henry Benjamin Decherd, Jr. He was born in Dallas on March 14, 1915, to Fannie Dealey Decherd and Dr. Henry B. Decherd. Ben's career with the newspaper began with part-time summer work during his school days. He attended public school in Dallas and participated in the schoolboy journalism of North Dallas High School as editor-in-chief of the school's bimonthly newsletter. He was a prolific letter writer all of his life, including childhood notes to friends and family from summer camp and during visits with his grandparents in their summer cottage in Arkansas. He composed long, imaginative, and humorous letters to his cousins Henry Allen Jackson and Rice R. Jackson, Jr., with whom he was close as they grew up. His letters turned his daily experiences into entertaining stories, and he concocted pet names for his recipients.

Later on, during his service in the war, Ben often wrote to his family and friends, including Hugh W. Ferguson, Jr., whom he alternately addressed as "My dear Froggie," or "Dear Little Frog Legs." Once, when responding to something in a letter from Ferguson, Ben opened with "My Dear Misguided Friend." Ben's names for himself as signer of the letters were equally varied and colorful, including "Bengie the Bee," when his duties were keeping him intensely busy, to "Hank the Yank," when writing from London.

Ben was slender and handsome, and he had an original mind, which he used to its fullest, not only in his studies, but in everything he undertook. He was deeply engaged by life and a high achiever in all of his endeavors. He consistently ranked at the top of his high school class, and he was a leader in the North Dallas High School ROTC, achieving the rank of cadet colonel. From high school he went to the University of

Texas, where he excelled in his studies, with a major in government, and he was elected to the scholarly fraternity Phi Beta Kappa.

Ben was accepted at the Harvard Graduate School of Business, where he hoped to continue his studies, but his grandfather, G. B. Dealey, had other plans for him. G. B. had closely followed Ben's career through school with great interest, and he recognized Ben's exceptional abilities. The Great Depression had taken its toll on the company, and G. B. had a heart-to-heart talk with Ben, asking him to forego further studies and to come into the company, where he was greatly needed.

Ben joined the full-time staff of the *Dallas Morning News* on September 29, 1936, shortly after his graduation. At the company, he was first a reporter for both the *News* and Belo's afternoon newspaper at the time, the *Dallas Journal*. His editors soon noted that his writing abilities were exceptional, but Ben was not one to be easily satisfied with himself. He soon decided to try his hand at another newspaper, where he was not part of the family. He spent a year as a trainee at the *Baltimore Sun*, where he was able to achieve similar feedback on his abilities. Following that experience, he returned to the *News* and joined the advertising department staff to broaden his experience.

On December 17, 1938, he married Isabelle Lee Thomason of El Paso, Texas, whom he had met as a student at the University of Texas, where she had been highly regarded both as a student and as a campus beauty. She was from a prominent family in El Paso, and her father, Robert Ewing Thomason, was a U.S. congressman and good friend of House Speaker Sam Rayburn. He later served as a federal judge for the Western District of Texas. Ben and Isabelle married in El Paso, then returned to Dallas to make their home. Ben's mother, Fannie Dealey Decherd, whose daughter Ruth had died only two years earlier, saw to it that Isabelle was introduced to other young women of her own age among the families with whom the Decherds were friends.

After the United States entered World War II in December 1941, following the Japanese attack on Pearl Harbor, Ben joined the U.S. Army as a second lieutenant on February 7, 1942. He was soon appointed aide-de-camp to General Walter B. Krueger, whom he served for twenty-seven months, earning four battle stars and the Bronze Star. He was promoted to captain, then to lieutenant colonel, and later he was named chief of the liaison branch of the War Department's Bureau of Public Information.

When he was reassigned to the War Department, Ben put his wit and his writing skills to work composing an entertaining how-to manual for his two successors, who were to serve General Krueger. In it he gave detailed, step-by-step instructions on how to do the job, infusing each entry with his characteristic good humor. The manual is forty-three typed pages, and on the cover page, after the title, "Beans, Bullets and—Mail," he describes the contents: "Being a fireside chat on how to be an Aide-de-Camp with the minimum wear and tear on the Boss, the Chief of Staff, the Army Staff, and yourself, including a few household hints on how not to harass the troops. . . ."[4]

At the end of the section labeled "Utilities," after explaining the requirements of keeping the general happy when the power goes out, he adds, "These moments are extremely tense and always take a few weeks or months off your normal span of life. Also, these moments contribute materially to the loss of hair or to the graying of that which is left." At one point, he offers an aside: "Incidentally, aides are never supposed to sleep anyway." General Krueger and Ben maintained a warm personal relationship until the general's death in 1967, regularly exchanging letters and family visits.

Ben's experiences serving one of the army's most important generals during wartime were good training for his upcoming role as aide-de-camp, or as it was termed, "assistant to the president," his uncle, Ted Dealey. That was the role he was assigned shortly after returning to the *News* on January 1, 1946, just before G. B. Dealey died at age eighty-six in February.

Ben and Isabelle had been married for eight years before their first child was born on January 10, 1947. The couple was delighted with their baby daughter and named her Dealey in recognition of Ben's family heritage. Dealey's maternal grandfather, Ewing Thomason, proudly handed out cigars in the House of Representatives in Washington, D.C., in honor of his granddaughter's birth. Four years later, the Decherds welcomed the arrival of a son, Robert William Decherd, who was born on April 9, 1951.

Ben took great delight in his children and was actively involved in their upbringing. The quality of life in the Decherd home is evident in a warm, newsy letter to his former boss and regular correspondent, General Krueger, dated March 29, 1952. Ben wrote of his five-year-old daughter and one-year-old son, "We are enjoying these two children immensely and do not regret one moment that we devote to their entertainment, training and happiness."[5] In the same letter he tells of a garden planted with his daughter, Dealey, in which they are growing onions, tomatoes, radishes, carrots, Kentucky Wonder beans, chives, and lettuce.

Ben was a personable, good-humored man with a gift for administration, which enabled him to move immediately into substantive work at the company when he returned after the war. Being the eldest of the four boys, and the first to join the company, he was also the first to take on some of the more significant management challenges following his grandfather's death. Of particular interest to him was the enhancement of the G. B. Dealey Retirement Pension Plan, which would enable older workers to better afford retirement. He had been on hand when discussions of the plan were initiated, and he took up the challenge as soon as he returned to work to help ease the overcrowding as soldiers returned to their jobs.

The next of the boys to join the *News* staff was Ben's first cousin Walter Allen Dealey, Jr. Al arrived on June 30, 1937, with a fresh Bachelor of Business Administration degree from the University of Texas. He was a smart, hardworking young man who had been a member of the National Honor Society at North Dallas High School and achieved Eagle Scout rank in Boy Scout Troop #73 in Dallas. After his father died during Al's sophomore year at Texas, Al worked full-time and attended classes full-time because his inheritance of stock in the company was not accessible.

Upon joining the *News*, Al was assigned duties in the accounting department as bookkeeper, when all such records were still kept by hand. Not as polished or as conventionally handsome as Ben, Al was, however, methodical and focused, and the accounting work suited his temperament well. In 1939, he married a young woman from his mother's hometown of Palestine, Texas, but the union soon ended in divorce. Maintaining his job at the *News*, Al enlisted in the Texas Defense Guard, in which he was serving as an officer when the United States entered World War II. In November 1941, he resigned from his commission in order to enlist as a private in the U.S. Marine Corps Reserve, and he was sent for basic training to San Diego, California. Making a good showing at boot camp, Al was subsequently sent to officer training school in Quantico, Virginia. Following his training, he was assigned to duties on the Quantico Base, where he was serving when he married for the second time.

Al's bride was Mary Alice Cockrell, a lovely and lively young woman, whose family was among the first and most important in early Dallas history. Mary Alice, who became better known as Mackie, had also graduated from the University of Texas, and she attended graduate school at Texas Woman's University. At the time of her marriage she was interning in nutrition studies at Johns Hopkins Hospital in Baltimore, Maryland. Their wedding on March 2, 1943, was held in the Marine base chapel at Quantico, and the ceremony was low-key, with the bride's sister and brother-in-law the only attendants. Al and Mackie continued to live in Virginia, where Al's posting kept him until later in the war, but as the war in the Pacific grew more heated, Al was sent overseas, where he took part in the Okinawa campaign. He returned to the United States on December 31, 1945, and was released to inactive duty as a captain. He later retired from the Marine Reserve as a major.

Coming back to the *News* after the war, Al joined Ben for his apprenticeship in the company that they were to inherit along with their other cousins. Ted confided in him that since Al had lost his father and Ted had lost his first son, he would regard Al as his own son, alongside Joe. Ted promised to provide him all the advantages of the other three "boys." And even beyond that commitment from the president of the company, Al was a naturally talented financial manager, as his father had been. He soon made his mark in the business operations of Belo, and in the spirit of his grandfather, G. B. Dealey, Al became deeply involved in local community-service efforts as well.

The third of the four boys to come into the company was Ted's son, Joseph MacDonald Dealey. Joe first joined the *News*'s full-time staff as a sports reporter in January 1942. He had recently graduated from the University of Texas with a bachelor's degree in English and minors in history and economics, which he selected as preparation for a newspaper career. On May 4, 1942, Joe didn't show up for a baseball game he was assigned to cover. When he arrived at the newspaper later, his editor proceeded to chew him out for missing an assignment. When Joe was able to respond, he explained that he had been issued a draft summons, and at game time he was being sworn into the U.S. Army Air Corps.

Joe was born in Dallas on July 18, 1919, to Ted and Clara MacDonald Dealey. He grew up knowing he would be a newspaperman, and like his father he loved to write: "I never knew anything else. I just never had any other desire to do anything else."[6] Joe was a quiet, introspective young man, very fond of reading. For more than ten years, as he was growing up, Joe's mother took him and his sister, Patsy, to spend the summers with their MacDonald grandmother in California. During many of those same years, his cousins Ben Decherd and Jimmy Moroney went with their own mothers to spend summers with their Dealey grandmother at the Dealeys' two summer cottages in Winslow, Arkansas.

Joe worked as a part-timer in the mailroom of the *Dallas Journal* in 1937, before he graduated from Highland Park High School. Following high school, he continued the family tradition by going to the University of Texas at Austin. Then, in 1940, while Joe was a student at Texas, a momentous shift occurred at Belo. His now legendary grandfather promoted his father to president of the *Dallas Morning News*, which also meant that Ted became president of A. H. Belo Corporation, as the office applied automatically to both institutions at the time.

Ted had served under his father for twenty-five years by that time, and no one other than G. B. Dealey had ever headed up the Dallas newspaper. Although G. B. would continue to keep a close eye on things by not relinquishing his role as chairman of the Belo board, it was a time of great anticipation for Joe as he completed his studies, knowing that his father was expecting much of him.

Immediately following his graduation from the University of Texas in 1941, Joe spent a few months at the Southwest School of Printing, where he learned the mechanical side of the newspaper business. Then, as an officer in the Army Air Corps, Joe was a dashing figure, serving four years in aircraft maintenance. Following his officer training, he was stationed at first in Dallas at Love Field, and then served in occupied Germany and France. He was discharged from the service in May 1946 with the rank of captain. He returned to the *Dallas Morning News* in September of that year, where he joined Joe Lubben and his cousins Ben Decherd and Al Dealey.

Joe's first job upon his return from active duty was reporting on business news, which he enjoyed because it enabled him to get to know the city and the business environment, where many of his friends had begun to establish themselves. However, the view of most editors and newspaper managers at the time was that reporting on business was not wise for a newspaper. Joe recalled that business news "really wasn't considered all that important in those days. Out in the strict news department, they pretty much took the view that we were prostituting the news columns and giving companies free publicity." In spite of that, he stayed with the business news department as a reporter for the next several years, learning his way around and developing relationships that would stay with him forever.

On January 18, 1947, Joe married Doris Carolyn Russell of Dallas, and their wedding sparked a great many parties in their honor, many of which were reported in the society pages of the *News*. Their first child was born on December 1 of that same year, when they welcomed a son whom they named Joseph MacDonald Dealey, Jr. Three years later a second son was born, Russell Edward; the two boys were joined by a sister, Pamela Carolyn, in 1953, and another, Frances Patricia, in 1956.

Joe was a dignified and formal young man who was universally liked by employees, townspeople, and ultimately civic leaders and newspaper executives nationwide. He always spoke with modesty and equanimity, and he chose his words carefully. But it wasn't easy being the president's son. Even late in life, he spoke with circumspection, as though trying to avoid making any statement with which his father might have taken exception. His private papers are full of notes and memos from his father in which Ted criticized Joe's activities and pursuits and the decisions he made.

The intense father/son relationship also affected those around the pair, who later told of heated arguments in raised voices. Joe said in a 1986 interview, "I've often told people that my father was less of a father and more like a brother to me than you might expect. We got along well together. We had our arguments, and sometimes they were pretty spirited arguments, and maybe they served some purpose. But they were never wrenching or so severe as to cause a disruption." Those spirited arguments, however, gave Joe a lifelong aversion to any form of confrontation, which did not always serve the company's best interests.

A few months after Joe joined the staff of business news, the quartet of cousins was complete when James McQueen Moroney, Jr., joined the company's full-time staff in late 1946. Jimmy's father, who was second in command after Ted, gave Jimmy the task of reading the various trade publications looking for items that would be of interest or beneficial for the senior executives. So Jimmy set himself up at a desk in the JJAB room, along with his cousins, and started reading. Years later he said, "Well, that got a little bit dull after about three days." So he went to the newsroom and found assistant managing editor Felix McKnight and said to him, "Felix, if I am going to stay in this business, I've got to learn something about it, and I want to go to work up here in the news department."[7]

Of course there was no question about his staying in "this business." Like his cousins in the shared office, he had been nudged along throughout his life toward the ultimate moment of entering the family business. So, Felix McKnight put him to work at the city desk across from city editor Jack Krueger, a stern taskmaster who treated him like anyone else. Jimmy started in the lowest staff position in the newsroom, but that didn't bother him as he answered phones, took obituaries, and dealt with whatever came in—if he didn't know how to handle a matter, he got it to someone who did. And, like his cousins, he seemed to have a natural aptitude and a genuine enthusiasm for the business.

Jimmy was born in Dallas on July 10, 1921, to G. B. Dealey's youngest child, Maidie, and her husband, James M. Moroney. He was their third child, the baby of the family behind two sisters, Mary Elizabeth, always known as Betty, and Jean. His family lived in Highland Park, and he attended public schools there before going away to St. John's Military Academy in Delafield, Wisconsin. During childhood summers, he spent time in Winslow, Arkansas, at his grandfather's cabins, where he played with his cousins who might be there at the same time. He recalls G. B. spending four or five weeks in Arkansas in the hottest part of the summer, getting the newspapers delivered to him daily, so that he could keep an eye on everything.

In high school and during his college years, Jimmy worked during the summers to earn a little spending money. He worked in circulation, helping distribute newspapers around the city at four in the morning, and at other times he worked in the broadcast side of the business, arriving at the Santa Fe Building penthouse studios of WFAA Radio in time to activate the switchboard and turn on equipment for the 7 a.m. program start. Jimmy was affable and outgoing, and he enjoyed interesting work.

He arrived at the University of Texas a year or two behind his cousin Joe, but they sometimes shared books and studied together, getting to know each other better than when they were growing up. In 1943, Jimmy graduated with a bachelor's degree in business administration, in preparation for his career at Belo. But rather than going back to Dallas immediately, he enlisted in the U.S. Navy and served aboard the cruiser *Quincy*, which saw action in both the Atlantic and Pacific theaters during the war. Rising from ensign to lieutenant (jg), Jimmy was onboard when the *Quincy* was the first ship to be fired upon in the Normandy D-Day landings. And later, he was onboard in January 1945, when the *Quincy* provided transportation and temporary headquarters for President Franklin

D. Roosevelt for the Yalta Conference with Winston Churchill and Joseph Stalin.

Following active duty, Jimmy returned to Dallas for a few months of rest before joining the company to begin his lifework. That Christmas, in December 1945, his mother, Maidie, hosted a large gathering of the family, with G. B. and Olivia reigning over their large brood. Maidie proposed that her father put aside his normal teetotaler stance, which he had assumed in 1934 when Walter died, in special recognition of the safe return of all eight of his grandsons from World War II. He replied, "I think I will," so she prepared him a tall glass of eggnog laced generously with bourbon whiskey. Jimmy recalls that he had never seen his grandfather take a drink before that evening, but nevertheless, "he turned it right up and drank the thing down." Not only was G. B. grateful that his grandsons were all home safely, he was clearly happy to have a good reason to celebrate with a little whiskey.

Jimmy spent nearly two years on the city desk, eventually taking the education beat and doing general reporting. Following that firsthand experience in the newsroom, he moved to the advertising department, where he gained valuable experience selling ads for the newspaper and helping make up the pages in the composing room. His father gently guided his progress, recommending areas where he felt Jimmy would benefit from the knowledge gained, as well as from the relationships he would build. Jimmy then spent time in the circulation department, in-house this time rather than distributing papers in the middle of the night. And he followed that with work in the promotion department, assisting in efforts to increase readership, circulation, and advertising sales.

Almost exactly two months after the Christmas homecoming celebration for his returning soldier grandsons, G. B. Dealey died at his home on February 26, 1946. His last words were recorded as "Don't worry . . . everything's . . . going to be all right. . . ."[8] He left confident that his beloved A. H. Belo Corporation would ultimately pass intact to his four remarkable grandsons, and he had already put in motion much of the work that would be accomplished in the next several years. The project on which he had spent most of his efforts during the last few years of his life was the planning of a new home for Belo and the *Dallas Morning News*.

By the late 1930s, G. B. Dealey knew that his rapidly growing newspaper needed more space for operations than was possible at the original site on Commerce Street between Lamar and Austin streets. He introduced the topic to his company officers in a memo dated March 23, 1937, and he began to investigate locations and architects. To make his decision about where to relocate the *Dallas Morning News*, he went back to the Kessler Plan of 1910.

It was G. B. who had urged the city's leadership to bring George E. Kessler to Dallas in the first place, and Kessler's City Plan for Dallas had been integral to Dallas's development since its adoption by the city. The Kessler Plan called for a grand Union Station on Houston Street, facing a one-block landscaped park, and it specified that the park should be surrounded with "monumental" buildings on the other three sides of the park.

By the time G. B. was planning a new home for Belo and the *News*, Union Station was a lively rail center, and Ferris Plaza was a green oasis with a glorious multicolor lighted fountain in the center. A hotel occupied the property north of the Plaza, and other businesses lined up along the eastern edge. However, the property on the south side of the Plaza was undeveloped. It was owned by the Frisco Railway System, and it was contiguous to active rail lines, which G. B. knew would be beneficial to the newspaper operation. But then World War II intervened, and the newspaper was in no position to consider spending on a new building, so the project was put aside for a time.

When it was clear that the war would soon be over, G. B. Dealey sought to acquire the property he had identified earlier. He wrote a letter to the president of the Frisco Railway, dated October 14, 1944, in which he told him:

> We have been looking around for a site for a couple of years and finally decided that the one that we want more than any other is the one that is owned by you. It would be ideal for our purposes, and if we secure it we would put up a building which would add very much to the beauty of the entrance to Dallas through the Union Station and the little park in front.

He continued:

> George E. Kessler, in 1910, when he made the city plan for Dallas,

> had the idea of making that a beauty spot, with the little park in front of the station and with monumental buildings on the other three sides. So if we get your property, we would put up a building that would be in keeping with his thoughts and one that would be a valuable addition to that end of the town.[9]

His plea was successful, and when the property was secured, G. B. turned to architect George L. Dahl, who had formed his own firm in 1943. Before that, Dahl had been a partner of LaRoche and Dahl, which had been Belo's architect since 1898, through nine contracts to remodel and expand the original 1885 building. Dahl's charge from G. B. was to create a building for the future of the *Dallas Morning News*, for fifty to 100 years out, and to make it "monumental." In his instructions regarding placement of the building on the site, G. B. told him, "Put it back far enough so we can have a front yard and landscape it with grass, shrubbery, and trees, and put up two flagpoles. Let's add to the beauty of the plaza in front of us, and in no way detract from it."[10]

Dahl was by that time a well-known architect with a national clientele. He had designed several other monumental buildings in downtown Dallas, including the Titche-Goettinger Building and the Neiman Marcus Building. He had designed twenty-four buildings for the University of Texas at Austin. And, perhaps most important of all, he had been the chief architect of the 1936 Texas Centennial Exposition, supervising the entire design and construction of Fair Park, one mile east of downtown Dallas.

Over the next year, Dahl prepared designs for the building with G. B. Dealey's guidance. However, before the plans were final, G. B. died, leaving it to his son Ted and son-in-law Jim to make the final decisions. Honoring G. B.'s vision, Ted and Jim completed the planning process with Dahl within another few months. Jimmy Moroney recalled in a 1986 interview, "almost the first day I was there, they were completing and approving the plans for this building that had been growing for some time."

A groundbreaking was held on October 17, 1946, with Ted and his very dignified eighty-three-year-old mother, Olivia Allen Dealey, wielding the shovels in a public ceremony. As preparations were underway and invited dignitaries began to gather near a tent erected for Mrs. Dealey and other officials, Ted spied a small earthmover on a nearby construction site and talked the crew into loaning it to him to use in his groundbreaking.

As the gathered civic leaders and company employees watched, Ted revved up the small bulldozer and drove it over the rough terrain from the project on which it was engaged to the site of the new building, nearly capsizing along the way. He finally arrived on the Young Street site for the newspaper's photographers to capture his stunt for posterity.

The cost of the building was more than any of the executives at the time could fathom, coming in at $6 million. The company was making very little money at the time, and they had to borrow much of the funding needed to build. The company's main banker, First National Bank in Dallas, was reluctant to lend so much money, as the country was rebuilding after the costly war. However, after further discussions among the Belo directors, financing was secured from a combination of sources, and the project proceeded. Southwestern Life Insurance Company provided two-thirds of the funds necessary; the First National Bank in Dallas and the Republic National Bank of Dallas provided the remaining one-third.

Borrowing money was a shocking experience for the Belo executives and directors, but there was essentially no alternative if the company were to keep up with the growing community and the newspaper's increased circulation. The newspaper had been forced to turn down advertising for more than a year because of its limited press capacity. And outside pressures mounted when the *Wall Street Journal* announced plans to launch publication in Dallas in the spring of 1948. The *News* already competed daily with the afternoon *Dallas Times Herald*, which historically had led the *News* in display ads and in circulation within the city of Dallas.

Following G. B.'s earliest admonitions to George Dahl, the building was designed to serve the company for fifty to 100 years. It included state-of-the-art soundproofing around the pressroom, as well as foundation supports to handle adding additional floors as they were needed in the future. The construction was arduous, including deep excavations for the basement under the pressroom where the newsprint rolls were moved into position for loading onto the presses. During the digging, the workers came upon an artesian spring, which filled the site with water before they could figure out a way to divert the flow.

The building was completed and dedicated two and a half years later, on May 13, 1949. It fulfilled G. B. Dealey's dream of making a significant, permanent contribution to the "beauty spot" of Kessler's imagination. In a story by Kenneth Foree that appeared in the paper on May 22, 1949, the first paragraph gives a hint of the pride the employees had in their new home: "Stand in Texas' handsomest lobby in the *News*' new stone palace, glance toward the rear and upward and there juts a second floor lobby that looks for all the world like a walnut bridge on a black marble ship."

The "walnut bridge on a black marble ship" overlooked a two-story, horseshoe-shaped lobby space with a 175-foot-long by seventeen-foot-high oil-paint mural created by Perry Nichols, one of Texas's foremost artists. The mural had been commissioned by Belo to depict its history in Texas, from 1842 on the barrier island where it was born, to the towering pine forests of East Texas where it helped establish the South's first newsprint production operation. It also depicted the WFAA Radio tower, signaling from its location miles from the studios in downtown Dallas, and the Texas farmers who benefited from the newspaper's focus on agriculture issues. The mural was painted on artist's canvas in strips about forty-eight inches wide by seventeen feet high, which the artist attached like wallpaper to the three long walls around the upper levels of the *News* building lobby.

The central image of the mural, which was directly above the front doors of the building, and directly across from "the bridge," depicted a giant, idealized nude figure of a man, along with symbols of Texas history and the six flags under which it had been governed. The depictions of Belo's history began on the far left, where the panel was dated 1842, and the narrative images continued toward the right, telling of the Galveston newspaper. The Dallas newspaper was chronicled beginning on the far right, starting with a panel dated 1885, and those images continued to the center moving right to left. It was a spectacle that drew many visitors over the twenty-two years it was in place in that original location.

Kenneth Foree's last paragraph in the story announcing the new build ing pays tribute to the man whose vision was made manifest that day:

> . . . the late, great George Bannerman Dealey who came to this country with his parents in 1870 as an immigrant boy of 11, who was with the *Galveston News* and the *Dallas News* for seventy-two years, who helped build Dallas and Texas, who was a kindly, simple, dignified, handsome and wonderfully wise little gentleman who appeared to have stepped out of a portrait, who planned the great new palace of the *News* and whose greatest regret as the fatal pains circled his heart was without doubt that he would not live to see this day and the palace of his dreams.[11]

Of course, G. B. would have blushed for that description of him to appear in his own newspaper, and he likely would have been uncomfortable with the description of the building as "the great new palace of the *News*." However, he would have been pleased that the legacy of his mentors, Willard Richardson and A. H. Belo, was memorialized on the front of the new building, even though the tribute isn't clear. The words chiseled in the stone of the three-story façade towering over the beautiful "front yard" are an edited version of G. B. Dealey's words spoken to the entire staff of the newspaper on October 1, 1906.

The occasion was the twenty-first birthday of the *Dallas Morning News*, and his words referred to his two great predecessors, Richardson and Belo. He said, "They built the *News* upon the rock of truth and righteousness, conducting it always along the lines of fairness and integrity, and acknowledging the right of the people to get from the newspaper both sides of every important question." For the façade of the new building, G. B.'s 1906 tribute to his predecessors was converted into a statement of the principles by which the company was to conduct its business:

> BUILD THE NEWS UPON
> THE ROCK OF TRUTH
> AND RIGHTEOUSNESS
> CONDUCT IT ALWAYS
> UPON THE LINES OF
> FAIRNESS AND INTEGRITY
> ACKNOWLEDGE THE RIGHT
> OF THE PEOPLE TO GET
> FROM THE NEWSPAPER
> BOTH SIDES OF EVERY
> IMPORTANT QUESTION
>
> *G. B. Dealey*

Moving the company to the new building was a monumental task, which required precise planning in advance. Company executives had watched closely as construction evolved over three years. The logistics of moving the operation to the new site had to be perfect, because one missed step could mean missing an edition of the newspaper. That was not an option. The planning was assigned to longtime mechanical supervisor Leven Deputy, who had managed the entire construction project. Deputy mapped out an elaborate staging plan that avoided missing a press run.

Tom Simmons recalled being on duty to put out the Sunday paper on March 19, 1949, the Saturday night that the move was accomplished:

> I was make-up editor at the time, and it was my job to be in the composing room to oversee the make-up of the pages. I remember the composing room was on the third floor of the western side of the building on Commerce Street. And a hole was knocked in the third floor wall, so that, one by one, as we finished with a big piece of machinery, such as a linotype machine, which would weigh a ton or more, it could be put on a hoist and lowered out and through the window down to the truck, which was waiting below to take it the five or six blocks over to the new building, where the process was reversed. And slowly, during the night, up to midnight, as we felt we could release the machine, why, it would be hauled off. By the time the paper had been put to bed at 2:00 a.m., the machinery was just about all gone, and we went over Sunday night to the new building—there it was—and we put out the Monday paper.[12]

The new presses had been acquired earlier and stored until the new pressroom was ready. By the time of the move, the new presses were already in full use, following a "divided effort between the old plant and the new," which had begun on November 17, 1948.[13] Jimmy Moroney recalled being on hand for the complex process and hearing typesetters comment that the lead was still hot when they sat down to their machines installed at their new location. When everything was in place, the company held a series of public events to welcome readers and advertisers to the new building. More than 5,000 visitors were given guided tours of the state-of-the-art facility.

The late forties and early fifties were a time of gradual but steady transition within A. H. Belo Corporation, as the grandsons found their places in the company and the older generation gained confidence in them. Sol Katz commented on those days: "Anybody who had any sense knew who they [the grandsons] were, but *they* didn't tell you. They just worked here really, just like we did. They showed up every day on time, did their work, went their way."[14]

The elder Jim Moroney supervised the management of the broadcast stations, as well as the business operations of the newspaper, and although he regarded the broadcast operations as merely an entertainment adjunct to the newspaper, rather than serious business, he had recommended that Jimmy spend some time there, in addition to his newspaper duties. So, unlike Ben, Al, and Joe, who focused entirely on the corporate management and the newspaper business, Jimmy also spent time in the broadcast side of the business, where his warm nature and outgoing personality made him a popular colleague.

With the company's early success in radio, executives had been tracking the changing technology of communications, and back in the late 1930s, they had experimented with something they called "facsimile radio." Specially designed radio transmitters were used to send edited versions of pages of the *Dallas Morning News* to homes equipped with a dedicated facsimile receiver. That receiver printed out large pages, about half the size of a standard newspaper page, with the edited stories. The experiment was great for showmanship at the State Fair of Texas, where the company demonstrated it, but it was a bust with the public, because the machines were bulky, expensive, and ultimately unnecessary so long as one could subscribe to the newspaper itself.

After that expensive failure, the head of the broadcast operations lost his credibility altogether when he touted the emergence of FM radio as more significant and more profitable than television. At his recommendation, Belo postponed applying for a television license while it ramped up its FM radio investments. In September 1947, Belo increased the power of its FM radio station, originally called KERA, to 14,000 watts, and simultaneously changed its call letters to WFAA-FM.

In December 1947, when Belo applied to the FCC for a television license, there were numerous competing bids for licenses already under consideration, and Belo was not awarded the first one in Dallas.

The first license awarded in Dallas was for station KRLD, and it was acquired by the *Times Herald*, but that station didn't go on the air right away. The first station on the air in Dallas was KBTV, which raced ahead, going on the air on September 17, 1949. However, the owner of that station, a Tyler, Texas, oilman by the name of Tom Potter, who also owned four radio stations in East Texas and Louisiana, had invested in the new technology without knowing much, if anything, about it. Within only a few months, the operation was costing him $1,000 a day more than it was making.

While Belo awaited word from the FCC on its application for a license, Potter inquired if the Belo executives might be interested in buying out his stake and taking over the license. Belo welcomed the chance, because it put them in the game that was already well underway in North Texas. By then, the *Times Herald*'s KRLD had signed on, and the first station on the air in Texas, Amon Carter's WBAP in Fort Worth, was serving the same market.

The negotiations with Tom Potter began in December 1949, and the Belo directors approved the purchase for $575,000 on December 31, 1949. The funds for the purchase came from the issuance of $600,000 in debenture bonds bearing 4¼ percent. On March 1, 1950, Belo closed the purchase of KBTV, which included the building on the corner of Harry Hines Boulevard and Wolfe Street and all of the equipment. Most of the employees stayed on, as well. The sale gave Potter an approximate profit of $100,000 over his investment.

Belo began operating the station on March 17, 1950, and changed the call letters to WFAA-TV on May 21, 1950. By then, WBAP-TV in Fort Worth, the first licensed station in Texas, had been on the air for more than a year, since September 1948. According to reports at the time, it was also losing money, but conditions quickly were turning in favor of television operators, as more and more people acquired sets and advertisers realized the great potential.

The first broadcast under Belo's ownership of KBTV signed on at 2:45 p.m., March 17, 1950, with live coverage of the company's annual Roundtable Dinner for WFAA and *Dallas Morning News* employees, which was underway at the Automobile Building at Fair Park. The broadcast featured a speech by Ted Dealey and entertainment by the performers from WFAA Radio. That event had traditionally been covered by WFAA Radio, and the management at the time saw little difference between the two forms of broadcast. Like the radio station before it, WFAA-TV was tagged "A Television Service of the *Dallas Morning News*." Continuing the focus on service to the community, WFAA-TV began regular news broadcasts at 6:00 p.m. and 10:00 p.m. in 1951.

Only a month before the company's first television broadcast, on February 13, 1950, Ted had said to the stockholders and directors, "It must frankly be admitted that in 1949 we were skating on thin ice." The company had been challenged to fund the new building for the *Dallas Morning News*, and moving its 900-employee operation had been complex and expensive. For the year 1949, Belo grossed $8,746,457, and in Ted's words, its "take home money was only $68,724," less than one percent of revenue.[15] One year later, however, the tone was completely different, when he remarked: "We were fortunate in getting into TV when we did. While it lost a lot of money in 1950, the trend of revenue is definitely and firmly upward. In other words, TV is our anchor to windward at the present time just as AM radio was in the Depression days of the early thirties."[16] Indeed, his pronouncement soon played itself out, when television profits increased 51 percent from 1953 to 1954, leaving everyone "slack-jawed."[17]

In 1950, Ben Decherd was already "assistant to the president," a position he held for many years, gradually taking on responsibility for the day-to-day administration of the company. Ben's duties and responsibilities were increased considerably when one of the key executives, treasurer Myer M. Donosky, "resigned to pursue other interests." Behind that standard euphemism was a conflict that everyone knew about but was powerless to resolve. Donosky had gotten crosswise with Ted when he stood up to him regarding what Donosky believed was a shortsighted and costly decision on an important newsprint purchase. Ted wrote about the flap years later, revealing his innate mean streak, but using the editorial plural, "We let him sweat it out for a month or so, after which time he resigned."[18]

Donosky went on to other accomplishments and maintained good relationships with most of his Belo colleagues over the years. When he left Belo, many of his responsibilities were given to Ben, including oversight of the G. B. Dealey Pension Fund, the company's retirement policies, and supervision of all the production departments. With the increased administrative authority, Ben set up the company's first personnel department and organized the company's first promotion department. Many of the areas Ben organized over the next few years were still in place largely unchanged thirty years later, when the company began its modernization and transformation to a public company.

Also in 1950, Joe was named assistant secretary and, like his father before him, he moved reluctantly from the newsroom to the executive suite. He maintained his relationships with the news and editorial departments, however, and in 1955 he was given the official role as liaison between those departments and the executives.

Jimmy was named assistant to the business manager, Joe Lubben, in 1950, which gave him continued association with the broadcast side of the business in a very important time, as well as increased involvement in the newspaper's business operations. By 1954, Jimmy was providing information on broadcast operations to the president for his annual reports.

In 1950, Al Dealey was making his mark in the company as assistant treasurer, and that year he was elected the "Outstanding Young Man of the Year" by the Dallas Junior Chamber of Commerce. He was serving on the executive boards of the Community Trust and several other service organizations, and he had become active in the Presbyterian Church. About that time Ted sent around a memo directed to the department heads, but he included the four boys in his request that everyone cut back on their community involvement, so that they could pay more attention to their respective jobs. Ted explained that he never was able to find any of them when he wanted to call a meeting, and that their allegiance was to the newspaper, not the community.

The memo from his uncle challenged Al's sense of duty and commitment to the service organizations in which he was involved, and it caused him to do some soul-searching. As Al recounted thirty-five years later, he was beset with conflicting emotions about Ted's request. By then he had already realized that he would not have the clout in terms of shares to rise to the top of the institution, although he had grown up expecting to spend his life at Belo. The personal satisfaction he found in community service was compelling. And then a solution to the dilemma presented itself to him while he was attending a Texas-Baylor football game in Waco. "When we were sitting at the football game that afternoon, I got up with the crowd, and I sat down with the crowd, but I don't suppose I yelled a lot because I was wrestling: What are you going to do? Well, the ultimate solution was that I was going to quit what I was doing, and I was going to re-educate myself in the ministry."[19]

By then the first of Al and Mackey's three sons had been born, and Al took a leave of absence from Belo in December 1950 to attend seminary in Austin, and to see if his call to the ministry was authentic. Joe recalled that "Al was at that time considered one of the best newspaper accountants in the business, and it was a real loss when he decided that he wanted to stick with the ministry."[20]

Al's son John, who was born while Al was still a junior executive at the company, remarked at Al's funeral service in 1999 that his father had had the longest leave of absence Belo had ever allowed one of its employees.

Al was ordained to the ministry at the Preston Hollow Presbyterian Church in March 1955. He later served at the Marble Collegiate Church in New York under Dr. Norman Vincent Peale, before returning to Dallas and forming the Churchill Way Presbyterian Church in 1956.

Al and Mackey eventually divorced, and Al's ministerial career devolved into pastoral counseling, after he returned to school for a master's degree in pastoral care from Andover-Newton Theological School. Al later married and divorced a third time before marrying a fourth time and being widowed when she died. When Al died in 1999, he left behind his fifth wife.

When it became clear that Al was not returning to the company, his financial responsibilities went back to Jim Moroney, Sr., and Jimmy was promoted to assistant treasurer. In 1954, Bill Smellage joined the company as controller after several years working at Peat, Marwick, Mitchell, which handled the company's audits. Bill took over the financial management of the company, and he worked closely with the three grandsons over the next ten years to put in place more modern business practices.

In 1952, as Jimmy was finding his place within the management ranks, he met a lovely young woman on the golf course at the Dallas Country Club and started up a conversation. He was surprised and delighted to learn that she had recently joined the cast of WFAA Radio's popular daily broadcast "The Early Birds," as a featured singer.

Born Helen Claire Wilhoit, she was a graduate of Northwestern University, and she had taken the stage name Lynn Hoyt as a professional singer. WFAA had hired her away from the Teddy Phillips Orchestra, where she had been a lead singer. She and Jimmy began to see each other often over the next year, so Jimmy was surprised again when she announced that she was leaving WFAA to return to singing with the orchestra. She told him that since he hadn't seemed all that interested in her, she had accepted a marriage proposal from the orchestra's leader, Teddy Phillips, and was moving to Washington, D.C.

Both Lynn Hoyt and Teddy Phillips were well-known popular entertainers, and a few weeks after she left WFAA the announcement of their engagement and impending wedding ran in the *Dallas Morning News*, where Jimmy's mother, Maidie, saw the notice. Jimmy recalls that his mother commented to him that she was disappointed that he had not liked Lynn well enough to pursue a more lasting relationship. That did it for him, and he immediately flew to Washington, where he persuaded Lynn to change her mind and marry him instead.

Lynn was born and grew up in Maryville, Tennessee, where her family still lived, but she was already well known in Dallas because of her celebrity status with WFAA Radio. Their wedding at the Holy Trinity Catholic Church in Dallas on March 2, 1954, delighted all of their friends and both sets of parents. They wasted no time in starting their family, with daughter Mary Molly Moroney born on January 3, 1955. Next came James M. Moroney III, who was born on September 4, 1956, followed by Melinda (Mindy) Moroney on October 25, 1957, and Michael Wilhoit Moroney on July 15, 1959.

In the late 1940s, after G. B. died, Ted moved to a downtown hotel for several years. Joe had just joined the company, and his sister, Patsy, was married and starting her own family. In explaining his move to the hotel to his colleagues and friends at the time, Ted said that his wife, Clara, was too critical of him, drank too much, and was unpleasant to live with. He soon divorced her and married Trudie Lewellen Kelley on June 29, 1951.

His new bride was eleven years younger than he, quite pretty, and she immediately took over his time. He liked to tell friends that he had found her selling umbrellas at Neiman Marcus, which was across the street from where he lived while separated from Clara. In fact, that was the truth, and Trudie clearly knew that she had landed a prize, wasting no time before persuading Ted to adopt her daughter, for whom he provided generously both during his lifetime and in his will. In a 1965 listing of beneficiaries of a trust Ted set up principally for his grandchildren, his adopted daughter and her three sons are shown with equal holdings to those of his grandchildren by Joe and Patsy.

According to several family friends, Joe and Patsy had great difficulty accepting their parents' divorce, and Clara lived only eighteen months beyond Ted's marriage to Trudie, dying on December 3, 1952, at age fifty-seven. When Ted brought Trudie into his social life, friends and family alike found her demanding and often unpleasant, but the couple thrived for eighteen years until Ted's death, enjoying round-the-world travels and other shared interests. Trudie survived until 1995, never managing to endear herself to her husband's family.

In 1952, grandsons Ben Decherd, Joe Dealey, and Jimmy Moroney were elected directors of the company. Their election was a matter of routine, and they had already attended meetings as guests for several years. Joe Lubben had been elected a director in 1948, and Maurice E. Purnell, who was a grandson of Eugene Locke and had taken his grandfather's place as the company's chief legal counsel, had been elected to the board in 1950.

The makeup of the board following the 1952 election comprised thirteen directors, counting Mrs. G. B. Dealey. Ten of the directors were employees, and the outside directors were George Waverley Briggs, a former employee and one of G. B.'s original partners in the company, and Maurice Purnell. Ted maintained strict control of the business decisions and the editorial positions, even with all of the new faces in the boardroom. In his report to directors for the year 1952, he ended by making this grand statement:

> The *News* is pulling as a team now more than it ever has. No longer is it a business alone. It has become by all standards an institution capable of wielding great power. We should work untiringly that this power will be dedicated in the final analysis to the people who we serve—that it never swallows us into the impotent darkness of conceit and self-satisfaction.[21]

In the early 1950s the country was in the midst of heightened Cold War rhetoric, and as early as 1948 Ted had announced to his board, "The struggle for world peace, the clash between Communism and Democracy and the fear of even greater inflation have been naturally reflected in our own operations, and it has been necessary for all departments to make further adjustments in this troubled postwar era."[22] The right-wing, anti-Communist John Birch Society, which had been founded by Robert Welch of Massachusetts, had developed a large contingency in Dallas, which supported the organization's Southwest regional headquarters office.

In those difficult days throughout the country, friends took sides against friends in the Communist paranoia that was ubiquitous. The *New York Times*'s senior executives were "very distracted and disturbed by the intrusive tactics of a Senate subcommittee that was investigating Communism in the press. . . . It was a strange, awkward, embarrassing time for the paper, one of suspicion and conflict, anger and compassion."[23]

In Dallas, the suspicions and conflicts were fueled by the *Dallas Morn-*

ing News itself. Exerting his will and promoting his own politics through the newspaper's editorials, Ted directed the *News* to provide editorial support for Sen. Joseph McCarthy in the senator's relentless search for Communists through the House Un-American Activities Committee. The *News* was one of the few daily newspapers in the country to support that campaign of intimidation and coercion, mainly of intellectuals, writers, and artists, but it spoke to a large constituency within its readership. Even the Democratic U.S. congressman-at-large from Dallas, Joe Pool, was openly supportive of the McCarthy hearings, reflecting the ultraconservative leanings of his constituents in Dallas.

Internally, those editorial positions took a toll on reporters and editors and their credibility as a reliable source of news. In his summary of the activities of 1954, managing editor Felix McKnight wrote, "Never had the integrity of the news department been so severely challenged. . . . It is a constant problem and the importance of honest, down-the-middle news editing is stressed. The public does not separate editorial opinion and straight news. Our job is to make our news exhibit foolproof."[24]

Waving his own anti-Communist banner in Dallas, Ted also waged a war of words against Southern Methodist University for employing professors and inviting to campus speakers whom Ted believed to have Communist leanings. He went so far as to accuse President Willis Tate of being a Communist, on the theory that if he allowed them on campus, he must be one of them.[25]

During the early 1950s, as Belo struggled to pay off the debt incurred in building the new Young Street headquarters and took on the responsibility for operating a television station, dividends were affected and the executives were hard pressed to maintain G. B. Dealey's characteristic level of community philanthropy. While community involvement was not among Ted's priorities, the other officers and directors prevailed in 1952 to set aside a small fund as an endowment for a private non-profit foundation to be called the G. B. Dealey Foundation. In more recent years the foundation's name has been changed to the Belo Foundation. Their plan was that the fund would be invested and the company would add to its corpus each year, so that it would grow into a sizeable endowment. In time, the fund could be used to provide the cash necessary to maintain the company's local philanthropic efforts, even if business profits were not substantial enough to do so.

Corporate profits, however, began to rebound, and by 1955, Belo's overall net earnings were up 45 percent over the preceding year, representing an all-time high. Those earnings were in spite of the company's funding a new broadcast tower at Cedar Hill, air-conditioning the newspaper pressroom, and substantially reducing its bonded indebtedness. Directors in 1955 also approved sizable contributions to both the G. B. Dealey Foundation and the G. B. Dealey Retirement Pension Plan.[26]

The pension fund was in need of a boost significant enough to support more retirees. Although the days when employees who wished to remain on the job indefinitely were accommodated, even for life, were gone, introducing mandatory retirement was a fairly shocking change for employees, and those affected were not always agreeable to retiring. However, Ben Decherd reported at the end of 1958 "that retirement progress has been good and that the facts surrounding the retirement philosophy were being gradually accepted by most of the employees."[27]

Upon G. B. Dealey's death in 1946, A. H. Belo Corporation had entered what Jimmy Moroney called the "formative years" between 1946 and 1956. During those ten years Belo took on its first-ever major debt to erect the new building at 508 Young Street; it imposed retirement policies on workers who had expected to work as long as they lived, as their predecessors had; and it embraced the future by establishing an FM radio station and three years later purchasing its first television station. When that formative period concluded, the investments made by the company in itself over that decade were poised to pay off handsomely in the company's long-term financial stability.

Chapter 4

THE DARK DAYS OF DALLAS

1956–1964

After the economic downturns of the mid-1950s, Belo's financial position began to rise again in the late 1950s, and the directors sought ways to maximize that growth. In 1957, the *Dallas Morning News* instituted its first major change in the circulation department in thirty years, when it shifted from using employee district managers to a system that many newspapers were turning to at the time, the use of independent contractors. The purpose was to continue the paper's "all-out campaign" for circulation dominance over the *Dallas Times Herald* within Dallas County. The *Times Herald*, as the afternoon newspaper, had led in that category for years, while the *News* had held dominance in its statewide circulation over all newspapers in Texas. That arrangement had been fairly well accepted by both Dallas newspapers, and the relationship between the two papers was cordial, even while it was highly competitive. But the competition for circulation numbers to support higher advertising rates was heating up, and changes were made to promote more aggressive circulation sales.

In that same year, the *News* took a shocking blow in its relationship with the cross-town newspaper, when its longtime managing editor, Felix McKnight, resigned to become vice president and editor of the *Dallas Times Herald*. Years later, after the *Times Herald* went out of business, McKnight said of his leaving the *News*, "It was without doubt the biggest, most troubling decision I've ever made in my life. I was perfectly happy, and I thoroughly respected the institution and certainly its people. . . ." But "out of the blue" came an offer from the *Times Herald* by way of a third party, a prominent local businessman. A longstanding unwritten agreement between the two papers declared that neither would attempt to hire away the other's key personnel. By sending their offer by way of a third party, the *Times Herald* hoped to avoid hard feelings with the owners of the *News*. The *Times Herald* offered McKnight a substantial advancement in his career, along with membership on its board of directors, and options to buy stock in the company. McKnight figured that such ownership opportunities, all of which Ted Dealey had dangled in front of him over his career at the *News*, were not going to be made available to him anytime soon, considering how many others were in line ahead of him. McKnight moved out of his office the night he delivered his resignation to Ted, in what he described as a "pretty tearful four-hour session."[1] Jack B. Krueger, who had been at the *News* for thirteen years and was assistant managing editor, was named managing editor to replace McKnight.

Another blow landed hard on Belo's financial position in 1957 when the National Broadcasting Company did not renew its affiliation with WFAA-TV. Until then, the station had contracts with both NBC and the American Broadcasting Company for programs, which was not an unusual arrangement at the time. The aim of the station management had been to end its split network affiliation and to contract with NBC full-time. Losing NBC completely was doubly troubling for that reason, and it meant that WFAA had to act quickly to develop its relationship with ABC instead, spending "huge sums of money" to promote ABC programs and to buy or produce additional programming to fill empty programming hours.

In late 1958, furthering Belo's effort to improve its financial position, the directors passed a resolution that "A. H. Belo Corporation voluntarily adopt the terms and provisions of the Texas Business Corporation Act, passed at the regular session of the Fifty-Fourth Legislature of the State of Texas," in order to enable the company to reorganize its capital structure eliminating the preferred stock, which had been issued when the company was organized in 1926. The target date for the reorganization was April 1, 1959, at which point all of the preferred stock was to be redeemed at $103 per share, plus the quarterly accrued dividend of $1.25

per share. Ultimately, the company redeemed $925,000 of preferred stock outstanding and paid $124,297 to stockholders in dividends.

In early 1959, Ted addressed all of his newspaper department heads, requesting that they revisit their budget projections for the first six months of 1959 and that they apply the business principles he had posted around the building: "Dollars Saved Are Dollars Earned, and a Profitable Business Stays in Business."[2] He reminded them that Christmas was over and that budgets should reflect what each department had to have, rather than simply what it would like to have, for 1959.

As part of its reorganizing efforts, with the company still stinging from the loss of McKnight to the *Times Herald*, Belo instituted the company's first-ever stock option plan. It was extended to fourteen key employees in the company's management. In reporting on the effect of the stock option plan later, Ted said that "it ignited sparks of aggressive competition along the entire broad front of corporate business activity, and undoubtedly helped dawn what well might be the first day in a new era of success and accomplishment."[3] Indeed, that year corporate net profits doubled over the previous year, and 1959 turned out to be the most successful financial year in the company's history, with increases in all phases of corporate activity—newspaper publishing, radio, and television. Henceforth, those executives holding options were invited to attend the stockholders' meetings, which had been closed to them before.

Another milestone for Belo was reached in 1959, when the company negotiated the sale of its original television headquarters building and the land surrounding it at 3000 Harry Hines Boulevard, in order to relocate both the television and radio operations to a new building to be built at the corner of Young and Market streets, next to the Dallas Morning News Building. The Harry Hines property was sold to the Area Television Educational Foundation, operators of public television station KERA, for $400,000. On the last day of 1959, construction began on the new $2,500,000 facility, next door to the *News*, on land acquired earlier for that purpose.

The year 1959 was the first full year for WFAA-TV's new station manager, Myron F. (Mike) Shapiro, who set about to reorganize the television operations and launched a career that would become legendary by the time of his retirement a little more than twenty years later. In a statement to management after his first full year on the job, he said: "I can only assure you a concerted effort by one and all to provide you with the best broadcast properties in the country."[4]

Mike had joined Belo in 1952 as a salesman at WFAA-TV and had become station manager in 1958. By 1960 he had been promoted to general manager of both WFAA-TV and WFAA Radio, and in 1961 he launched a half-hour live show called *Let Me Speak to the Manager.* The idea for the show came after Mike refused to air a network program that contained strong language. The station was deluged with letters from viewers wanting to know why the show wasn't aired. Ward L. Huey, Jr., retired vice chairman of Belo, who started his career as a cameraman for *Let Me Speak to the Manager,* said that "[Mike] was one of the early pioneers to speak out for programming standards."[5]

Inside Television, as the show was renamed, continued for the next eighteen years. Mike answered mailed-in questions from the station's viewers, and in so doing he made it known that Channel 8 had lofty standards for both programming and commercial advertising. He was a hard-nosed, straight-talking executive, and he wasn't afraid to criticize networks or even the station's competitors, if he felt they had transgressed ethical standards. Huey described him as "strong, tough, and aggressive, but innovative, fair, and softhearted." Before Mike's retirement twenty-three years later, many in the company and throughout the industry believed he had fulfilled his early assurances many times over.

By 1959 Belo's enhanced retirement system enabled a large group of older workers to retire with full pensions to support them. Ben Decherd had been working for several years with a pension consulting firm whose representative, Robert T. Richardson, he hired in 1959 to further his efforts to liberalize the pension plan and formalize the retirement program. The plan began with the retirement of employees seventy years old and older. The following year all those who turned sixty-nine were required to retire, and thereafter the age went down one year at a time until age sixty-five became the standard.

In his treasurer's report for the year 1959, Jimmy Moroney wrote, "1959 will probably be remembered as one of the outstanding financial years in the history of A. H. Belo Corporation." The year ended with a 62.2 percent increase in newspaper earnings; an increase of 190.7 percent in radio earnings; and a spectacular increase of 1,200.1 percent in television earnings.

Following the financial triumphs of 1959, in February 1960, Ted created great turmoil within the executive ranks of Belo and throughout the entire company with his coarse handling of career promotions for "the boys," G. B. Dealey's three grandsons, Ben Decherd, Joe Dealey, and Jimmy Moroney, who were then junior executives. Everyone expected that the three young men would be moved into higher-level positions, but the timing and succession plan were not part of general management discussions. As it turned out, Ted used his mother's death on January 28, 1960, to trigger the changes. At her death, Mrs. G. B. Dealey was ninety-six years old, and she had held the title of chairman of the board since G. B.'s death in 1946.

Shortly after Mrs. Dealey died, Ted wrote a memo to Belo stockholders making "some suggestions" for executive changes to be acted upon at the upcoming meetings of the stockholders and directors. About three weeks before the scheduled meetings at which new Belo officers were to be elected, Ted distributed his memo, dated February 19, 1960, requesting that he not be reelected president, but rather that he be named chairman of the board, replacing his mother, and that he also be named publisher, a title which no one had held formally since A. H. Belo died in 1901.[6]

At the time of the memo, there were several executives with the necessary tenure and expertise who were in line for consideration to succeed Ted as president of Belo. The highest ranking of the candidates was Ted's brother-in-law Jim Moroney, Sr., who had flourished in his management responsibilities at Belo for twenty-six years, and who was a couple of years younger than Ted. Jim was the senior vice president with executive authority for the company's finances, as well as direct authority for the broadcast side of the business. However, in his memo, Ted summarily disqualified Jim from higher office at Belo, not only at that time but at any time in the future, on the basis that he was "of the Roman Catholic faith." And along with Jim Moroney, Ted banned Jim's son Jimmy from ever advancing to Belo's highest office.

Ted's memo read, "For a Roman Catholic to be chosen as president of A. H. Belo Corporation would be extremely detrimental to the institution, if not ultimately suicidal, because Texas is predominantly a Protestant state . . . ." He went on to say that he held no such prejudices personally, but that he had to be practical and face the facts. On the same basis, and in the same paragraph, Ted also disqualified Joe Lubben, the third most senior company officer who managed all of the advertising departments. Lubben was a Belo director and controlled the largest block of Belo shares outside the G. B. Dealey Trust.

Joe Lubben's father, John F. Lubben, had joined A. H. Belo & Co. in 1881, and he had been G. B. Dealey's closest associate and partner in the acquisition of the company from the Belo heirs in 1926. He had served as an executive and director of the company until his death in 1938. Joe Lubben himself had been at the company his whole working life, rising through the ranks on his own merit. But Ted's memo forthrightly ignored merit as a factor in his decision, and Joe Lubben did not protest.

That left two possible candidates, both grandsons of G. B. Dealey. The one whom many believed Ted was grooming for the position was his nephew Ben Decherd. Ben already carried much of the responsibility of the presidency, having served for more than ten years as "assistant to the president," while Ted spent more and more time on his personal interests and serving on industry boards. Ben was the oldest, most accomplished, and best educated of the three grandsons in the company ranks. He had joined the company in 1936 before serving under General Krueger in World War II, and he had since won the unqualified admiration of his colleagues with his abilities as a manager of people and an insightful member of the Belo board of directors. In addition to his corporate leadership positions, two years earlier, in 1958, Ben had been appointed to take the place of George Waverley Briggs as a trustee of the G. B. Dealey Trust, joining Ted and Jim Moroney.

The last of the possible candidates for president was Ted's son Joe, who had joined the company full-time in 1946. Joe had been appointed assistant secretary of the company in 1950 and elected to the Belo board in 1952 along with Ben and Jimmy. At the time of the memo Joe was secretary of Belo Corp.

Ted did not attend the meetings of shareholders and directors on March 15, 1960, at which his suggestions were to be presented. He explained in the February 19 memo that he and Trudy had a long-planned vacation trip to Europe that prevented his being there. Instead, Ted had arranged for his memo to be distributed after he left the country, and for it to be read into the minutes of the meeting by the elderly Leven Deputy. Leven had been an employee of Belo since 1904 and a director since 1940, but even in his dutiful delivery, Ted's words were characteristically blunt: "In my opinion, Joe M. Dealey should be named as the next President because he bears the name of Dealey."

The memo went on to explain Ted's assessment that the public wouldn't understand if someone with a name other than Dealey were to be given the top position in the company. It concluded by saying that his recommendations had nothing to do with "the fact that he is my son, nor because of my natural affection for him. . . . Emotion does not enter in." He cited his respect and love for the institution as his "entire motivation." The memo concluded with a coy disclaimer: "I realize, of course, that my nomination of Joe M. Dealey to assume the reins as head of the institution is entirely advisory. It is merely a suggestion to the Board."

Several who were directors at the time recalled later that Ben was noticeably stunned by Ted's elevating Joe over him. When the memo was circulated several weeks before the meeting, Ben pleaded with the other directors to support him rather than Joe for the presidency, or at least to postpone the vote until he had time to deal with his uncle on the matter. However, all of the other directors had seen Ted in action enough times to know that his "suggestions" would be imposed one way or another, and no one dared to go on record acknowledging the inequity of the situation.

In private, the directors apologized to Ben and counseled him to be patient. Even Joe Lubben, who had the shares to stand up to Ted and support Ben, was cowed by Ted's bullying and his history of taking vengeance on those who did not obey. So long as Ted maintained control of the G. B. Dealey Trust, largely by intimidation, he controlled the important decisions of Belo Corp., no matter what anyone else may have wanted.

The next day, Joe sent a letter to his father in France, showing no awareness of the inequity of the situation and little understanding of the controversy surrounding his election to the presidency:

> Dear Dad:
>
> Well, the big day arrived and now is past. Everything went off smoothly and in a manner you would have liked.
>
> Today, the day after, what with the stories in the papers and the announcements that were quite naturally made over radio and elsewhere, our phones around here have been ringing off the hook . . .

> Of course, I am extremely thrilled and happy. I think the others are, too, now that the initial shocks have worn off. Quite naturally there was some disappointment, but for the most part it has been drowned in renewed spirit of cooperation among us all . . .

He concluded:

> Despite our occasional disagreements I still believe that you are the best newspaperman in this neck of the woods, and I only hope that what I do here now and in the future will at least emulate the great pattern you have set for me. You are the greatest Dad in the world.
>
> Lots of love to you all.[7]

Joe clearly believed that the best man had won in a fair contest.

Ben Decherd also sent a letter to Ted at the Hotel Meurice in Paris on March 16:

> Dear Ted:
>
> Yesterday, as you know, the board of directors carried out your wishes.
>
> To the end I opposed any action now. I shall continue throughout my life to oppose those things which, in my own conscience, I do not believe to be right, but I want you to know that I'll support Joe as president of the *News* with everything I have to offer.
>
> Sincerely,[8]

By all indications, Ben honored that pledge for the rest of his life.

Acting on Ted's further suggestions, the board elected Jim Moroney, Sr., to the new position of vice chairman of the board. Joe Lubben was elected senior vice president; Ben Decherd was named vice president, secretary, and assistant treasurer; and Jimmy Moroney was named vice president, treasurer, and assistant secretary.

For his part, Ben was gracious in his intense disappointment, as evidenced in his letter to Ted, as well as in his undiminished public commitment to Belo and the *Dallas Morning News*, and particularly to his cousin Joe. However, executives and others close to him at the time commented that the rebuff broke Ben Decherd's heart. They recalled that Ben withdrew from his work emotionally and continued to be troubled for the rest of his short life by what many saw as a betrayal of his trust in his uncle and of his rights.

On March 15, 1960, Joe Dealey became president and chief executive officer of Belo, which titles also applied to the *Dallas Morning News*. Following the death of Alfred Belo, Jr., in 1906, the position of president had held the highest power and authority in the company, and that phenomenon would not change for another twenty-six years, when in 1986 Ben Decherd's son Robert William Decherd was elected chairman of the Belo board, and a profound shift in power from the presidency to the chairmanship of the board was accomplished.

The year 1960 was a turning point for Belo in another way, when four new directors were elected to the ten-member, close-knit board. There was only one vacancy created that year, when Mrs. G. B. Dealey died. As part of Ted's February 19 memo of "suggestions," he also proposed enlarging the board with four new directors whom he had selected. Two were from inside the company, and two were from outside. All four director-nominees were unanimously elected to the board on March 15, and Ted was named chairman and publisher, even though the bylaws of the company had no mention of a publisher among the officers listed.

The two new directors from within the company, Sol Katz and Jack Krueger, were both longtime *News* employees. Sol had joined the company at age sixteen in 1929 and steadily worked his way up through the ranks of the circulation department. He was highly regarded throughout the company for his wisdom and good sense, as well as for his organizational skills. Jack was a newsman who came to the *News* in 1944 from the Associated Press. He was appointed managing editor when Felix McKnight left to join the *Times Herald* in 1957, and the newsroom never missed a step when he took over. He had been credited with reorganizing the news department into much more efficient divisions and improving coverage of controversial issues.

The two nominees from outside the company were prominent Dallas business and civic leaders, A. Earl Cullum, Jr., and D. Gordon Rupe. Both men were well known and well regarded by the other Belo directors, although Ted had not consulted anyone else before nominating them. Earl Cullum, fifty, had worked at WFAA Radio for three years, beginning in 1924 when he was just fourteen years old, following which he earned a Bachelor of Science degree from the Massachusetts Institute of Technology in 1931. In 1948 he was awarded a Presidential Certificate of Merit for work he accomplished at the Radio Research Laboratory at Harvard University during World War II, and he went on to have a distinguished career in the Dallas firm he founded, A. Earl Cullum & Associates, a radio and television engineering company.

Gordon Rupe, fifty-seven, was a self-educated financial executive who joined his father's investment firm, Dallas Rupe & Son, right out of high school and was later credited with playing a large role in establishing Dallas as an international financial center, when the firm made a substantial loan to a company in Mexico City. He was equally well known for his civic and philanthropic activities in Dallas, including reviving the Dallas Symphony Orchestra after World War II, as well as projects in medicine, education, and city development.

The makeup of the board at their election included four old-timers and five younger members. The old guard included Ted, sixty-seven, the only remaining member of the original board formed in 1926; his brother-in-law, Jim Moroney, sixty-five, a member since 1934; R. M. Buchanan, seventy-one, an employee of the company since 1921 and a director since 1937; and Leven T. Deputy, also seventy-one, an employee since 1904 and a director since 1940. The next generation was represented by five members. The eldest of them was Joe Lubben, fifty-four, who had been with the company full-time since 1928 and on the board since 1948. Next was Maurice Purnell, also fifty-four, who was elected in 1950, only the second outside director since 1926 and the grandson of Eugene Locke, the company's first general counsel. The remaining three directors were G. B.'s grandsons: Joe Dealey, forty; Ben Decherd, who had turned forty-five the day before; and Jimmy Moroney, thirty-nine. All of them had been elected to the board in 1952.

In 1961, the directors voted one more member into their ranks, the last to be added for another seven years. Bill Smellage, who was the same age as Jimmy Moroney, was elected to the board after having been in the management of the company since 1954. The three grandsons, in concert with Joe Lubben, had already begun to manage the company by committee, according to many who were around in those days. Their new executive positions, along with the influence of the new board members, enabled the modernization of the company to gain momentum moving into the new decade.

Ted was formally elected chairman of the Belo board, a role he had actively played for fourteen years while his mother held the title, and publisher of the *News*. In that position, with his son in the presidency, Ted continued to be a lightning rod. But instead of deflecting the damaging bolts, Ted managed to include his son and the entire company in the public criticism he attracted.

In advance of the 1960 presidential election, the *News* editorialized that John F. Kennedy was unfit to be president because he was a Catholic and beholden to the bishops and the pope in Rome. Repeating the line of thinking Ted had used within the company earlier in the year, the newspaper's proclamation reflected a general intolerance that was widespread in Texas at the time. After the 1960 election, the *News* editorial said, "Kennedy made 220 promises. The *News* neither hopes nor expects that the new President will be able to make good."

Describing Ted's editorial influence in his book *Death of a President*, William Manchester said, "As the most venerable voice in Dallas, the *News*, under Dealey's leadership, had made radical extremism reputable in the early 1960s."[9] The ultraconservative tone of the *News*'s editorials of the 1950s and early 1960s was widely held as contributing to the anti-intellectualism and anti-liberalism that was the norm in Dallas at the time. Manchester comments that ". . . the thunder of moral indignation is clearly evident in the editorials of the *Dallas Morning News*, whose anti-administration crusade was the key to Big D's absolutism."[10]

The staff of the editorial page had not changed throughout the 1940s and the 1950s. All of them were veterans at the *News*, having spent their entire careers there, and all but one of them were about the same age. The editor of the editorial page during those years was William B. Ruggles, a former sports editor at the *News* in Galveston and Dallas before joining the editorial page staff; and the key editorial writers were Lynn W. Landrum, whose writing was the chief source of the "moral indignation," and Sam Acheson, who had written the history of the newspaper, *35,000 Days in Texas*, in 1938 under the guiding hand of Ted Dealey. All of them had grown up at the paper alongside Ted, who had worked as an editorial writer before moving to the business side of the company. The junior member of the writing staff was C. Richard West, and he had been writing editorials under that staff since 1937, shortly after he joined the company upon his graduation from the University of Texas.

Dick West had his chance to prove himself in 1958, when Ruggles was required to take his accumulated eight weeks of vacation under the new personnel policies, and Dick was given temporary authority over the page in his absence. He was made assistant editor in 1959, at which time it was announced formally that he would have the editor's job in 1960, when Ruggles would be required to retire in keeping with the new retirement policy. Dick had come of age in the editorial department admiring the harsh, unforgiving tone of Lynn Landrum's byline columns, and once Ruggles retired, he put that tone into the institution's editorials as well. Ted clearly supported Dick's angry, mean-spirited rants, but the other executives cringed in private, knowing how those editorials affected the reputation of the newspaper. In his annual report on activities for 1960, Dick reported that the editorial highpoint of the year was "our vigorous political campaign." He continued proudly, "The endorsement editorial for Nixon and Lodge was reprinted in some 80 newspapers; more than 400,000 copies were distributed."

On April 7, 1961, *Time* published an article critical of the *Dallas Morning News*'s editorial positions, which it noted were Ted's personal views, and it further noted the right-wing drift of the once moderate and even-handed *Dallas Morning News*. In response, Ted wrote letters to a far-reaching mailing list saying, "We all here at the *News* office feel that it is a compliment to us when *Time* disagrees with us and criticizes us. There is an obvious slant in practically every page of the magazine, and as a matter of fact, I think *Time* purposely sacrifices accuracy and fairness to a kind of a pert style which is supposed to attract readers." Ted signed most of the letters, but a few were produced on Joe's letterhead for his signature. Joe had been implicated in the magazine's biting criticism, as his father's successor as president, and his willingness to sign some of the letters demonstrated Ted's ongoing control.

Ted himself might have been accused of using a "pert style," if by that he meant impudent or disrespectful. In fact, he was a prolific writer and completely unrestrained in what he wrote, using crude anecdotes and cruel descriptions of persons he knew, which he would note were "only for private consumption." He seems to have been compulsively driven to tell whatever he knew about other people, other institutions, even recounting rumors, carefully labeling them as such. His published writings, as well as his internal documents, provide abundant evidence of his compulsion to write what he called the unvarnished truth about everything and everyone.

In a thick file he created in 1965, as he reminisced in journal-like writings about his fifty-year career, he created character sketches of longtime company employees who had been lauded by Sam Acheson in his book *35,000 Days in Texas*. In Ted's words, while Acheson's characterizations were appropriate for his book, "I think it is interesting in evaluating individuals . . . to outline their virtues but also to explore their faults."[11] He continued, ". . . after all, a record of this sort is supposed to tell the truth and nothing but the truth, letting the chips fall where they may." He then provides lurid details of improprieties, on the job and off, of many of his longtime management employees. Of one highly regarded managing editor whom he had fired, he wrote, "His downfall was on account of whiskey, women and racehorses," but he added, "we remained friends until his dying day."

In addition to his private writings, Ted self-published, through the *Dallas Morning News*, several books and booklets about his travel experiences. He used the booklets to promote his values and view of the world, explaining in a foreword of one such booklet, *Travels in a Troubled World*, that "the primary duty of any free lance reporter is to give an accurate report of his travels to his readers so that they will know what they are getting into when once they make up their minds to visit distant and foreign lands." With the same sensibility with which he had described Port Moresby in New Guinea as lousy, in another of the booklets, called *Sunset in the East*, he recounted the surrender of the Japanese aboard the battleship *Missouri* on September 2, 1945, which he had witnessed. As was typical of the day, he wrote disparagingly of the appearance of the surrendering soldiers, and then he added grandiose comments about the cultural superiority of the countries that made up the Allies.

But in terms of business operations at Belo, Joe reported to stockholders in his first president's report on April 19, 1961, "Overall corporate activity [in 1960] bordered on the spectacular. . . . In the space of two short years, then, financial results have grown nearly 25 percent." He ended his report with "In conclusion, there is a new spirit and vigor throughout the entire organization."

Later in 1961, after the *Time* article appeared, and nearly two years after Ted had promoted Joe to the position of power in the company, Ted took advantage of an invitation extended to the newspaper by the White House. The *News* was invited to send a representative to a luncheon with the president of the United States, at which newspaper publishers from across Texas would be able to chat with President Kennedy and his cabinet. Rather than allowing his son, ostensibly the head of the company, to attend, Ted seized the opportunity to go to the White House luncheon on October 27, 1961, along with nineteen representatives of other Texas newspapers. After some remarks by President Kennedy, the guests were invited to comment or ask questions. Ted stood up at the table after being recognized and read from a long text he had prepared in advance. The following brief excerpt is the part most widely quoted in later news accounts:

> The general opinion of the grass roots thinking in this country is that you and your administration are weak sisters. Particularly is this true in Texas right now. We need a man on horseback to lead this nation and many people in Texas and the Southwest think that you are riding Caroline's tricycle.[12]

His remarks, and particularly the forum in which he expressed them, created an uproar of disapproval from his fellow publishers around the table, and then around the country, as word of the White House incident spread. Reports of his behavior were published everywhere, and Ted received piles of letters in response to them, including some from right-wing extremist groups offering to sign him up for membership. Ted laughed about the extremists, and he responded to every letter that supported his view. In a letter to the editor of the Borger, Texas, *News-Herald*, which supported his stance, Ted wrote, "I used the expression 'weak sisters' and 'riding Caroline's tricycle' in a deliberate attempt to swipe some headlines, and apparently in that I was eminently successful."

Clearly enjoying the publicity, he kept the headlines going by publishing on the front page of the *News* his own account of the incident, along with the full statement he had read and his reasons for reading it. In that account, he described the president's reaction to his presentation at the luncheon:

> I explained to the President that my memorandum was not an expression of personal opinion but was instead a reflection of public opinion in Texas as I understood it and as it had been presented to me. The President assured me that he was not mad, but he added, "Don't subscribe to that paper. I'm tired of reading its

editorials."To which Mr. [Pierre] Salinger replied,"But I HAVE to read them."[13]

The Associated Press picked up Ted's account of the event, and it was reprinted widely. Soon, the White House put out its own version of the incident in which the description of the president's responses differed significantly from Ted's report of them. At that point Ted launched an investigation into the background of the author of the White House account, Charles Bartlett. Ted wrote to numerous conservative publishers with protests that Bartlett fabricated Kennedy's responses, and he added that Bartlett was Kennedy's "boyfriend and fellow millionaire playboy."[14]

The week following the luncheon, Ted sent a telegram to all nineteen Texas publishers who attended, asking: "Do you vote with me or against me concerning my remarks to the president last week? Are there any comments you would like to make? Please wire us collect."[15] He received fifteen responses with sharp rebukes of his behavior and praise for the president's restraint under the circumstances. One publisher, Dorrance D. Rodrick of El Paso, said, "Probably Harry Truman would have taken your plate away from you."

Four of the publishers whose comments Ted solicited did not respond at all, but George Baker, a West Texas publisher who had not attended the luncheon, copied Ted on a letter of apology sent to the president by way of Pierre Salinger. In the letter he expressed regret for not being able to attend, then, he added, "I regret further that I was not present to express my views on the manner in which Mr. Dealey presented his controversial statement." He went on to say that "the manner in which it was done certainly is not representative of the Texas way of accepting hospitality and going about changing things."

James F. Chambers, Jr., president of the *Dallas Times Herald*, whose paper was also editorially conservative, responded to Ted with a telegram stating, "I think you were rude to President Kennedy. We were his guests in his home. You could have had your say in your paper, in a letter, or at a regular press conference without embarrassment to anyone." Pat Taggart of Waco wrote, "Your truculence and phrasing were inappropriate under the circumstances." Dudley Dougherty of Beeville responded with "Did not agree with you as remarks made were boorish and rude to one's host. . . . So, why ruin opportunity you had by insulting him?" Dougherty ended the telegram with "Best Personal Regards." Houston H. Harte, Jr., publisher of the *San Angelo Standard Times*, sent a succinct message: "Please let the matter die. Texas has been embarrassed enough. I cannot condone rudeness to President personally nor to the office he represents."

Col. B. J. Horne, publisher of the *San Antonio Light*, responded on behalf of his newspaper and all of Hearst newspapers, saying, "Vote very definitely against you concerning your remarks to the President of the United States." And John T. Jones, Jr., president of the *Houston Chronicle*, telegraphed, "I did not vote at the President's luncheon last week, nor will I do so now. The Chronicle's editorial page reflects its opinions."

But even after memos from circulation manager Sol Katz regarding canceled subscriptions and fifteen letters from his fellow publishers condemning his actions, Ted wrote a paper that he titled "Rebuttal."[16] The paper is typed on pink paper, which means that his secretary prepared it from his handwritten copy. Ted wrote by hand in red ink across the top, "Not printed—just comments and thoughts." The "Rebuttal" is a rationale and personal justification in which he criticizes his fellow Texas publishers for allowing themselves to be awed and brainwashed by the president. Shortly thereafter he proclaimed in a personal letter to a friend that he had received "almost unanimous approbation of my stand."[17]

Clearly obsessed with the whole matter, he further asked the *News*'s Washington Bureau chief, Bob Baskin, to try to get copies of the guest lists for upcoming publishers' luncheons at the White House so that he could call up the ones he knew to try to bring them around to his way of thinking before they arrived in Washington. Baskin reported that he was unable to get any information, because security had been tightened at the White House after the visit by the Texas delegation. Then, for weeks thereafter, Ted published letters sent to the newspaper supporting his stance—all on the front page.

Manchester quoted President Kennedy commenting on the experience, revealing that Kennedy had looked into Ted's background, too, after the disturbing incident: "After that exhibition he put on in the White House I did a little checking on him. He runs around calling himself a war correspondent, and everybody in Dallas believes him."[18]

In general, Ted seemed to prefer ascribing his opinions to others in the framework of "reporting" what the "grass roots" were thinking. He used it in communications with his directors, as well as in his remarks to the president. Over the years since his father had died, Ted had increasingly identified himself and the *News* as southern and partisan with the South and its narrow causes. That positioning was in sharp contrast to his predecessors, Alfred H. Belo and G. B. Dealey, whose belief was that the newspaper should be solidly nonpartisan and committed to equanimity.

Through both Lynn Landrum's columns and Dick West's editorials under Ted's supervision, the *News* had taken on a tone of self-righteousness that would never have been allowed before 1946. Ted's absolutist, us-and-them approach led to a loss of nuance and subtlety in the ideas presented in the *News*'s editorials for years to come. In his second president's report to stockholders, loyal son Joe said on May 1, 1962,

> Our editorial page continues to be the very best published by any newspaper in the South or Southwest. A hard-hitting staff of expert editors helps produce a vigorous and fearless editorial voice which goes far in shaping the destinies of the people of Dallas and of Texas, if not the entire southwestern area.[19]

But by the stockholders' annual meeting the next year, on March 19, 1963, Joe seemed to be growing aware of the disconnect between the *News*'s editorials and the thinking of its readers, as he tried to rationalize the extremism of the newspaper's positions:

> While we have not been, by any stretch of the imagination, altogether successful, we do detect a growing trend among ever increasing numbers of people to hew to our long published editorial policy. . . . We attempt to state our official stands without fear or favor, knowing at times we might assault the opinions of the majority.[20]

However, while he acknowledged that the *News* was out of step with the majority of its own readers, Joe did not acknowledge that his father's ideas, and therefore Dick West's editorials, might be wrongheaded.

Then, eight months later and only two years after the incident at the White House, the country and the rest of the world found another reason to criticize the *News*, and by extension the family that owned it, when President Kennedy was assassinated in Dallas, in—of all places—Dealey Plaza. That morning the *News* had published a full-page, black-bordered advertisement criticizing President Kennedy's foreign and domestic policies. (See Appendix D for the full text of the ad.) The ad had been placed by a group of ultra-right-wing Dallas businessmen, including the organizer of the local chapter of the John Birch Society. Speaking of that time, Stanley Marcus made these comments years later:

> The *News*, in my opinion, was almost single-handedly responsible for the prevailing [ultraconservative] state of mind in Dallas at the time of the assassination. . . . Ted was a difficult person to voice your differences to, because he was part of the bigoted crowd himself. . . . Had G. B. Dealey been at the helm, he would have said, "We cannot permit a racist or a bigot of any type to stand up and twist the community into a false position."[21]

A clerk in the accounting department in those days, who was on hand the day before the assassination, recalled later that the ad in question was delivered to the newspaper at the last possible moment, obviously by prior arrangement, and that it was paid for with cash. She recalled that all of the normal approvals were bypassed when only an inexperienced, part-time copy boy was left on duty to take the ad. The young man, as he had been instructed, delivered the ad directly to the composing room, where it was placed in the next day's edition, without a review by management.[22]

Years later, Joe commented on the running of the ad. He was not at the paper the day the ad was delivered, as he was traveling home from a weeklong newspaper conference in another city: "I didn't know a thing about that ad until I saw it in the paper the next morning. . . . The ad should have been turned down. . . . I would have killed it."[23] In another interview a few years later, Joe said, "If the assassination had not occurred, we probably would have been criticized for running that ad. Since it did occur, we were *really* criticized, and the criticism had merit, frankly."[24]

The former clerk, Mildred McLerran, recalled that several people in the composing room lost their jobs or were reassigned for placing the ad without proper authorization and disclaimers. Joe revealed in the 1983 oral history that he confronted his father over the matter, and without directly accusing his father of participation in the acceptance of the ad, he told him that publishing the ad was like throwing a pie in the face of a guest you had invited into your home. His father responded that the ad reflected the editorial position of the paper, confirming his complicity in the setup.

Immediately after the assassination, the Federal Bureau of Investigation came into the newspaper's offices and insisted on going through the company's files, and Mildred McLerran recalled being assigned to help them locate materials. She and several others interviewed also recalled that reporters from all over the country swarmed into the newsroom looking for material that might provide background on the story. She said that the newspaper's morgue had to be closed when visiting reporters, including Dan Rather, ransacked the files and were found to be carting away materials and records. Over the next several weeks, she recalled, armed guards were posted on the roof of the *News* building, as the paper received thousands of scathing letters, which she screened for the executives. Among the letters and telegrams were multiple threats, which led authorities to issue identification cards for *News* employees to present in order to enter the building.

By the time Joe delivered his report to stockholders for the year 1963, only four months had passed since the assassination. His report opened, "From the corporate or overall standpoint, 1963 was by far the best operating year in our history." In fact, the company had not only experienced its highest profits on record, it had also built a new paper warehouse beside the railroad track behind the pressroom, and it had acquired a group of small community newspapers in the suburbs around Dallas County. The only mention of the events of November 1963 came near the end of his report, when Joe said, "Special mention should be made of the splendid record of achievement by our newspaper in covering in depth all of the events leading up to, surrounding and following the assassination of the President."[25]

The first Pulitzer Prize won by a Dallas newspaper was awarded to *Times Herald* photographer Robert H. Jackson in May 1964 for his photo capturing the moment Lee Harvey Oswald grimaced in reaction to being shot by Jack Ruby. The *News*'s photographer Jack Beers had also been there at the time, and he had captured the moment before the shot was fired. Beers's astonishing photo, showing Jack Ruby lunging toward Oswald with his pistol in his outstretched hand, was run the next morning, taking up most of the front page of the *News*. However, Jackson's photo, taken one second later, ran in the *Times Herald* the afternoon of the shooting and won the prize.

Joe's report on the company's activities during 1963 concluded with a paragraph about "rebuilding efforts" in the editorial department, filling vacancies created through the retirements of the remaining longtime members of the staff, resulting in "the youngest and most inexperienced staff in the history of the *News*." He continued, ". . . while this is being written approaches are being made both inside and outside the building in an effort to bring our editorial staff to full strength." However, Dick West remained firmly entrenched as editor of the page, and he maintained his power over the editorial opinions of the institution until his retirement in 1977. Joe was able to justify the rigid, even snide, editorial page by pointing to the bottom line, year after year, remaining oblivious to the concerns of those around him about the harsh tone and the absence of equanimity.

Inside Belo's business operations during 1963, several developments kept the company moving forward. A new subsidiary was established in that year when the company acquired several small suburban newspapers, converting all of them to afternoon papers to capitalize on the growing populations of the surrounding communities and to undercut the advertising potential of the *Times Herald*. The new company was called News Texan, Inc. None of the small papers was profitable for the first two years, but after that they began to provide modest income to Belo's earnings.

The active management of Belo continued under the same four key executives: Joe oversaw the news and editorial operations of the *Dallas Morning News*. Ben handled all personnel matters, companywide, and all subsidiary operations, as well as strategic planning for the company's future, although it wasn't called that at the time. Jimmy headed up companywide finance operations, production, and plant management of both the *News* and WFAA. Joe Lubben oversaw the *News*'s advertising.

Even though Ted's personality, his decisions, and his actions had set the tone for the company for twenty-three years, his own private interests took up much of his time and often kept him away from the newspaper during those same years. In addition to his hunting trips and foreign travels, he was active in industry initiatives throughout his career. Ted held many of the highest posts in newspaper organizations nationwide, including the Associated Press. He was among a handful of publishers who established the Southland Paper Company in Lufkin, Texas, the first newsprint plant in the South.

At home, Ted was a founder of the Dallas Zoological Society and its first president in 1955. He later donated a collection of 2,000 volumes of books on wildlife and the outdoors to the Dallas Zoo. He was an ardent supporter of the Dallas Museum of Natural History, to which he donated his collection of Dorothy Doughty porcelain birds, as well as wildlife paintings by artist Reveau Bassett. He helped establish the Dallas Society for the Prevention of Cruelty to Animals, and after his marriage to Trudie, he became a nationally renowned breeder of dogs, particularly Airedales and Welsh terriers. But, as was noted in Ted's lengthy, unsigned obituary, "he was known less nationally for such work than for the controversy he occasionally aroused. When it came to speaking his mind, he was courteous but blunt. He believed in nothing less than complete honesty."

Ted's blunt speaking and ideological narrowness cast a pall over the company throughout the fifties and early sixties. In 1964, the Belo management finally was able to still his voice editorially, in a bitter battle with him over an endorsement of Lyndon Baines Johnson for president. The entire editorial board of the *News* and the company's other senior executives voted to endorse President Johnson in the 1964 election, rather than the ultraconservative Republican candidate, Senator Barry Goldwater. However, Ted, who had followed Johnson's early political career in Texas, had never forgotten the accusations of voting irregularities in Johnson's 1948 election to the U.S. Senate, and considered him "a crook."[26]

Ted refused to condone the Johnson endorsement and threatened to publish his own list of reasons that Johnson should not be elected president. The conflict was resolved only when the editorial board and company executives backed down, compromising with him by not endorsing either candidate. Ted's concession was to relinquish his seat as chairman of the Belo board to his brother-in-law, Jim Moroney, whom he had earlier attempted to disqualify from higher office because he was Catholic. As part of that rearrangement of executive authority, the board created an executive committee and elected Ben Decherd to be its chairman. The purpose of the committee, which included Ted, was "to consider and advise with the president on important matters of policy affecting the corporation."[27] The move took Ted out of the company hierarchy and put Ben in line to succeed Jim Moroney as chairman of the board. However, the real power remained with the president of Belo and the *Dallas Morning News*, and Ben still had only the power to advise the president, his cousin Joe.

Even with the younger generation firmly in place, Ted's looming shadow long continued to obscure the changes put in place in the newspaper's editorial positions by his successors. The harsh tone and political

...als positions had nearly overwhelmed the legacy of more ...rs of distinguished journalism. Stanley Marcus put it suc- ...e *Dallas News* failed in its responsibility to be a good mirror ...mmunity]. I think they had a cracked mirror." He referred to ...d between G. B. Dealey's control of the company and his grand- ...ally taking over as the "interregnum" of Belo. Internally, the *News* staff was fond of Ted, and he in turn had great affection for his "*News* family." Former *News* advertising executive Leland Renfro seemed to reflect the ambiguous attitudes of most *News* employees toward Ted when he said that Ted was easy to talk to, and "he just couldn't have been nicer. I could tell you a story about Ted, but I'm not going to tell that because, after all is said and done, it's a little off color."[28]

Alfred Horatio Belo, for whom the company is named, died in 1901 at age sixty-two.

George Bannerman Dealey and his wife, Olivia Allen Dealey, had five children. Pictured (*from left*) are Annie, Ted, Olivia, G. B., Maidie, Walter, and Fannie.

The Dealey family traveled to Pikes Peak in Colorado in 1899.

Walter Allen Dealey (*left*) was his father's intended successor, but after Walter's early death, his brother Edward M. (Ted) Dealey was pressed into service.

Ted Dealey poses with his sisters and mother. *From left*: Ted, Annie Dealey Jackson, Mrs. G. B. Dealey, Maidie Dealey Moroney, and Fannie Dealey Decherd.

G. B. Dealey's grandchildren posed together for this portrait of the next generation. *From left*: Rice R. Jackson, Jr.; Gilbert S. Jackson; Gordon D. Jackson; H. Ben Decherd; Joe M. Dealey; Henry Allen Jackson; Ruth Decherd; Walter Allen Dealey, Jr.; and (*front*) James M. Moroney, Jr.; Jean Moroney (Laney); and Betty Moroney (Norsworthy). Not pictured is Patricia Dealey (Brooks), Joe Dealey's younger sister, who was born soon thereafter.

Company executives posed in the pressroom in celebration of the fiftieth-anniversary issue of the *Dallas Morning News* on October 1, 1935. *From left*: G. B. Dealey, John F. Lubben, Ted Dealey, Jim Moroney (who had joined the company the year before), Leven Deputy, John E. King, James Q. Dealey (G. B.'s brother), and E. B. Doran.

In early 1951, as the three grandsons of G. B. Dealey were finding their way around the company, they were paid a visit by a fellow newspaper heir-apparent. Ben Decherd, Joe Dealey, and Jimmy Moroney stand behind Amon Carter, Jr., holding the *News*. Carter's father was publisher of the *Fort Worth Star-Telegram*.

Posing in front of the Douglas Chandor portrait of their grandfather in the Dallas Morning News Building are *(from left)* James M. Moroney, Jr.; Joe M. Dealey; and H. Ben Decherd on the occasion of their election to the board of directors of A. H. Belo Corporation, February 22, 1952.

In 1956, Jimmy Moroney, Joe Lubben, and Ben Decherd posed for a photo to illustrate a story in the in-house employee magazine, *Sparks*, announcing their being elected officers of outside organizations.

Doris and Joe Dealey, with Ted and his second wife, Trudie, attended an ANPA convention in April 1961, just as *Time* magazine published an article critical of the *News*'s editorial positions, which they blamed on Ted, and by extension, his son Joe, who had recently been named president of the company.

Chapter 5

A NEW ERA DAWNS

1965–1972

The year 1965 might be considered the year that most everything began to speed up, and the media business was at the forefront of changes worldwide. The world, in general, had begun to seem smaller, as technological advances made communications more immediate, no matter the distance. Newspaper editors and television news directors experienced the phenomenon every day, when there was more available news to report than ever before, and not enough space or time to report it.

At Belo in particular, 1965 was the year that WFAA-TV converted to all-color transmissions, donating its old cameras to public television station KERA-TV, which occupied WFAA's original headquarters building. The *Dallas Morning News* installed its first computer systems that year, beginning with payroll administration and classified advertising. The Dallas Morning News Building had been planned with extra space to be finished out only when it was needed. That year, another 60,000 square feet was finished to accommodate the growing newspaper operations. Among other needs, room was needed for the mainframe computer and the new department called data processing, which had been created to service and to build on the new computer systems.

In early 1966, Joe Dealey made especially prescient, almost fearful, comments to the Belo stockholders about the coming electronic revolution. He said, "The computer alone with its swift and silent magic has only just begun to revitalize this business and our industry. The potentials inherent in this type of technological sophistication stagger some and will cause us all to take fresh and thoughtful looks at the processes which, until now, have served us well." He further alluded to the effect that everyone feared computers would have in displacing employees, saying ". . . approaches [to retraining and reassigning employees] must be perfected with equity to all . . ."[1] In midyear he commented to the Belo directors that "the pace of our business has undoubtedly accelerated and accelerated greatly. . . . [I]t is certainly not the same leisurely affair it might have been twenty years ago."[2] Of course, those who were in charge in 1946, when Joe came back from World War II, probably didn't consider their workdays all that leisurely, but the company was certainly experiencing unprecedented change in the mid-sixties.

Dallas was changing too, as it continued to reel from the worldwide perception that it was a city of hate that somehow had contributed to the assassination of President Kennedy. Under the influence of Ted Dealey, the *News* had supported Dallas's ultraconservative U.S. congressman Bruce Alger since 1956. However, in 1964, with Ted's voice muffled somewhat, the *News* shifted its editorial support to Alger's opponent, Dallas mayor Earle Cabell, who had been recruited to run for Congress by city leaders striving to project a more moderate image of the city. Cabell easily won the election, in part because the Civil Rights Act of 1964 had energized the electorate in the still-segregated black neighborhoods of the city.[3]

Cabell had resigned his seat as mayor in order to run for Congress, and he was replaced as mayor by J. Erik Jonsson, who in December of 1965 launched a program to engage the citizens of Dallas in a series of discussions about the future of the city. His program was called "Goals for Dallas," and it included residents from throughout the city neighborhoods in discussions and planning for the future. Goals for Dallas has been credited as an important factor in Dallas's relative stability during the volatile decade beginning in 1964, while other cities around the country experienced much greater turmoil.[4]

Dallas and Belo did not escape the protests and counter-protests of those years, however. Among other incidents during 1965, civil rights marchers gathered at Ferris Plaza across the street from the Belo companies to protest racial inequities in all Dallas institutions; on another occasion, the American Nazi Party rallied in the same location, trying to keep everything as it was. Three bomb threats were called in to the *News* in the fall of that year, presumably reacting to news coverage of the national civil rights movement. A heightened sense of Belo's vulnerability led management to install much tighter security around the offices and printing plant.[5]

In 1966, Joe took on a highly visible role in the community when he volunteered to chair the annual United Fund Campaign. His leadership that year resulted in the most successful public fund-raising campaign in the local United Fund's history, and launched Joe's lifelong career in community involvement. Rather than supporting community initiatives strictly through the editorial product and remaining behind the scenes personally, as G. B. Dealey had done, Joe took on leadership of numerous fund-raising efforts, which made him a highly visible figure. That gave his father another opportunity to criticize his son, whom Ted often chided to pay more attention to his job and to stay out of community projects.

Joe deflected the fatherly criticism, and he surely felt justified in his personal volunteer work when he won the statewide Headliner Club's Publisher of the Year Award for 1965, and then the 1967 Linz Award for exceptional community service in Dallas. The Linz Award was presented annually by the Linz jewelry company in association with the *Dallas Times Herald*, which made it even more precious to Joe. His almost full-time career in volunteer community service kept him out of the office a good bit of the time, and thus out of the direct line of his father's fire throughout the sixties. Even after Ted died, Joe continued his community work until his health failed, years after his retirement. He made his philosophy clear in addressing a civic group in 1968: "Newspapers, like other local institutions, are citizens of the community served. They should behave like citizens and, through their publishers, involve themselves wholesomely in public and civic affairs."[6] He reiterated that philosophy, almost verbatim, nearly twenty years later in an interview conducted two years after he had retired. In the long run, he had become better known, and loved, by more people in the community for his volunteer work than for his running of the A. H. Belo Corporation.

Over the five years from 1960 to 1965, the number of employees of the Belo companies had increased only 10 percent, while net earnings per share had increased 149 percent. The increase in advertising sales during 1965, up 8.4 percent over 1964, added more than 400 pages to the news hole of the *Dallas Morning News* for the year, and managing editor Jack Krueger noted to his boss that the additional space was accommodated with one fewer newsroom employee than the previous year. He also commented that it was becoming increasingly hard to recruit experienced talent to the newsroom, as competition for those jobs was growing nationwide, and salaries were rising faster in other industries, as well as at other newspapers and in other parts of the country. However, Joe's characteristic focus on maintaining expenses at the lowest possible level year after year usually meant that salary increases or additional personnel were secondary to accommodating the steadily rising costs of newsprint and ink.

At the same time, newspapers all over the country had begun to notice that the younger generation wasn't as committed to reading newspapers as their parents had been. The analysts blamed the trend on the rapid proliferation of television, and in 1962, Joe had delivered a speech at the national meeting of the American Newspaper Publishers Association, titled "The Sustainability of the Newspaper Business in Competition with Television and Radio." To combat the threat, newspapers took a cue from their advertisers and launched their own aggressive marketing campaigns, creating or enlarging internal departments for that purpose. Nothing could be taken for granted anymore.

At the *News*, Ben Decherd took the lead in making the promotion department a separate entity from the advertising department, where it had traditionally existed simply as a line in their budget, with no spending authority. At the time, the department was being run by a former city editor who had been sidetracked to that position from the newsroom to make way for someone else, which was a typical practice in those days. Over time in the promotion department, the former city editor had created an adversarial relationship with the newsroom, where editors and reporters felt that he was not respectful of the division between the business side of the newspaper and the news side.

When the department was made independent, Ben put it under the direct supervision of Joe Lubben, a second-generation Belo executive and head of advertising. Joe hired the newspaper's first professional promotion manager, Dick Jeffrey, who had been with a New York advertising agency for eight years before joining the *News*. Dick was given the charge to improve the newspaper's public visibility and to repair the rift that had occurred with the newsroom. Soon after Dick arrived, Joe Lubben attended a newspaper meeting in Florida, traveling with his wife and a few colleagues and their wives. They were boarding a train on a rainy day, when Joe slipped on the wet platform, fell, and broke his leg.

The broken leg was already stiff from a childhood automobile accident that destroyed his knee; this time, the thigh bone snapped. As an ambulance was called, Joe insisted that the party of travelers board the train and continue their itinerary. His friends and colleagues were impressed with Joe's stoicism, as he insisted that they shouldn't stay on the platform to fuss over him, and the story was added to many others about his strong character. His wife Rene stayed with him on the platform, and the two of them remained in Florida for another two weeks while Joe recovered in the hospital. Even after returning to Dallas (in an ambulance), Joe was unable to work for several more weeks.[7]

Ben filled in for Joe and worked directly with Dick Jeffrey while Joe recovered. Dick recalled in a 1986 interview that Ben "had a real interest in promotion and an insight that probably was more incisive than most of the others." It was Ben who recognized that promotion of the newspaper would be crucial in difficult economic situations, and that it had to be independent of the revenue-generating departments to be effective. Ben gave Dick the responsibility to budget for promotion of the paper and the authority to spend the money. Ben told him, "There might be times when we will want to cut the general budget but raise the promotion budget."[8] For the first time, promotion was recognized as crucial to maintaining Belo's profitability.

In January 1966, the *News* added to its push for young readers by publishing a tabloid designed for teenagers, but it failed to attract advertisers sufficient to support it and was soon dropped. Forty years later, throughout the newspaper industry, efforts to attract young readers continue unabated, as the predictions about falling readership of print editions bear out. Of course, television and radio aren't the cause, as everyone had feared. The proliferation of online sources of information that has captured the attention of young audiences has newspaper publishers searching for ways to apply their high-principled form of journalism to this seemingly limitless and largely unfiltered electronic playground.

When Belo's astonishing financial results for the year 1965 were confirmed, Joe proposed to the board at their final meeting of the year that a group of fifty key employees be given a one-time bonus to acknowledge the extraordinary year. The bonus raised morale and inspired renewed efforts, all of which contributed to the upward trends continuing the following year. The news hole of the paper continued to increase over the prior year, with an average of 6.2 more pages per day supported by advertising sales; the paper added a new press to its pressroom; and computers were introduced into other areas, including typesetting, which necessitated extensive training of those employees who were willing to learn. While computers reduced the number of employees needed at the newspaper, WFAA-TV management doubled the size of the news department, from ten to twenty people, and replaced its one color camera with four new ones.

The year 1966 was the beginning of the Dallas Cowboys craze, which fueled readership of the newspaper's sports section that continues today; and two of the *News*'s most beloved writers, Paul Crume and Frank Tolbert, kept readers' attention with their lively columns. Paul Crume's Christmas column titled "Angels Among Us," which has been reprinted many times over the years, including on December 24, 2005, was first published on that date in 1967. Many longtime familiar bylines were lost during those years, however, as the company enforced its newly imposed retirement policies.

The younger writers and editors who took over the vacated slots expected and received salaries at the higher levels that had been achieved over time by the veterans. The mid-sixties also brought unrest among the trade unions that operated at both the *Dallas Morning News* and the *Dallas Times Herald*. The two newspapers continued their long-customary joint negotiations on contracts with all of the unions, and on several occasions arbitration was required for the newspapers to come up with agreements, particularly with the union representing the pressmen.

Competition between the *News* and the *Times Herald* had always been keen, both for readers and advertisers, but it had also been cordial, with each more or less conceding the other's dominance in its primary demographic and geographic targets. While a great many Dallas residents routinely subscribed to both the morning and the afternoon newspapers, the *News* had more of the affluent white readership and more of the black readership. The afternoon *Times Herald* was perceived to be the favored newspaper of so-called blue-collar workers, and the *Times Herald* advertisers tended to be those that aimed for that clientele. For example, during 1967 the *News* had 77 percent of Neiman-Marcus's advertising, but only 16 percent of Montgomery Ward's. The mid-range department stores, such as Sanger-Harris and Titche's, split their advertising almost equally between the two newspapers, with a slight preference for the

Times Herald, which had enabled the *Times Herald* to lead the *News* in total retail advertising.

On the other hand, the *News* had always dominated in classified advertising, which Dick Jeffrey's department promoted heavily every day. In a 1986 interview, Jeffrey described running into the *Times Herald*'s advertising director, John Wolf, at an event where Wolf questioned him about spending so much money promoting classified advertising. The *Times Herald* position, to let classified ads sell themselves, had been established by its early publisher Edwin J. Kiest and maintained faithfully ever since. Jeffrey responded, "John, every dollar I run promoting classified advertising is building business for the *Times Herald*. We [the *News*] are going to get more of it, because I'm doing the promoting, but if you were doing your job properly, you'd be promoting classified advertising, and then we'd get some of your promotional benefits."[9]

Another distinction between the two papers had existed since 1885, when the *News* began publication calling itself a statewide newspaper from day one. The *News* carried more state and national news, while the *Times Herald* focused on its local coverage, another reflection of Kiest's philosophy. For many years, those distinctions had enabled the *Times Herald* to dominate the *News* in local circulation and in total paid advertising, although the *News*'s total circulation was higher, with its subscribers in areas outside Dallas, and it always led in classified advertising.

Records at the *News* show that the management constantly discussed ways of overtaking the *Times Herald*'s leads in both Dallas County circulation and overall advertising. In the mid-sixties, the *News* began to achieve significant increases in its advertising linage, such as the 10.2-percent jump from 1965 to 1966. In the same time period, the *Times Herald* linage grew 7.8 percent, but it was enough to maintain its lead in total paid advertising over the *News*. The heartening increases in the *News*'s advertising sales brought attention to the manager of the retail advertising department. Soon, John A. Rector, Jr., was promoted to director of advertising and was challenged to overtake the competition. John had joined the *News* in 1947, beginning as an advertising salesman, and he had earned the respect of management with his exceptional competitive spirit and accompanying sense of humor, about himself and about his chosen profession.

By that time, in keeping with Joe Dealey's abhorrence of debt, Belo had paid off its loan to build the Dallas Morning News Building, and with its new mandatory retirement policy reducing costs of keeping people on the payroll for life, the company found itself in a more profitable position than ever before in its history. Belo had cash to spend on diversifying its businesses, and in 1966, the directors voted to invest in two new, unrelated startup companies with what they believed were justifiable connections to media operations.

One of the companies was called Big D Productions, and it was the creation of the well-known big-game hunter Herb Klein, who planned to produce a series of thirty-minute wildlife films for sale to the national networks. Joe had known Klein through his longtime association with the Dallas Museum of Natural History, which his father, Ted, had supported before him. Big D Productions seemed to bring together Klein's expertise as an animal expert and Belo's expertise as the developer of original programming, which had begun with radio and continued in television.

The other venture was called Weather Warnings, Inc., and it had been founded by local meteorologist Dale Milford to package and sell weather forecasts to newspapers, radio stations, and television stations. WFAA-TV and Radio and the *Dallas Morning News* were already clients of Weather Warnings, so the investment seemed practical, as well as promising. Unfortunately, while both companies seemed poised to take Belo into new, forward-looking enterprises, both of them failed. Belo ended up writing off its original investments, as well as several loans made to the two companies.

Belo maintained its conservative approach to business through 1967, and though still quite profitable, the *News* lost ad linage to the *Times Herald* that year. WFAA-TV suffered as well, when ABC had a low-ratings year, and both AM and FM radio stations were unable to find what worked with the emerging rock 'n' roll generation. However, several national and local civic events led to important changes within the company.

That year Dallas elected its first black member of the Dallas Independent School District board of trustees, Dr. Emmett J. Conrad, who would go on to serve for ten years, while the DISD struggled with federal desegregation orders and court-ordered busing. Waking up to its responsibility to be a leader in the civil rights debate, in 1967, the *News* hired its first black columnist, Julia Scott Reid, who gave voice to a community that largely had been invisible to the newspaper's white readership.

The *News* began to serve its non-white readers better in another way, too, by running the notices from minority communities about debutante selections, special social events, and other items of public interest, and, for the first time, taking wedding announcements, notices of engagements, and other such ads from the African American community. It also increased reporting on the civic events of the minority community, which by then accounted for more than 20 percent of the Dallas population. By 1969, the *News* was supporting a variety of minority issues editorially, including helping to elect the city's first black member of the Dallas City Council, George L. Allen, and its first Hispanic council member, Anita Martínez. Its white readers reacted in letters to the editor, with many supporting the broadened coverage and many others objecting to it, reflecting a community in transition.

In May 1968, WFAA-TV was the first station in the Dallas/Fort Worth market to hire an African American on-air reporter, when former Dallas Cowboy football player Frank Clarke joined the Channel 8 news staff as a sports reporter. By 1970, the station had a minority training program focused on putting more representatives of the minority communities on the air and in management positions behind the scenes. Between 1965 and 1971, the WFAA newsroom went from ten employees to fifty-four, of whom eleven were female and eight were minority. And by 1977, the region's first minority news anchor, Iola Johnson, who had joined WFAA in 1973, led the six and ten o'clock weekday news programs.

The changes made across the company during the sixties reflected the shift in power that began in 1962, when the G. B. Dealey Trust was at last in the hands of the three grandsons. By that time, Ben Decherd had succeeded G. B. Dealey's good friend George Waverley Briggs as trustee in 1957; and Joe Dealey and Jimmy Moroney had succeeded their fathers in 1962. However, Ted continued to monitor their every move and readily made his opinions known.

On his own, Joe eventually developed a warm relationship with President Lyndon Baines Johnson. Before LBJ decided not to run in 1968, he invited Joe and the *News*'s managing editor, Jack Krueger, to visit him in the White House on two different occasions. As he did with other publishers, he presented firsthand his positions on the war in Vietnam and on domestic issues. President Johnson, with the help of Joe Dealey and Jack Krueger, attempted to win over Ted to the president's side during that time. At the president's bidding, one afternoon the *News* executives quietly left the downtown office, taking Ted with them, and drove to Love Field, where they boarded President Johnson's private plane and flew to his Texas ranch for a personal tour and barbeque. Ted reportedly objected at first, but was amused by the ploy, and ultimately had a whopping good time. However, he continued to oppose LBJ politically.

Even in the context of greater community involvement, openness, and tolerance, the conservative tone of the editorial page continued to define the *News*, just as it defined a great many of the newspaper's readers. Editorial director Dick West's young heir-apparent, Jim Wright, won the top award in 1967 from the conservative Freedoms Foundation at Valley Forge for his editorial titled "Why Do You Stay?" The editorial urged those who burned their draft cards and refused to bear arms for their country in Vietnam to take up residency elsewhere. West reported at the end of the year that the *News* was the only newspaper in the country ever to have won the top award from the Freedoms Foundation twice: the first award had been given to him in 1961. That record was to stand for many years, and West reported it annually while it stood. Later, in 1976, he proudly reported that a Freedoms Foundation award had been given to Joe Dealey, Jr., who was by then a member of the editorial writing staff with a byline column.

Internal management changes continued at Belo in 1968, with Jack Krueger's promotion to executive editor of the *News*, which opened the way for Tom Simmons to be promoted to managing editor. Tom had started his career with Belo in 1931, straight out of Sunset High School in Oak Cliff, south of downtown Dallas. He started as an unpaid apprentice on the Oak Cliff edition of the *Dallas Journal*, but he was hired as soon as a spot opened up, and with his innate intelligence and quick mind, started his climb to the top newsroom position.

At the March 1968 meeting of the Belo board of directors, the elder generation of family members, Ted Dealey, seventy-five, and Jim Moroney, seventy-three, formally stepped aside and took emeritus status. Ted became publisher emeritus, and Jim became chairman emeritus. Their changes in status opened the way for Ben Decherd to be voted chairman of Belo at age fifty-three. Although at the time the chairmanship did not outrank the office of president, the position Joe had held since 1960, Ben's election to chairman was a personal triumph nonetheless. It also seemed to finally acknowledge that as a shareholder he outranked Joe, since his shares in the G. B. Dealey Trust would not be divided with a sibling as Joe's would.

Ben's enthusiasm upon his election was kept in check by his having lost his mother, Fannie Dealey Decherd, only a few weeks earlier, when she died on February 5 at age eighty-one. Then, in September, Chairman Emeritus Jim Moroney died as well. Ted and his sister Maidie Dealey Moroney were the last surviving of the five children of G. B. Dealey. The following September, Ted wrote a letter to Ben in recognition of Ben's thirty-third anniversary with the company. By that point, Ben had been chairman of Belo for eighteen months, and it must have been cold comfort for him to read:

> Dear Ben:
> . . . I have always found you to be broad-minded and fair in connection with all the problems of the business. In addition, I find it easier to talk to you about the perplexities that sometimes arise than I do with any of our other executives, with no disparagement to them. Perhaps this is because we seem to think alike and because I feel more comfortable during our chats than I find it possible with some others who are more dogmatic and more stubborn in their convictions than you are.[10]

He concluded, "Anyhow, you are a meticulous workman insofar as the details of the company's operations are concerned and, on top of that, you have vision, imagination and most excellent judgment. . . . Good luck always, Ted."

At their meeting in March 1968, the Belo directors had passed a resolution to increase the number of directors from twelve to fourteen, immediately nominating two new directors, Mike Shapiro and Dick Blum. Both were company executives who had shown great loyalty and leadership abilities over many years, Mike at WFAA-TV and Dick at the *Dallas Morning News*. Richard D. (Dick) Blum had joined the newspaper staff in 1957 as an administrative assistant in the executive offices, working largely with Ben Decherd on labor relations. He had moved to Dallas in 1955 to be production manager of the southwest edition of the *Wall Street Journal*, where he had been employed for several years. His specialty, which he had developed while working at the *Journal*, was negotiating with the various labor unions, which were becoming more vocal and politically charged in the late 1960s.

The newly constituted board, all of whom were shareholders, immediately faced the growing concern of the beneficiaries of the G. B. Dealey Trust following Fannie's recent death. They had grown increasingly mindful of the restrictions placed on their inheritances by the terms of G. B. Dealey's will, as well as by bylaw 25 of the company's governing documents.

Internal records show that discussions regarding the implications of bylaw 25 were a constant in all stockholders' dealings over the years of its existence. Bylaw 25 continued to impose restrictions on the sale or other disposition of any Belo stock; it further required voting rights in some instances to be vested in a trustee other than the beneficial owner; and it authorized the company to buy back stock in certain circumstances at a price fixed in accordance with a formula spelled out in the bylaw.

The value per share of stock in the A. H. Belo Corporation on February 29, 1968, was $14.434, using the formula in bylaw 25, and stockholders' equity by that formula was $20,103,952.47. In early 1969, the company officers and directors discussed the possibility of taking the company public, which would effectively reorganize the entire stock structure. And on July 1, 1969, a 100-percent common stock dividend was issued, having the effect of doubling the number of shares outstanding and halving the value of each share.

Meanwhile, Belo continued its revenue growth and with cash in hand negotiated the purchase of another broadcast television station, the CBS affiliate in Beaumont, Texas, KFDM-TV. Belo closed its purchase of KFDM in early 1969, putting in place the Belo business practices in an effort to improve the station's ratings and profitability. During that year, WFAA-TV took over the number one position among Dallas/Fort Worth television stations for both its 6 and 10 p.m. news slots, and its annual profits shot up over those of 1968, reflecting Mike Shapiro's dynamic leadership.

At the *News*, 1969 revenues hit an all-time high, but even more importantly, the *News* closed the gap between its total paid full-run advertising and that of the *Times Herald*, moving up to 50.5 percent from its position at 48.79 percent in 1968. Ad sales supported an increase of 733 pages in the news hole of the *News* over 1968, and Jack Krueger announced a plan to build the newspaper's staff of investigative reporters, a move that was roundly supported by the directors and cheered by the newsroom staff.

Then, on September 15, 1969, the *Dallas Times Herald* ran this headline on page one above the fold: "Times Herald, Times Mirror Propose Plan for Merger." Along with the story, the paper ran a group photo with Otis Chandler, vice chairman of the Times Mirror Company and publisher of the *Los Angeles Times*; Dr. Franklin D. Murphy, chairman and chief executive officer of the Times Mirror Company; James F. Chambers, Jr., president of the Times Herald Printing Co. and publisher of the *Dallas Times Herald*; and Clyde Rembert, chairman of the board of the Times Herald Printing Co. and president of KRLD Television. In the photo, Murphy, Chambers, and Rembert are seated at a table looking straight into the camera with suitably proud, businesslike faces, while young Otis Chandler sits off to one side, looking slightly away from the camera, laughing.

All employees of the *Times Herald* received a memo that morning, before the news story came out in the afternoon, saying, "The purpose of this memorandum is to assure you that our properties will continue to be operated by the present management with our own Board of Directors." It was signed by Clyde W. Rembert, Chairman of the Board, and James F. Chambers, Jr., President and Publisher.[11]

The story in the newspaper that afternoon stated, "The Times Mirror Company will issue a new series of 1,800,000 shares of convertible stock to *Times Herald* shareholders in exchange for assets of the Times Herald Printing Company." It continued, "Each share will carry a .70 annual dividend and will be convertible into 1.111 shares of Times Mirror stock, listed on the New York Stock Exchange. The transaction will require a total of 1,999,800 shares to be reserved for conversion." It further explained that based on the value of stock at the time, which was $45.50 per share for Times Mirror common stock, the total market value of the underlying *Times Herald* common stock was approximately $91 million. Later in the news story, Times Mirror chairman and CEO Dr. Franklin Murphy said of the so-called merger that he saw it as "an association of $90 million worth of people with a few buildings, some transmitters and equipment thrown in as a bonus."[12]

The management of the *News* had heard rumors that the *Times Herald* might be for sale, but they had no concrete information. At the time, the shares of the Times Herald Printing Company were in the hands of about ninety individuals, many of whom were the children or other heirs of former employees, and most of them had no other connection to the company by then. In a 1961 unpublished history of the *Times Herald*, Reginald C. Westmoreland recounted the interesting story of how the employees came to own the *Times Herald*.

When the principal owner of the newspaper, Edwin J. Kiest, died in 1941, he had been publisher since 1896, and he had no descendants. In his will, he had divided his shares of the company among eight loyal employees, including men from the executive management ranks to production and maintenance. Two of those men, Albert Swinsky and E. K. Mead, died within a few years, and their shares went to their heirs. The remaining six men, Tom C. Gooch, John W. Runyon, Clyde Taber, B. C. Jefferson, Allen Merriam, and Dennis A. Greenwell, found themselves instant millionaires, on paper anyway.[13]

According to former *Times Herald* officer and director Robert Solender, the rules then in place at the *Times Herald* prohibited nepotism. That meant that no relative of any employee, including the new owners of the paper, could come to work there. And that meant that when those six men died, their shares went to their heirs, who were not otherwise affiliated with the newspaper. Solender explained that in 1969, the directors of the Times Herald Printing Company voted to sell the company because of litigation or the threat of it from some of those ninety or so shareholders, who were dissatisfied with the share price and with the lack of a public market for their shares.[14]

Principal among those stockholders who were dissatisfied was a former employee who had acquired shares during his tenure with the company. *Times Herald* editorial page and book page editor A. C. Greene had filed suit on March 20, 1968, against the eleven members of the board of directors of the Times Herald Printing Company. He had sued in both state district court and federal district court, charging the directors with undervaluing the stock in a reorganization of the company in 1965.[15] The proxy statement issued to shareholders by the Times Herald Printing Company on November 14, 1969, outlined the particulars of Greene's suit and explained that the company had made it known to Greene that the "pendency" of his litigation would stand in the way of a merger that the Times Herald Printing Company was discussing with an unnamed buyer.

Greene agreed to drop his suit when he learned that the terms of the sale meant for him, as it did for the other stockholders, that the value of his holdings would be roughly four times greater than the 1965 valuation of the stock, a fact that certainly confirmed the rightness of his protest. The proxy further explained that if the sale didn't go through, Greene had the right to reinstate his litigation.[16]

Two days after the public announcement, president and publisher James F. Chambers, Jr., wrote to the shareholders: "I would like to stress that we will maintain our editorial and programming independence and will also have our own board of directors, which will be made up in the main by the same people who are serving you today."[17]

Appealing to the community at large, all of the top officials of the Times Mirror Company came to Dallas and spent about three weeks, appearing before the city councils of Dallas, Fort Worth, and Denton. They pledged to their various audiences to maintain the local focus of the newspaper's coverage. The local newspaper executives set up close to forty meetings with various civic organizations in Dallas, as well, where they appeared along with the Times Mirror executives to assure the local readers of their continued commitment to serving Dallas and the North Texas region. In an editorial run on September 16, 1969, the *Times Herald* called the proposed sale a "Partnership for Progress," and the editorial stressed the merits of such a "merger" and the benefits to "the resulting company." The executives in place at the time, including Felix McKnight and Robert Solender, were given contracts for five years or up to retirement age of sixty-five, and in some cases, for five years thereafter, as consultants.

The day of the announcement, Joe Dealey was in a private airplane returning to Dallas from a trip to Newfoundland with friends. As they flew at cruising altitude, the pilot handed out copies of the *New York Times* and the *Wall Street Journal*. Joe first saw the announcement at the bottom of the front page of the *Journal*, and he thought to himself, "My Lord, what are we faced with now? Here comes a deep-pockets organization in there." And then, discussing the announcement with his traveling companions, he said, "It's not going to be the same from here on in."[18]

The *News*'s executive editor, Jack Krueger, said that the announcement didn't make much of a ripple in the upper ranks at first, except that everyone thought things would become more interesting, and the heightened competition "shook the *News* loose from some cobwebby ideas."[19] But on the frontlines in the newsroom, managing editor Tom Simmons said,

> When we learned that the *Times Herald*, which had been our hated competitor for all these years, was being bought by the *Los Angeles Times*, the news department felt a sense of insecurity that we were going along, making a nice profit, but here was the *LA Times* coming in with its millions of dollars of resources, and we could just see that they would pour these millions into the *Times Herald* and just beat us by the mere feat of spending money. This made us much more determined to do our job much better not only in the news department, but in all other parts of the building.[20]

At the *News*, the newsroom, circulation department, and advertising department ramped up their efforts to combat the impending threat from the "deep pockets" coming to town. Joe closed the year with an address to the directors that began, "1969 was a time of wars, of civil unrest, of a greatly expanding economy, . . . a time of great change for all the world's people." And without naming the interloper, he concluded, "The news department is aware that we may have a new visitor in town before long, and it looks forward to the confrontation."[21]

The purchase of the Times Herald Printing Company by Times Mirror became final on July 1, 1970. The Federal Communications Commission required the new company to sell either their Dallas television station or their Dallas radio stations, KRLD-AM and KRLD-FM. In a magazine supplement published by the *Times Herald* on May 6, 1979, in celebration of the newspaper's centennial, the text explains that the company retained television station KRLD-TV, renaming it KDFW-TV, and it sold its two radio stations to Philip R. Jonsson, son of J. Erik Jonsson, for $6,750,000.[22]

When the proceeds from the sale of its radio stations were soon thereafter used to purchase Lyndon Johnson's Austin television station, KTBC, the *Times Herald* directors "discovered" W. Thomas Johnson, Jr., working for LBJ's family as executive vice president of their broadcasting company. Tom Johnson, no relation to the president, was a Harvard MBA, and he had served President Johnson as a White House Fellow during his presidency. Thereafter, he helped President Johnson with his memoirs and supervised the building of the LBJ Library on the University of Texas campus in Austin. Johnson was named executive editor and vice president of the *Times Herald* in August 1973, and in 1975 he succeeded Chambers as publisher.

At the closing in 1970, *Times Herald* publisher James Chambers was elected to the board of directors of the Times Mirror Company, and *Los Angeles Times* publisher Otis Chandler joined the board of the Times Herald Company along with Times Mirror chairman, Franklin Murphy, and its president, Albert V. Casey. That opened an era of great expectations for the *Dallas Times Herald*.

Soon after, Times Mirror realized that the *Dallas Morning News* was gaining, rather than the other way around, as they had expected, and it wasn't long before they began tinkering with the local focus of the paper, which had been its historical advantage. Felix McKnight recalled that after a couple of years, the new owners increased the news department staff from about 112 to 275, increasing salaries as well as headcount, and openly declared their intent to put the *News* out of business. Betraying their promises to local readers, Times Mirror brought in outside managers and editors who, McKnight said, "attempted to mold the image of the *Times Herald* into sort of a national configuration type [of newspaper], which it wasn't and never was and never should have been."[23]

Of course, what the outside influence did for Dallas and for the readers of both of its daily newspapers was quite extraordinary. The "foreigners," as the incoming *Times Herald* owners and management were called by a great many Dallas people in the mid-1970s, stimulated both newspapers to make improvements that were long overdue and were widely appreciated by readers of both newspapers. In fact, the new *Dallas Times Herald* was welcomed and embraced particularly by the key demographic group, younger readers, as it began to give voice to an emerging liberal political sensibility in Dallas.

At the *News*, in a characteristic demonstration of misreading the times, editorial page editor Dick West hired a new editorial writer in 1973 whom he described as "a talented and scholarly writer who lacks only a few hours of having his doctor of philosophy in history." His name was Bill Murchison, and that year the *News*'s editorial page won three more awards from the conservative Freedoms Foundation.

The circulations of both newspapers continued to grow, with the *Times Herald* gaining at a slightly higher rate, especially among young professionals, who were streaming into the city as the first wave of Baby

Boomers was graduating from college and launching their careers. The competition for both readers and advertisers was fierce, as the *Times Herald* went after the typical readers of the *News*, while also gaining ground with the coveted younger readers.

As the competitive environment between the two newspapers ramped up, in 1970 the public television station KERA initiated a daily program called *Newsroom*, hosted by Jim Lehrer, at the time a disaffected former reporter at both the *Times Herald* and the *News*. Responding to the newspapers' lack of depth in coverage of sensitive or controversial topics, such as the growing civil rights debates, Lehrer covered topics that editors of both papers had avoided because they tended to reflect badly on Dallas and its institutions.[24] The immediate popularity of *Newsroom*, and its success in achieving funding from the Ford Foundation, added to the frenzy at both daily newspapers to attract readers and viewers among the increasingly anti-establishment younger population. That early success at KERA in Dallas launched Jim Lehrer's distinguished and still ongoing career with the Public Broadcasting System.

Internally at the *News*, the changes across town at the *Times Herald* led to increases in the number of news department employees and in their salaries, at last, when reporters and writers became unwilling to carry on with the old business-as-usual stance. Other big changes to occur at the same time included a huge leap in printing technology, when the cold-type process using photocomposition replaced the hot-lead typesetting machines at both newspapers. At the *News*, the last of the huge, bulky hot-type machines were removed, and the operators who were willing to retrain in the new process demanded, through their union, and were given a substantial increase in their wages. That change was accompanied by the installation of the first individual computer terminals, known as CRTs (cathode ray tubes), for use in the circulation department, and the resulting space shifts around the building enabled management to undertake a $1.75 million remodeling of the twenty-one-year-old building.

Late in 1970, the seventeen-foot-high by 175-foot-long mural by Perry Nichols, which depicted the history of Belo from 1842 to 1949 when it was installed, was removed from the grand two-story entrance to the Dallas Morning News Building. The ceiling of the entrance was lowered to create 1,000 square feet more office space above it on the second floor. The Nichols mural, along with hundreds of bound volumes of the *News* and the *Dallas Journal*, was donated to the University of Texas System, which was then developing the Institute of Texan Cultures in San Antonio, where the mural was to be put on permanent display and the bound newspapers were to be housed for the benefit of future generations.

Complicating the competitive environment for Belo in Dallas, as WFAA-TV approached its mid-1971 deadline to apply to the FCC for renewal of its license to operate Channel 8, a strike application was filed by a company called WADECO. Jim Wade, brother of then Dallas County District Attorney Henry Wade, formed a shell corporation specifically to challenge WFAA license renewal and take over the operation of Channel 8. The firm had no assets, and its challenge was based solely on the FCC's rumblings at the time about the perils of media cross-ownership, and on the recent success of a similar takeover in Boston. In Boston, the challenger had been awarded the license and taken over operation of the television station with no cash payment to the original operator of the station other than for its building and equipment.

Likewise, on the radio front, Maxwell Communications, owners and operators of the Dallas independent television station Channel 33, filed a civil antitrust lawsuit against Belo that challenged its licenses to operate its two radio stations. Both matters were ultimately decided in Belo's favor, but not for almost ten years, and not before the broadcasting managers had spent incalculable hours assembling materials, year after year, to support the company's applications for license renewals. In addition, Belo spent millions of dollars over the years in legal fees and other related costs.

Even as shareholder challenges had led to the sale of the *Dallas Times Herald*, Belo was experiencing its own version of shareholder unrest. After exploring the advantages and disadvantages of taking the company public in 1969, Belo's directors determined that it was not good timing for the company. Instead, Ben Decherd began an active program to communicate more regularly and individually with those shareholders who were most vocal about wanting a public market established. The most insistent of those was Gordon Jackson, whom Joe Dealey had already asked not to come to the corporate offices because of his penchant for shouting and using foul language when Joe was not immediately forthcoming with information about financial and operations matters.

The key difference between the shareholders of the Dallas Times Herald Company, who sold the paper to Times Mirror, and those of Belo at the time was that the beneficial owners of Belo stock were almost all first cousins and direct descendants of G. B. Dealey, or they had been active in the management of the company for years and years. In several cases they were both. And all of them shared a strong, common interest in working things out, although Gordon's impatience and impulsiveness strained relations on occasion. Jimmy Moroney characterized the Belo shareholder situation during those times as one of intently working through difficulties and maintaining communications among the principal shareholders, as much as possible, until compromises could be worked out:

> I think there were those of us who were in the third generation who felt very strongly about wanting to preserve the company as much as we could as a family entity and a local institution, and we were able to get along—now that's probably the most important thing—we were able to get along.[25]

That third generation of G. B. Dealey's family, which Jimmy noted was "able to get along" in the long run, included eleven first cousins: Jimmy Moroney, Jr., and his sisters, Betty Moroney Norsworthy and Jean Moroney Laney; Joe Dealey and his sister, Clara Patricia Dealey Brooks; Ben Decherd, whose only sibling had died young; brothers Henry Allen Jackson, Rice R. Jackson, Jr., and twins Gordon Dealey Jackson and Gilbert Stuart Jackson; and Al Dealey, who was an only child. The terms of the G. B. Dealey Trust would eventually make those cousins, along with the Lubben family members, the primary shareholders of the company, in their various percentages as determined by G. B.'s will.

G. B. Dealey had left equal portions of his Belo stock to each of his three daughters, who were never part of the operations of the company, and to his surviving son, who had been included as an equity partner in the 1926 reorganization of the company. All of G. B.'s Class A common stock was left in trust, with each of the four surviving children to receive dividends on $^{15}/_{64}$ths of his 68 percent of the company's stock. The dividends on the remaining $^{4}/_{64}$ths were to go to the only child of the late Walter Dealey. As it turned out, the terms of the will meant that the descendants of the daughters, including the four Jackson children, the three Moroney children, and Ben Decherd, would one day collectively own more of the company than the descendants of the two sons, who had been included as partners in the company from the start. Furthermore, Fannie's only surviving child, Ben, would become the largest individual shareholder.

The division of shares held in trust had been clear since 1946, but it was not clear when the cousins would be able to realize their inheritances, or what the value would be when the Trust expired. When Ted died on November 26, 1969, at age seventy-seven, he left one surviving sibling, his youngest sister, Maidie Dealey Moroney, who lived for another twenty one months, until August 25, 1971. According to the terms of the Trust, the eleven cousins would become owners of their shares exactly five years after Maidie's death, as she was the last remaining of G. B.'s five children. However, according to bylaw 25, if they wanted to maintain their ownership of the shares (rather than sell them back to the company at a price determined by the formula in bylaw 25), they too would be required to put them in trust for their heirs, which trusts would be required to last for at least twenty-one years following their own deaths.

The only way to repeal bylaw 25 was by "the unanimous consent of all holders of the Class A common stock of the corporation and all persons owning the equitable title of or beneficial interest in any of such stock." Until then, the various attempts to reach unanimous agreement among the beneficiaries of the Trust and the other Class A common stockholders had failed. At least some of those shareholders always preferred the status quo over the unknown outcome of shareholder freedom. And from all accounts of those days, it was all about shareholder freedom rather than money.

The first annual meeting of shareholders after Maidie Dealey Moroney's death was held on March 28, 1972. It was the first meeting at which all eleven cousins were in attendance, including Al Dealey, Patsy Dealey Brooks, Betty Moroney Norsworthy, Jean Moroney Lancy, and the four Jackson brothers, in addition to the three who were company officers and directors, Joe Dealey, Ben Decherd, and Jimmy Moroney. The various trustees, acting on behalf of the beneficial shareholders of the numerous trusts represented by then, reelected the members of the existing board of directors, which numbered eleven after the deaths of Jim Moroney in 1968, Ted Dealey in 1969, and Gordon Rupe in 1970.

The G. B. Dealey Trust was represented by trustees Ben Decherd, Joe Dealey, and Jimmy Moroney. Additionally, Joe was trustee for the Ted Dealey Residue Trust, as well as for the trust for the Walter Dealey family, and other Dealey family interests; Joe Lubben was trustee for the Lubben family interests; and Jimmy Moroney was trustee for the Moroney family interests. Although the informal discussions, that is, those that did not lead to votes or resolutions, were not recorded in the minutes of that meeting, it is likely that while gathered for that meeting the cousins continued their long-running discussion of the restrictions placed on them by the continuation of the 1926 contract among shareholders and by bylaw 25.

By then, Ben had learned that he had advanced lung cancer, and he had been in treatment for the disease for almost a year. Coming to terms with his own mortality, Ben put his mind to building consensus among the Class A common stockholders in order to end the tyranny of bylaw 25. He worked closely with directors Maurice Purnell, the board's legal advisor, and Bill Smellage, who was also an officer of the company, to accomplish that important change in the company's governing documents. Ben knew that he had to succeed so that when the G. B. Dealey Trust expired on August 25, 1976, and the shares were divided among the cousins and his own children, they would not be subject to the restrictive terms that had effectively held the company intact for thirty years.

Ben surely recognized that among the key stockholders, he was the one most likely to be able to reconcile the diverse points of view. He had maintained his friendships with all of his cousins through the years, including the Jackson brothers, and he had earned the respect and admiration of the company officers and other inside stockholders with his practical and equitable administration of the company for thirty-six years. And by then, he surely knew that he would not live much longer.

Behind the scenes, Ben held numerous individual conversations with his cousins, with company management, and with the lawyers representing Belo. The lawyers prepared a written consent to dissolve the shareholder contract and repeal bylaw 25, leaving blanks for the signature of the shareholder and the date it would be signed. The document was sent to all shareholders on October 25, 1972, along with a letter from Joe Dealey calling a special meeting of shareholders for November 6, 1972. Joe's letter strongly encouraged shareholders to attend the meeting for further discussions of the matter, but he also encouraged them to sign the unanimous consent and return it in advance of the meeting even if they planned to attend.

The minutes of that Special Stockholders' Meeting held on Monday, November 6, 1972, note that "Upon roll call, it was determined that all of the issued and outstanding common stock, being 2,880,658 shares, was represented by proxy or in person." The minutes further record that the shareholders unanimously consented to cancel the 1926 contract and to repeal bylaw 25, both to be effective on January 1, 1973. The beneficiaries of the G. B. Dealey Trust would be free at last to access their inheritances when the Trust expired, and to plan their futures in the meantime.

The resultant enthusiasm and optimism among shareholders was short-lived, however, when less than two weeks later, on November 18, 1972, Ben died of lung cancer at age fifty-seven. Ben had been the channel of communications for everyone involved in company ownership matters—the board of directors, the officers of the company, the family shareholders—for all of them with each other, but especially with the Jackson brothers, whom the others knew less well.

Joe Dealey and others long had been affected by Ted's harsh attitudes toward the Jacksons, stemming from his uneasy relationship with their mother, his sister Annie. Joe and the others viewed Gordon Jackson's interest in creating liquidity in the Belo stock to be unreasonable and threatening to the company's stability. Gordon's increasingly frequent requests for information about the company were routinely snubbed by the ever circumspect Joe. Ben, on the other hand, respected the Jacksons' right to have more information about the workings of the corporation of which they were to be significant shareholders, and he saw their interest in establishing a market for Belo shares as only reasonable, under the circumstances. Without Ben, communications with the Jacksons would be difficult, if not impossible, considering the existing rancor between them and other Belo directors.

Then, only six days after Ben died, Maurice Purnell died. He was the second most senior member of the board and its most longtime and trusted legal advisor. Maurice, sixty-six, had served twenty-two years as a board member. At the final meeting of the board that year, which was held less than a month later, on December 19, 1972, the directors passed the usual resolutions recognizing each man for his contributions to the company. The resolution recognizing Maurice Purnell recalled his "more than a third of a century" serving as the company's legal counsel, as well as his service as a director. It particularly noted "his successful defense of the Belo Plan for newsroom employees of the *Dallas News* before the United States Supreme Court," noting that the Belo Plan "served the newspaper industry well for many years" after that victory. The second paragraph of the Purnell resolution reads,

> It was particularly tragic that the loss of Maurice Purnell should follow by less than a week that of his fellow-board member, our Chairman of the Board, H. Ben Decherd. Without their guiding talents this Board will find its tasks much more difficult.[26]

Those words were more than the standard rhetoric written in commemoration. They proved prophetic, as the other directors struggled with increasingly complex shareholder issues and increasingly impatient shareholders, particularly Gordon Jackson. And all the while, the company had to be run better than it ever had been, as the *Times Herald* went after the *News*'s readers and advertisers as never before.

But the year 1972 held one more surprise and distraction for Joe Dealey. Joe's older son, Joe Dealey, Jr., who went by the nickname "Scoop," given to him by his grandfather Ted Dealey, had already graduated from Trinity University in San Antonio and returned to the *News* to work in the news department as a writer. He was the first member of his generation of G. B. Dealey descendants to come into the company, and with him in mind, the company executives had created a three-year management training program. Joe had entered the program at the beginning of 1972, beginning a planned rotation through the various departments of the company. His chief interest was in writing, particularly for the opinion pages, and his name sometimes appeared in the paper as a byline on articles or columns he composed.

On the same day as the year's final meeting of the Belo directors, December 19, 1972, two Garland, Texas, brothers kidnapped Joe Jr.'s beautiful young bride of less than two months, Amanda Mayhew Dealey. They sent a ransom note to Joe Dealey, Sr., rather than to her husband, Joe Jr., or to her own wealthy father, Charles Mayhew. Joe Sr. immediately contacted the *News*'s key editors and his friends at the other local media outlets and put a news blackout on the story while he and Charles Mayhew assembled the $250,000 demanded by the kidnappers. On December 22, the ransom was paid, Mandy was released, and a few hours later, the kidnappers were captured in their home counting the loot.

That night WFAA-TV ran a special half-hour report called "Mandy's home for Christmas," preempting a network show, and the following day the *News* devoted its front page to the story, plus four more pages inside. The local news blackout in the early hours of the kidnapping, then the extensive coverage in the Belo media properties after the kidnappers' capture, led to criticism of Joe Sr. among the company's own journalists. They believed that the story should have been played as any other socialite kidnapping would have been played, which at the time would not have been given five pages in the newspaper or a special half-hour on television. Ultimately, the community showed how it felt about the coverage, though, when a local jury gave the brothers each 5,005 years in prison after finding them guilty at their trial less than four months later.

Chapter 6

ENTER THE FOURTH GENERATION

1973–1976

Most of the business of the final meeting of company directors in 1972 dealt with assigning Ben Decherd's considerable operational responsibilities to other officers of the company. Joe Lubben was elected a trustee of the G. B. Dealey Trust to replace Ben, but no new directors were elected, and no new chairman was named. In fact, the board did not replace Ben as chairman for another seven years, such was the effect of his loss on his two cousins and fellow directors, Joe Dealey and Jimmy Moroney, and on the other Belo directors. Joe presided at the meetings.

When Ben died, he was survived by his wife, Isabelle, and their two children. Their daughter, Dealey, and son, Robert, were the heirs of his 15/64ths of the G. B. Dealey Trust. The older of the two children was Dealey, who at the time was living in El Paso with her husband, H. David Herndon, and their three-year-old son, Ben. She was four months pregnant with their second child, Bryan.

Her brother, Robert William Decherd, was a senior at Harvard College, majoring in American history and serving as president of the *Harvard Crimson*. He had already begun interviewing for jobs as a reporter at newspapers in Baltimore, New York, and Washington, D.C., looking toward his May 1973 graduation. The night before his father died in Houston at M. D. Anderson Hospital, Robert's mother called to say he should come home immediately. He traveled all night, arriving three hours before Ben died with Isabelle, Dealey, and Robert by his side.

That morning also marked the beginning of a remarkably close, lifelong bond between Robert, Dealey, and Jimmy Moroney. The door to Ben's hospital room opened at about 9:30 a.m. and Jimmy walked in; he had flown from Dallas simply to say good-bye. After a few minutes at Ben's bedside, Jimmy signaled Robert to step outside the room with him for a talk. Sitting on the concrete steps of the hospital's internal stairwell, Jimmy spoke fondly of his cousin and friend since childhood. He told Robert that from that day forward Robert could always count on him; then, he headed back to Dallas. Robert never forgot Jimmy's graceful act of love toward his father and his family, and he soon found himself relying heavily on Jimmy's support of him and Dealey.

Neither Robert nor his sister was fully aware of their father's extensive financial interests in Belo, because their parents had never made an issue of their legacy. Like the other beneficiaries of the G. B. Dealey Trust, Ben had never had real access to the wealth represented by his interest in the company. While the family lived very comfortably on Ben's salary and his income from the Trust, the children were not raised in great wealth. In an interview in 1987, Robert said, "It sounds almost incredible in retrospect, but when my father died in 1972, I was a senior in college, and I couldn't tell you I had a sophisticated understanding at all of this company—what the institution was, and what it represented, or what his [Ben's] role in a family sense was at the *Dallas Morning News* or the Belo Corporation."[1]

Until his father's illness progressed to an incurable state, Robert had never questioned him extensively about the family business, nor had he ever seriously considered coming back to Dallas immediately after graduation to work at Belo. His father's early departure from the scene changed everything. While in Dallas over Christmas break that year, Robert made an appointment to meet with Joe and Jimmy. He told them that he and his sister, Dealey, wanted to determine as quickly as possible what their roles should be with their combined 16-percent interest in the company.

At the same time, Joe Jr. was progressing through the management training program at the *News*, and the next generation of management leaders was rising on the broadcast side of the business. After graduating from SMU in 1960, Ward L. Huey, Jr., spent a brief time at Glenn Advertising in Dallas, before joining WFAA-TV as a camera operator. With his innate talent for salesmanship and his enthusiasm for the future of television, Ward quickly scaled the ranks to sales manager and was named station manager in late 1972. In mid-1972, another promising candidate for management, David T. Lane, who had been on-air as sportscaster and news anchor at WFAA, was sent to the Beaumont station, KFDM, to bolster the efforts there, and by the end of the year he was made station manager. In 1973, Ward hired Marty Haag to come to Dallas as news director, and almost immediately the newsroom lit up with his energy and his passion for getting at the heart of the stories of the day. Marty hired Iola Johnson and WFAA soon climbed to the top of the Dallas/Fort Worth market.

The years 1972 and 1973 produced record profits for Belo. Joe reported to the stockholders that the 1972 profits were "plowed back in additions to the property, plant and equipment, and a reduction of debt, and dividends to shareholders."[2] He reminded them that "... the reinvestment ... into the business is a continuation of a long standing philosophy to keep our properties in the forefront of new and changing developments and industry environments." The figures for 1973 were even higher, as were the dividends. But in spite of profit growth year after year, Joe remained a frugal, fiscally conservative president, always reminding his officers that fixed costs were rising even faster than revenues, and that profits depended entirely on maintaining tight budgets, particularly in salaries. Furthermore, his passion for not taking on debt limited the company's ability to grow.

Robert Decherd attended his first Annual Stockholders' Meeting on March 27, 1973, a few months after his father's death. He was joined by eight of the ten surviving first cousins in his father's generation. The only cousins absent were the older two of the four Jackson brothers; however, their younger twin brothers, Gordon and Gilbert, were there. By then Robert had written a letter to Joe formally applying for a job at the *Dallas Morning News*, to begin after his graduation from Harvard.

At the annual meeting in March 1973, Joe nominated five new directors to the Belo board. His nomination of the five came without prior consultation with the shareholders who were not on the board, and he informed the non-family directors only a few days before the meeting, according to Bill Smellage, who was a company officer and director. Joe's announcement was a surprise, to say the least, considering that not only did it represent an unprecedented number of directors added to the board at one time, but it was also an unprecedented step toward bringing outside leadership into the governing of Belo. It was a bold step for Joe to take, but he needed the help, especially after losing Ben and Maurice.

In fact, the board had been reduced to nine members by the deaths of five members in fairly rapid succession, and all but one of the nine remaining directors were employees of the company. With the five new directors, the board was returned to its former size of fourteen members, but now with six outside directors. The directors elected in 1973 were Lloyd S. Bowles, Jr.; Robert E. Dennard; Patrick E. Haggerty; James J. Laney; and William H. Seay. (See Appendix B for a complete list of Belo directors from 1926.)

One of the new directors had a close family connection to the remaining ten cousins. James J. Laney had married one of the cousins, Jean Moroney, in 1942. At the time of his election to the board, Jim was also Belo's general counsel and president of the law firm Locke, Purnell, Boren, Laney & Neeley. In that regard, he might be viewed as replacing Maurice Purnell on the board, and as continuing the relationship with the firm that helped G. B. Dealey establish the A. H. Belo Corporation in 1926. He was familiar with Belo both as its longtime lawyer and as a member of the extended family for more than thirty years. Jim and Jean had two children, daughter Olivia Elizabeth, born in 1946, and son David McQueen, born in 1949.

Another new director had more distant family connections. Upon his election to the Belo board, William H. Seay was the chairman, president, and chief executive officer of Dallas-based Southwestern Life Insurance Corporation, one of the nation's ten largest stock life insurance companies. But he was also the grandson of one of G. B. Dealey's sisters. His grandmother Elizabeth Dealey Seay, along with her husband, C. M. Seay, had moved from Galveston to Dallas in 1885 when G. B. Dealey was sent to establish the *Dallas Morning News*. Bill Seay's grandfather had worked first at the *News* in Galveston, then at the *Dallas News*, for more than fifty years, always in a mid-management capacity under Leven Deputy in the composing room.

Bill Seay recalled growing up with the *Dallas Morning News* as a constant in his parents' home because of his grandfather's devotion to the company. But he did not become well acquainted with most of his cousins who were G. B. Dealey's grandchildren until he attended the University of Texas in the late 1930s and early 1940s. Bill and Joe Dealey were close to the same age, and they became good friends while both were students in Austin. Bill also became friends with Jimmy Moroney at that time, when Jimmy joined them at the university a couple of years later.

Bill was born in 1920 in Dallas and attended Woodrow Wilson High School, along with two other grandchildren of G. B. Dealey, Gordon and Gilbert Jackson, with whom he was close friends. At the University of Texas, he was an outstanding athlete, serving as a member of the sprint medley relay team that set a world record. He served as a captain in the U.S. Army during World War II, and after the war he joined his family's investment banking firm, Henry, Seay, and Black. In 1957, he was hired by Universal Life and Accident Insurance Co. as a vice president, and when it was acquired by Southwestern Life, he was made head of the combined company. Bill was also deeply involved in civic and charitable activities in Dallas, and his particular blend of expertise, relationships, and personal qualities of intelligence, humility, and quiet wisdom made him an important addition to the Belo board.

Another of the five new directors, Lloyd S. Bowles, "was chosen because he exemplified the business, civic and humanitarian leadership of the city of Dallas" that Belo was looking for in a director.[3] When he joined the Belo board he was chairman, president, and chief executive officer of the Dallas Federal Savings and Loan Association. He was also an active leader in many of the charitable and civic organizations that Belo and its officers had supported over the years.

Lloyd Bowles was born in Cherokee, Oklahoma, in 1916; attended Southern Methodist University, from which he received the Distinguished Alumnus Award in 1968; and served in the U.S. Army during World War II, leaving the service as a captain. When he joined Belo's board, Lloyd Bowles was also on the boards of five other major Dallas business institutions, as well as the boards of numerous industry organizations nationally.

Robert E. Dennard was president and a director of Dallas Rupe & Son, Inc., an investment banking firm founded by his wife Paula's grandfather, which he had joined in 1951. He was also president and director of the firm's parent company, Rupe Investment. Paula Dennard's father, D. Gordon Rupe, whom Dennard had succeeded at Rupe Investment, had earlier served as a director of Belo for ten years, from 1960 until his death in 1970. So, in addition to having distinguished himself in the Dallas community, Bob Dennard also had historical ties to Belo. Before joining Dallas Rupe & Son, he had founded an insurance company, Robert E. Dennard & Co., in 1947.

Patrick E. Haggerty, the fifth of the new directors, was chairman of the board of Texas Instruments, Inc. Haggerty was born in North Dakota and graduated from Marquette University in 1936 as an electrical engineer. During World War II, he served in the U.S. Navy as a lieutenant in the Bureau of Aeronautics in Washington, D.C., where he met J. Erik Jonsson and Cecil H. Green, whose Dallas company, Geophysical Service, Inc., made a successful bid proposal to develop electronic devices to detect submarines. Following the war, Jonsson and Green persuaded Haggerty to join them in Dallas to help build GSI beyond its wartime capabilities. Their partnership, along with the other GSI partners, Eugene McDermott and H. B. Peacock, ultimately grew GSI into the international powerhouse they renamed Texas Instruments.

Pat was a brilliant scientist as well as businessman, and Belo was only one of numerous boards on which he served nationwide. When he joined the Belo board, he was on the board of governors of the U.S. Postal Service, chairman of the National Council on Educational Research, National Fund Co-chairman for the American Red Cross, a member of the boards and executive committees of Rockefeller University and the University of Dallas, and a member of the International Advisory Committee of Chase Manhattan Bank. He already held honorary degrees from seven universities and was a Fellow of the Institute of Electrical and Electronics Engineers.

It was no coincidence that all five of Belo's new directors were prominent and widely known for their business acumen, as well as for their community involvement. In the news story announcing their election, the *News* reporter noted, "All 14 directors of Belo live in the Dallas area and base their operations there, accenting the company's tradition of an independent, locally controlled enterprise."[4] It was obvious that Joe's aim was to distinguish Belo's local governance from the outside ownership and growing outside influence at the *Dallas Times Herald*. And those five new directors started Belo's inexorable march into the modern world with their business expertise and insights.

Following the March 1973 annual meeting, Robert made two and a half pages of single-spaced, typed notes recording his impressions of the proceedings. He had been surprised by the way Joe managed to disregard the concerns of the non-management shareholders as he quickly went from one agenda item to the next without allowing time for questions or discussion. No doubt, Robert felt responsible for reporting on the meeting to his sister, who was not able to attend, and he was not happy about Joe's dismissive manner. He began his notes,

> As a contingent beneficiary of the G. B. Dealey Trust, I am deeply concerned about a wide range of problems which came to my attention prior to the annual meeting. I had anticipated that the stockholders' meeting would provide me an opportunity to hear some discussion of these problems; I do not think I am alone in feeling that the stockholders' meeting was a disappointment.[5]

The large turnout at the shareholders' meeting reflected the growing concerns of the non-management beneficiaries and shareholders about recent management decisions made without their knowledge. In particular, as part of the FCC license renewal challenge, the officers and directors had created a separate trust to hold a certain number of shares of common stock of the company. The trust was designed to function legally as the owner of Belo's broadcasting properties, because at the time there was no corporate distinction between Belo and the *Dallas Morning News*. The broadcast trust essentially separated the ownership of the television and radio stations from the newspaper. The Jackson brothers, as well as Robert and his mother, were expecting to hear an explanation of that decision. None was given. In fact, Joe quickly adjourned the meeting after concluding his perfunctory agenda, before inviting any questions from shareholders. Robert's notes continue:

> The Jacksons' grievances, and much of my concern, center on what appears to be a glaring lack of any free flow of information between management, beneficiaries and stockholders. . . . This circumvention of beneficiaries and stockholders, some of whom have holdings equal to those of anyone involved with the Belo Corporation, is insulting if not illegal. . . . More specifically, the intent of G. B. Dealey's will, it seems to me, was not to vest control of the corporation in the few, but to rely on the collective judgment of his descendants. So far as I can tell, recently collective judgment has been shunted and ignored rather than sought—and without cause or justification.[6]

Following the meeting, Robert and his mother, Isabelle, talked at length with Gordon Jackson, who commented to them that Ben Decherd and Maurice Purnell had been the only ones on the board who treated the Jacksons with respect. Reflecting on the situation, Robert noted that "[Gordon] will someday blow this whole business wide open if management does not begin to respond to his inquiries and suggestions with dignity." Two months before he graduated from college, Robert seemed resolved to take on the challenge of opening communications at Belo, so that the institution could survive the double threat of the competitive challenges to the business operations from the outside and the heightened stresses of generational change among the family owners of the business. His private notes on March 30, 1973, concluded,

> The time has come for the management of the Belo Corporation to realize that the beneficiaries and stockholders of this corporation are not stupid, that they are thoughtful and intelligent people representative of a great corporate tradition, and that they resent being treated like children. These people deserve to know what is going on in the corporation, how their substantial interests are being protected and administered. I suspect that most of them could provide perspectives which might well aid, rather than retard, the management of the corporation; indeed, the free flow of information cuts both ways.

Robert, with his sister's support and counsel, was forming his own management style as he reflected on Joe's modus operandi.

Remarking on those early days of the newly constituted 1973 Belo board, Bill Seay said in a 1992 interview that the five new outside directors kept quiet only briefly, becoming active right away in areas that seemed to need the most attention. Minutes of the meetings from those days reveal that at the first meeting after being elected, Bill Seay was the first of the new directors to speak up, recommending the appointment of an audit committee. He was acting on his knowledge of the records and documentation that would be expected of Belo if and when the time came to take the company public, and most likely he also recognized that the current stockholders required more detailed financial information immediately. He was supported vigorously by Pat Haggerty, who recommended that the audit committee be made up entirely of outside directors, and Jim Laney, whose additional recommendations led to overall better financial controls and a close review and improvement of the policies and business practices of the company.

Bill Seay further recalled that Joe and Jimmy were both completely open to his comments and recommendations, and that they never failed to heed the advice and guidance of the outside directors. Many years later, Robert Decherd commented about the five outside directors who joined the board together in 1973: "Their judgment and foresight, together with Earl Cullum's [the sixth outside director, elected in 1960], were largely responsible for the transition Belo achieved from a family company to a fully distributed, publicly held company with the same standards and values."[7]

Robert's insightful predictions about Gordon Jackson almost came true a couple of months later, when Gordon and his brothers, Gilbert and Henry Allen, filed suit against the company in May 1973. The suit attempted to block the newly created broadcast trust and sought a full accounting of the G. B. Dealey Trust Estate. The Jacksons quickly dropped their suit when the Belo directors were forthcoming with an explanation of the purpose of the new trust, which the Jacksons readily accepted as sound. However, Gordon's action was successful anyway, in that he and all the other beneficiaries of the G. B. Dealey Trust were given their first-ever detailed historical accounting of the assets of the Trust.

In a July 20, 1973, cover memo addressed to all beneficiaries and signed by the three trustees, Joe Dealey, Jimmy Moroney, and Joe Lubben, the first paragraph read: "For your use we enclose an accounting which itemizes each and every receipt and disbursement of the G. B. Dealey Trust from its initial funding on May 14, 1948 through the end of 1972."[8] The memo continues,

> Although none of us was a trustee during the early years of the Trust, we have undertaken to assemble and set forth on the attached Appendix A a detailed historical resume relating to the assets of the Trust and on Appendix B further information as to some of the items of receipt and expenditure which are not self-explanatory.

At last, the beneficiaries of the Trust had a detailed accounting history of the trustees' handling of the majority of Belo's stock. Appendixes A and B reflected exactly what the chairmen of the Trust had reported in oral summaries over the years; however, the written reports represented an important step toward a more sophisticated approach to providing information to those family shareholders who were not privy to the inner workings of the business.

Soon after the new board members were elected, and in conjunction with the creation of the broadcast trust, Belo formed a subsidiary, Belo Broadcasting Corporation, to separate the management of its television and radio operations from the newspaper side of the business. Internal documents explain the separation as growing out of the need "to meet increasingly stringent requirements of the Federal Communications Commission governing ownership and management."[9] The changing rules had sparked the costly challenge to WFAA's license renewal by WADECO, Inc., as well as the separate antitrust lawsuit by Maxwell Communications, both of which were still unresolved at the time. That was also the year that WFAA-FM Radio found a new voice, targeting the growing young audience. It changed its call letters to KZEW, calling itself "the Zoo," started playing rock 'n' roll, and made money for the first time in its history.

In those culturally volatile times, both the *News* and the *Times Herald* faced the necessity to make changes in their approaches to serving their readers. Dallas was finally growing out of its provincial status quo and beginning to experience more open racial conflicts. One such conflict was a galvanizing event, when African Americans joined Mexican Americans and many non-minority participants demonstrating their outrage following the killing by the Dallas police of a twelve-year-old Mexican American child while he was illegally restrained for questioning in July 1973. The citizens of Dallas could no longer ignore issues that both newspapers, as well as the local television stations, had routinely avoided in their unenlightened efforts to keep ugly truths in the dark.

But the era also included unprecedented growth for the region. The new Dallas/Fort Worth International Airport opened that fall; a groundbreaking was held for a new I. M. Pei–designed Dallas City Hall; and increasing tourism, partly fueled by the incessant interest in the assassination of President Kennedy, had led to an expansion of the Dallas Convention Center.

At that point, however, the citizens of Dallas had been unable to agree upon an appropriate memorial to President Kennedy at the site, Dealey Plaza, or at the Texas School Book Depository Building where the shots had been fired. Again reflecting the local tendency to avoid spotlighting unflattering images of the city, there was even discussion of tearing down the School Book Depository.

The only public acknowledgment that Dallas had any connections to President Kennedy was a privately funded fifty-foot square cenotaph designed by Philip Johnson that was constructed in 1970, two blocks away and out of sight of Dealey Plaza. It was intended as a commemoration of Kennedy's presidency, but it held no interpretive narrative. The only inscription was his name, John Fitzgerald Kennedy, engraved in gold on a plinth in the center.

The first obvious sign of change in the two dominant daily newspapers was at the *Times Herald*, when Tom Johnson took over the newsroom in 1973. At the *News*, the next generation of family members was moving into place, with Joe Dealey, Jr., and now Robert Decherd in the management training program.

Joe Jr. had enlisted in the U.S. Army after graduating from Trinity University in San Antonio. In 1971, upon completing basic training at Ft. Knox, Kentucky, Joe Jr. was awarded the American Spirit Honor Medal as the "trainee who 'best exemplified the qualities of loyalty, honor, initiative, leadership and high example to his comrades in arms.'"[10] Following that, he went through officer training and briefly considered a military career before returning to the *News*, as was expected of him. However, he remained in the military as a member of the Army National Guard for many years, while building his career with the company.

Robert had begun the program on September 17, 1973, and he and Joe were joined in 1974 by Joe's brother, Russell E. Dealey, and another recent graduate of Harvard, Jeremy L. Halbreich, who had been business manager of the *Crimson* the year following Robert's tenure as president. Jeremy's interests lay in the business management and marketing side of the newspaper.

The following year Belo continued its upward movement in net profits, in spite of a growing economic recession nationally. Both the print and broadcast properties managed to end 1974 on a high note, although there was unrest in the newsroom. Some of the reporters and editors at the *News* began a quiet revolt against low salaries and held discussions with representatives of the American Newspaper Guild concerning organizing at the *News*. The matter was dropped when the Guild spokesman failed to show for a meeting to move the plan forward, and soon thereafter another labor issue heated up dramatically. The Pressmen's Union decided to stand firm against management of both the *News* and the *Times Herald* over the issue of "manning" the presses.

National leaders of the Pressmen's Union, one of six that were in place at the *News* at the time, were at odds with the *News* and the *Times Herald* over the number of employees required to be at work at any one time on each press. The position of the newspapers was that the union's requirements were outdated, excessive, and unfair. Dick Blum explained the union's rigid manning regulations:

> The manning precluded men from transferring from one press to another, so that when you were running three or four presses . . . and one press broke down, . . . people who were working on the other presses would all stand around and watch those who worked very hard to do the work. They were not allowed to transfer and help.[11]

The *News*'s management, with the full knowledge and approval of the board of directors, offered contracts to the pressmen that guaranteed their jobs for life, if they would agree to reduce the manning regulations. The offer of stable jobs with no threat of layoffs was consistent with Alfred H. Belo's 1866 dealings with the National Typographical Union, and with G. B. Dealey's Belo Plan for wage and hour fairness, which was upheld by the Supreme Court in 1942. The pressmen, many of whom worked on both the morning and afternoon newspapers, were represented in the meetings with both newspapers' management teams by local union leaders and by a representative of the Pressmen's national organization, who was authorized to make the final decisions. A story published in the *News* reported, "On May 2, 1974, following 29 bargaining sessions which began July 2, 1973, the Pressmen's Union struck the *News* and the *Times Herald* and established picket lines at both papers."[12] As soon as the picket lines formed, the national representative of the Pressman's Union got on a plane and left, apparently considering that his job in Dallas was done.

Dick Blum recalled that when the pressmen emptied their lockers and walked out, he stood in the silent pressroom for a few minutes thinking about what would have to be done to publish the next day's paper without them. Luckily for the newspaper, and partly due to his skills as a negotiator, none of the other unions joined the strike, and most of the supervisors in the pressroom stayed, along with the foremen. Together, they worked with trained volunteers from throughout the company and other nearby non-union newspapers to continue to publish the paper. The *Times Herald* similarly continued publication without interruption.

Like other unionized newspapers, the *News* had sent non-pressroom employees to press training school during the year and a half leading up to the strike. They had spent up to six months at the training schools so that if necessary, they could fill in for the striking pressmen with no interruption in publication of the paper. When the picketers showed up, employees from advertising, circulation, promotion, facilities, and even the four members of the management training program stepped in to help put out the newspaper.

The stress caused by such a rift within the company ranks took its toll on everyone involved, but in his annual report for the year, Joe Dealey, in his typical understatement, said, "The pressmen's strike at the *News*, initiated in early May, continued throughout the year with no publication days lost because of it."[13]

All of the union members who left were replaced with others willing to work without the restrictions placed on the company by the Pressmen's Union. A dozen or so of the *News*'s employees who had trained for the fill-in positions decided to stay permanently in the pressroom, and non-union pressmen from other places came to Dallas. When the union members offered to return to work under the terms originally offered, they found that their jobs already were taken.

The following year and a half was remarkable only in that Belo companies held steady in the midst of a national recession, when businesses were closing and advertisers were cutting back budgets. Joe Dealey, Jr. Russell Dealey, Robert Decherd, and Jeremy Halbreich continued their management training, and eventually they were joined by a few others.

In January 1975, Robert married Maureen Healy, another Dallas native, who had graduated from the University of Texas at Austin in 1973.

Working together throughout 1973, 1974, and 1975, Robert and Dealey had privately lobbied Joe, Jimmy, and Joe Lubben, as trustees of the G. B. Dealey Trust, for a place on the Belo board, in recognition of their position among family shareholders. Joe politely but stubbornly dragged his feet and put off discussing the matter with Belo board members.

Robert and Dealey's plea was straightforward, supported by facts, as well as simple logic, and they patiently repeated their position year after year, since Joe required them to remind him, as though he had been too busy to give it much thought.

In a meeting in October 1974, Joe hedged about the matter by saying first that if he put Robert on the board the Jacksons would "go wild." Then he further commented that those in the management training program, presumably meaning Joe Jr. and Robert, in particular, would have to be patient and "win your spurs" before being considered for board membership.

Robert and Dealey were undaunted and pointed out that there was no basis for comparing their interests with the concerns of the Jacksons, particularly considering Ben's thirty-five-year career at the company and his long tenure on the board. Then Robert reminded Joe first of the substantial difference between his own stock interests and those of the others in the management training program, but more to the point, that his interest in a Decherd representative on the Belo board had nothing to do with his participation in the management training program.

Jimmy supported Robert and Dealey's position, and according to Robert's detailed meeting notes, several times during meetings Jimmy reminded Joe that Robert and Dealey were rightfully interested in a place on the board. Jimmy further clarified for Joe that Robert was not seeking family representation as a trustee of the G. B. Dealey Trust, which Joe seemed determined to misunderstand. His ongoing confusion was aided somewhat by Joe Lubben's immediate offer to step aside from both the Trust and the Belo board in favor of the Decherds' request. However, Joe's main objective seems to have been to avoid confrontation from any other interests, not just the Jacksons, but even his immediate family.

The Decherd family efforts were finally acknowledged on March 23, 1976, when, at the annual meeting of shareholders, Robert was elected a director, replacing Joe Lubben, who by then had reached the board's customary retirement age. Robert's mother, Isabelle, wrote a letter to Joe Lubben expressing her feelings upon his retirement:

> Dear Joe and Rene—
>
> Joy and sorrow have a way of walking hand in hand. So it is with me today. The contemplation of Belo without Lubben wrenches my heart, and is acceptable only in the light of what Belo has

> been with Lubben. . . . Belo and those who comprise it will forever be benefited by your years there.
>
> Robert's election to the Board is, of course, a source of great happiness for us all, and the fact that he is taking your seat has not only great meaning for him, but for Dealey and me as well. I am confident that he will discharge his duties in a manner that will justify your faith in him.[14]

Robert was about two weeks away from turning twenty-five when he joined the board, which was made up of thirteen members of his father's generation, including some of the most accomplished and powerful men in Texas.

Robert's sister, Dealey, recalled in a 2006 interview that getting Robert on the board was a way of "leveling the playing field" with his cousins, whose fathers would be looking out for them. She knew he could hold his own once he got there, because "once you level the playing field, Robert is going to win."

A day or two after the annual meeting, Robert received a handwritten congratulatory note from Joe Dealey, Jr., to which he responded, "I know you recognize the situation which resulted in my good fortune, and I want you to know how much your confidence and thoughtfulness mean to me. There are many good years ahead of us, and I hope that we both will always be as supportive of one another as you have been to me on this occasion."[15] Afterward, Joe Jr. continued his work as an editorial writer, keeping his distance from the management side of the business, which had never been his primary interest. However, whenever the opportunity arose, Joe Jr. was steadfast in his support of Robert's growing influence.

Robert also received a warm note from Jim Moroney III, who was still a student at Stanford at the time. In his note Jim said, "Though I realize it might be a 'trust motivated' move (referring to the large amount of Decherd stock) I don't think a better person could have been chosen. My proxy will hear no complaints from me."[16] And Robert responded to him, "I want you to know that your dad made the difference in this decision. He stood up for us and held firm to what he believed was right. None of us [the Decherds] will forget his part in our good fortune."[17]

Two other notes must have been especially gratifying to Robert as he stepped into his new role. His sister wrote, "Dearest Director, Here's to the future!! . . . We have great faith in you now as always. Let's hope this is only a beginning and one day we can all say the past years were worth it. If not, thank God you're the person you are and will succeed in a million other ways—we are all so blessed in that. With Love—Dealey."[18]

And his bride of fourteen months wrote, "The honor and great sense of pride you feel must be like that great feeling that I felt on the day you asked me to marry you. I love you with my whole heart and will stand beside you through the many challenges that lie ahead."[19] He was to need their support and encouragement through the coming years, as Belo began its inexorable movement toward becoming a modern business.

Robert's election to the board came while he was still in the management training rotation at the *News*, serving in the news department as assistant to executive editor Tom Simmons. However, he had already shown his practical nature and leadership ability during his school days at both St. Mark's School of Texas, where he graduated cum laude in 1969, and Harvard, where he graduated cum laude in 1973. While he acknowledged that his interest in newspapers was first engendered by his admiration of his father, he said that "the reality is that I started writing sports stories for my middle school newspaper, mostly because no one else wanted to do it, and I thought it was a great opportunity to proclaim the glories of our victories on the football, basketball, and soccer fields."[20] He further explained that in his efforts to excel at St. Mark's, with its focus on overachievement, "I went to my strength, as they say in sports, and that turned out to be the student newspaper. I ended up being the editor."

By the time of his senior year at St. Mark's, Robert had a firsthand, very personal experience with freedom of the press that he says has informed his life ever since. That year, his father, Ben Decherd, happened to be president of the board of trustees of St. Mark's, and the board faced a most difficult situation. The trustees voted to oust the headmaster of the school, and Robert was editor of the bi-weekly school paper. His father never asked him what the paper planned to do in its coverage of the matter, and as Robert and his fellow students covered the disruptive situation fully, no one tried to influence what they published.

In the 1987 interview, Robert said, "That experience had a very powerful effect on me, in terms of what it means to let a news process go on uninterrupted and uninfluenced by people who really have no standing in trying to influence it—but could, if they chose to."

When it came time to select a college, Robert applied to several schools—"at St. Mark's, you were encouraged to believe in the impossible"—and ultimately he had a choice, including Stanford, Yale, and Harvard, which he chose because of the opportunity to work at the *Harvard Crimson*. The *Crimson* is a freestanding corporation, organized and owned by the former editors, "and for a 17- or 18-year-old entering that environment [in 1969], when the world was turning upside down in universities all over this country, that really was an extraordinary experience. . . ."

Five months after Robert joined the Belo board, the G. B. Dealey Trust expired, on August 25, 1976. For several years, the directors had been fending off attempts by Gordon Jackson to create a market for his shares. One of the four Jackson brothers, the second oldest, Rice Jr., had died two years earlier, in May 1974. Although the eldest, Henry Allen, had not expressed concern about his impending inheritance, Gordon was more outspoken than his twin brother, Gilbert, and was impatient for a market to be established. He wanted to be free to trade his inherited stock, but even more importantly, he was concerned that his children would be faced with inheritance taxes and forced to sell without there being an established price and market for the shares.

Gordon was a bright and energetic man. He lived in Dallas with his wife, and they had raised two children, a son and a daughter, who were then in their twenties. He owned a successful manufacturing business, which he had created years earlier, and in the 1950s, he had read the law privately and passed the Texas Bar exam without going to law school. His knowledge of legal procedure in private companies was a powerful tool in his dealings with his cousin Joe.

Earlier in 1976, the Belo directors had hired the New York–based investment firm Morgan Stanley to study the company in order to come up with a value range for the corporation's stock, and to make recommendations regarding the development of a public market for the stock. One of the Morgan Stanley recommendations was a public offering. In April of that year, the company hired two Dallas investment banking firms to confirm the Morgan Stanley study or to make alternative recommendations. The two firms, Eppler, Guerin & Turner, Inc., and Rauscher Pierce Securities Corporation, worked independently of each other and without reference to the Morgan Stanley report.

A committee of Belo directors had been appointed to review the material prepared by the investment firms and to make recommendations to the full board about possible next steps. The Corporate Planning

Committee, as it was called, was chaired by Bill Seay, and the other members were Pat Haggerty and Bob Dennard. Their recommendations were presented to shareholders on August 19, 1976, at a special meeting called in anticipation of the expiration of the Trust a few days later.

At that meeting, which the minutes record was attended by the holders of 93.8 percent of the shares outstanding, including Gordon Jackson, Joe presented a review of activities undertaken by the company over the preceding months, outlining first the recommendations of Morgan Stanley, and then the findings of Eppler, Guerin & Turner and Rauscher Pierce. He summed up his report saying, "... your board of directors sincerely believes that a secondary offering of the Company's Common Stock represents the best and most reasonable solution to the concerns of the stockholders and would be in the best interest of the Company."[21]

In order to have enough shares available for the offering, at a recommended minimum of 500,000 shares, Joe and Jim both committed to sell 10 percent of their personal holdings, and the directors had approved participation by the company with up to 100,000 shares. The remaining would have to come from other shareholders. Those in attendance at the meeting approved further investigation, but in the final analysis the price per share estimated by the bankers was far below what any of the shareholders expected.

Several factors affected the perception of value of Belo's stock at that point, none of which the top executives of the closely held company had worried much about in the past. In fact, Joe had taken pride in several of the factors cited as detrimental to the stock valuation. He considered it a strength that Belo had maintained itself as a small company concentrated in one market, and that it had operated successfully without any real corporate structure. Until then, the senior officers of the *Dallas Morning News* were the top officers of Belo.

Frugality was always a chief aim of Joe's, and right behind that was maintaining the goodwill of the Dallas community toward the *News* and toward him as its recognized leader. Throughout the sixties, as others in the company brought him proposals to purchase newspapers and television stations in other markets, he rebuffed them. He resisted discussing important opportunities such as the *Austin American-Statesman* and the ABC affiliate in New Orleans. The company's two television stations, in his view, were not important assets, compared to the *News*, and so long as they were making money he didn't concern himself with them.

However, the perception in the public market was that Belo was highly vulnerable to being overwhelmed by its competitors in both publishing and broadcasting. The Times Mirror Company, one of the country's most powerful media entities, held exactly the same assets in Dallas/Fort Worth as Belo and made no secret of its plan to take over the market. Since Belo never made its financial affairs public, the bombast of Times Mirror and *Dallas Times Herald* executives' claims had skewed public perception about the strength of Belo in its home market. On top of that, the broadcasting environment was highly volatile all over the country. Belo was locked in the ongoing fight with WADECO over its challenge to WFAA's license to operate Channel 8, as well as with Maxwell Communications in the separate suit challenging Belo's cross-ownership of its radio stations.

A few years earlier, a strike application similar to the WADECO challenge had resulted in Boston's number two newspaper, the *Boston Herald-Traveler*, losing its license to operate its ABC affiliate to a local Boston group that took over operation of the $200 million asset without spending a dime beyond their legal fees. Ultimately, the *Herald-Traveler* was able to recoup a small percentage of its property's value by selling the new licensee its building, cameras, and equipment. That award on the part of the FCC reflected the government's growing wariness about cross-ownership of newspaper and broadcasting properties in a single market. Belo could be next. The shareholders and directors voted to regroup and work on Belo's perceived deficiencies before taking the company public.

Meanwhile, the G. B. Dealey Trust expired on August 25, 1976, and since bylaw 25 had been rescinded, 68 percent of Belo's Class A common stock was distributed to the beneficiaries of the Trust. In the spring of 1977, the A. H. Belo Corporation issued its first formal annual report for the fiscal year 1976. Senior vice president Bill Smellage and vice president/secretary Bob Richardson had a logo and design prepared for the report. The report was written, designed, and printed in-house, and only enough copies were produced to give one to each shareholder and to have a few for internal reference. The graphic design reflected the 1970s clash of tradition with modern language and style. The first page opened with the headline "The A. H. Belo Corporation: *what it is*," and that construction was repeated throughout to explain each of the individual properties.

The report contained a brief history of the company and descriptions of the *Dallas Morning News*; the *Texas Almanac*; News Texan, Inc. (publishers of the suburban dailies); Belo Broadcasting Corporation, with its subsidiaries WFAA-TV in Dallas/Fort Worth, KFDM-TV in Beaumont, WFAA-AM Radio, and KZEW-FM Radio; and Dallas-based Atlas Match Corporation, which in addition to manufacturing specialty book matches included printing operations called Optigraphics Corporation and Visual Panographics, Inc. (Atlas Match and the specialty printing operations were sold in early 1981.)

The 1976 Annual Report presented Belo's first public financial statements after the property descriptions, and it opened with Joe Dealey's letter to "Our Stockholders," juxtaposed with his full-page color portrait. He was posed sitting on the corner of his desk with a fountain pen in his right hand and an enigmatic smile on his face. The second paragraph of his letter read: "Net income for 1976 reached a record level of $7,368,207, a 56 percent increase over the previous year." The report also gave the first public listing of Belo's corporate officers and directors with color photos of all the directors. It was Robert Decherd's first appearance in a Belo annual report.

Deeper into the 1976 president's letter, Joe commented that the distribution of shares held in the G. B. Dealey Trust for thirty years "was undoubtedly a major occurrence in the career and development of the A. H. Belo Corporation." He continued, "While the event itself has not changed the actual operations of your company, it did broaden ownership to the extent that some 118 individuals or legal entities owned stock in the company outright when books were closed on December 31, 1976." He made no reference to the issues affecting Belo without the restrictions placed on its shareholders by their insightful ancestor fifty years earlier. However, he did acknowledge the challenges in the competitive and regulatory environments, as well as ". . . the uncertainty the future surely holds for us all." He closed with "Our purpose and responsibility to you is an objective of increased profitability, greater growth and even a higher degree of excellence. Your management pledges its best efforts to achieve all three."[22]

Chapter 7

COMPETITIVE GAINS AND RAPID CHANGE

1977–1981

While internal family ownership matters were taking up much of the Belo senior executives' time and attention in the late 1960s and early 1970s, the media world was rapidly changing all around them, and company managers were forced to keep pace. As broadcast media had matured and FM radio and UHF television had come into their own, the Federal Communication Commission had begun to voice concerns about the cross-ownership of print and broadcast properties in the same market, because of the prospect that one company's voice would drown out other voices.

Then, in 1975, the FCC enacted formal regulations that prohibited such cross-ownership. Belo and some other companies that owned radio and television stations along with newspapers in the same market were "grandfathered" into the new system, but the relationships changed.

By the time the new rules were in place, Belo had already built an imaginary wall down the middle of the driveway between the newspaper building and the television studios next door. That invisible wall created a highly charged competitive environment in which the *Dallas Morning News* and WFAA tried every day to outdo each other. The employees of the two properties were forbidden by management to confer with one another, and gradually, as personnel changed, they became strangers sharing the same driveway and parking lot.

Even as the *News* fiercely competed with its sister television station, its crosstown rival newspaper, the *Dallas Times Herald*, was ramping up its competitiveness as well. *Times Herald* management had spent 1976 beefing up the newsroom staff by recruiting writers and reporters from leading newspapers around the country, including the *Detroit Free Press*, *Philadelphia Inquirer*, *Miami Herald*, *Louisville Courier-Journal*, and *Washington Post*.[1]

Once the five-year contracts with the former *Times Herald* executives had expired, publisher Tom Johnson recruited Tom McCartin from the *Washington Post* to become executive vice president, focusing on the circulation and advertising side of the business. By the end of the year, the *Times Herald* had surpassed the *Dallas Morning News* in total Sunday circulation for the first time ever, with 320,727 subscribers to the *News*'s 318,705, as confirmed by the Audit Bureau of Circulation.

Responding to the heightened competition, Tom Simmons, vice president and executive editor of the *News*, commented, "The new atmosphere of being constantly on the offensive provides opportunities to take the newspaper further towards excellence in shorter periods of time. . . . The challenge is refreshing."[2] His attitude sums up the spirit of the entire *News* operation in those days, as it rallied to meet the *Times Herald* on its terms. While the *News* had always had a family feel, the challenge posed by increased competition seemed to enhance employee loyalty and commitment to the company, and particularly to improving the newspaper. Many of the reporters and editors present then have commented in interviews that it was an exhilarating time, a time when everyone became more enthusiastic about their jobs and about what the *News* might become with the increasing support of management behind their efforts. However, a series of events at the *Times Herald* over the course of 1977 presented some formidable obstacles to their achieving the objectives Joe Dealey had pledged to shareholders at the beginning of the year: "increased profitability, greater growth and even a higher degree of excellence."

In July, Tom Johnson left his publisher's post after only two years to become president and chief operating officer of Times Mirror's flagship newspaper, the *Los Angeles Times*. He was replaced at the *Times Herald* soon thereafter by Lee J. Guittar, forty-six, a Phi Beta Kappa graduate of Columbia University and most recently president of the *Detroit Free Press*. By then the *Times Herald* had conducted market research to gauge its progress against the *News* and found that although Dallas readers noticed the improvements in the editorial product at the *Times Herald*, too many of them continued to prefer a morning newspaper, no matter what. In other two-newspaper cities around the country, afternoon dailies were suffering, and some had already ceased publication or were operating under joint operating agreements with the morning newspapers. That trend made the solution to the *Times Herald*'s readers' complaints more than obvious.

The *Times Herald* had already begun publishing its Saturday edition as a morning paper in late 1975, but it was only available on news racks. Then, on August 1, 1977, at the annual meeting of the Texas Daily Newspaper Association at the Woodlands, near Houston, McCartin commented to Bill Smellage that the *Times Herald* was about to start a regular daily morning edition. He boasted that their new product would put the *News* out of business.[3] Shortly thereafter, the so-called "Texas Edition" of the *Times Herald* was launched within the city limits of Dallas, and the paper began calling itself "an all-day newspaper" in its promotional material.

With optimism at its peak in the executive offices and the newsroom of the *Times Herald*, and the new morning edition selling well, parent company Times Mirror began to show its true corporate commitment to Dallas. The Los Angeles executives refused to support the cost of adding home delivery for the morning edition, which greatly handicapped the promotion and sales of the product. The circulation department of the *Times Herald* already had a local reputation for being unreliable in delivery in comparison with the *News*. But it wasn't given an option to deliver the morning newspaper, which was sold only in boxes and at newsstands for more than four years. Years later, when interviewed for an article in the *Dallas Observer* by then-reporter (and later mayor) Laura Miller, former executive editor Ken Johnson said of the home delivery problem that "the approximate cost would have been $2 million. We were making profits of $10 to $12 million. It wouldn't have been a big sacrifice."[4]

However, back in 1979, when Lee Guittar was interviewed for the special centennial supplement to the May 6 issue of the *Times Herald*, he was still riding a wave of confidence that had been building over several years. When asked why he would leave the presidency of the sixth largest newspaper in America, the *Detroit Free Press*, to take on the competition with the *Dallas Morning News*, he answered: "Here I had a chance to be involved in all aspects of a newspaper that was determined to achieve greatness. The assignment in Dallas offered me an opportunity to get in on the ground floor and be part of that achievement." He further cited as one of his reasons the attitude he found in Dallas that "nothing can stop us."[5] That statement in 1979 may have been the crest of the *Times Herald*'s wave.

The sincerity and intensity of the campaign by the *Times Herald* to put the *News* out of business may have distracted the *Herald* executives and their bosses at Times Mirror from taking proper note of significant changes taking place at Belo beginning in 1976. As soon as Robert Decherd was elected to the board of directors, he became an object of great interest among media watchers locally, across Texas, and even nationally.

In the October 1977 edition of *Texas Monthly*, the "Reporter: Media" column carried the subhead "Decherd of Dallas: Sprucing up the *News*," and the writer speculated that Robert would take over the newsroom from the soon-to-retire executive editor Tom Simmons. The report praised Robert's influence on the content of the paper while he worked as Simmons's assistant and gave Robert credit for improvements in the arts and entertainment coverage, as well as coverage of women's issues, during his tenure in the newsroom. The report concluded by saying of Robert, "But wherever he goes in the *News* empire, that's where the action will likely be."

Another event in 1977, which wrapped up the era of the original Belo family in Dallas, occurred when their tenant in the Belo Mansion, Sparkman Funeral Home, decided to move elsewhere. That year Robert and other executives at Belo Corp. assisted the Dallas Bar Foundation in purchasing the Belo home from the descendants of A. H. Belo, Jr., for use as the Dallas Legal Education Center. The Dallas Bar Foundation restored the Mansion's main ground-floor rooms to resemble the décor and arrangement used by the family in 1900, and they converted the upstairs to offices and meeting rooms. When the home was restored, Belo Corp. placed on loan to the Bar Foundation large framed portraits of Belo and Belo Jr., as well as papers and artifacts from the elder Belo's Civil War days and his handwritten will.

At the *News*, newsroom staffers were encouraged by changes in quality-of-life issues that Robert addressed as he went about his daily routines working under Tom Simmons. Rena Pederson, longtime reporter and editorial page editor, recalled one day when Robert and she spoke in passing in the newsroom. He apparently noticed that she seemed a bit downcast, and he stopped to inquire if everything was all right. She remembers deciding to speak up about what was really bothering her, because she felt she could trust him. She explained that she was about to have to submit her resignation from her reporting job, because she had learned that she was pregnant.

The rules at the time required pregnant women to resign from the company; then, if they wanted to return to work after giving birth, they had to reapply and, if a position was open, they had to begin again as a new employee. Carolyn Barta had left for her second child's birth with an unofficial promise that her position would be held open for her. However, upon her return she found that it had been filled. She agreed to be hired in a lower-level position in order to resume her career. Robert listened intently to Rena's complaint and agreed with her on the spot that the policy was unfair. It wasn't long before the company instituted maternity leave.

But Robert's tenure in the newsroom was interrupted when he was recruited to take on a challenging situation that had been created by his fellow family shareholders. His father's first cousin and friend Gordon Jackson was adding fuel to his feud with his other cousin, Joe Dealey, playing out Robert's private speculation back in 1973 that "he will someday blow this whole business wide open if management does not begin to respond to his inquiries and suggestions with dignity."

Over the years, a great many publications have recounted the tale of how Gordon Jackson forced Belo to go public. But in fact, that is not true, and none of the stories ever captured Gordon's ultimate ambivalence or the sincerity of his effort to do the right thing by his grandfather G. B. Dealey and the company.

Long before the dissolution of the G. B. Dealey Trust in August 1976, Gordon had begun to push for the company to establish a fair market price for Belo shares, not so much to enable him to cash out, as to know the true value of his inheritance before his own children would have to deal with tax issues. His position was straightforward in his mind:

> The Trust, in effect, Grandfather's will, spelled out what we [he and his twin Gilbert] thought was a requirement that the trustees [of the G. B. Dealey Trust], there are three of them who are also officers [of Belo], ultimately receive the proper value of the stock. And my research indicated that the proper value was the fair mar-

> ket value, which assumed—Grandfather, I assume, just thought that the proper value should be arrived at through making a market in the stock—liquidity—and the only true value would be—and proper value would be—what the market would set on the stock.[6]

Over the almost ten years that he had tried unsuccessfully to obtain what he considered a fair hearing from Joe about his concerns, Gordon's passion to be heard on the matter had escalated to the point that he became incapable of compromise and unable to see that another interpretation of the wording of his grandfather's will might also be valid. By stonewalling Gordon over the years, even banning him from the corporate offices at one point, Joe inadvertently, but not unwittingly, made a committed adversary of his cousin.

Gordon, like his mother, Annie, was bright and creative, and also like her, he was stubborn and impulsive. He seems to have been largely unaware of his own power as a shareholder, and he apparently viewed the company as an extension of his cousin Joe rather than as an institution on its own. Ultimately, Gordon was unable to see when the little war he started with Joe was over. Furthermore, he failed to realize that he had won the war hands down, when he enthusiastically sold all of his shares and his children's shares for the highest price ever contemplated by the company or its shareholders.

The sequence of actions began when Gordon went head to head with Joe. As a beneficiary of the G. B. Dealey Trust, which held more than 68 percent of the company's stock, Gordon regularly pressed Joe for information about the operations of the company, and Joe steadfastly refused to give him any, considering it none of Gordon's business how the company was run so long as the dividends were paid on time. Three of the five branches of G. B. Dealey's family had access to operations detail as employees; two did not. But only Gordon seemed troubled by that. His cousin Al Dealey was more trusting and philosophical about his exclusion.

Over the years following Ben Decherd's death in 1972, Robert had been called on more and more by Joe and the Belo board to serve as what Robert called years later the "chief negotiator" with Gordon Jackson. His services were needed especially on those occasions when Gordon misinterpreted statements made by Joe or actions taken by the company. More frequently, Robert was called on when Joe refused to deal with Gordon at all, because of impatience or a lack of respect for the subtleties of Gordon's role within the family of beneficiaries.

After Robert was elected a director of Belo in early 1976, the board counted on him to maintain good relations between Gordon and the company, a task that took on a new life as soon as the G. B. Dealey Trust expired in August and the shares were distributed to the beneficiaries. By then the Belo board had begun to study the mechanics of taking the company public, which Gordon knew, but when nothing had happened after a couple of years, Gordon decided to take matters into his own hands.

At the annual meeting of shareholders in March 1978, five years after Robert had recognized the dynamics of the feud between Gordon and Joe, Gordon characteristically complained about the company's inaction toward establishing a market price for its shares and then announced his intention to seek a public market for his own shares, inviting other shareholders in attendance to join him. He had researched the matter and found that he could become a securities dealer, which he had already accomplished, and, acting as his own attorney, he registered his stock with the Securities Exchange Commission and the Texas State Securities office.[7]

As required by law, the SEC regional office sent a copy of Gordon's SEC registration to the president of Belo, Joe Dealey, explaining that Gordon was acting under SEC Rule 237 to offer a portion of his shares for sale to the public. At the same time, Gordon placed an advertisement in the Southwest Edition of the *Wall Street Journal* offering to sell 1,666 of his shares in no more than three-share lots at $30 per share. He had arrived at that price in consultation with the State Securities Board, which found his planned offering price of $35 per share to be unrealistically high.

On June 1, Gordon began responding to inquiries from his *Journal* ad by sending a prospectus, dated May 26, 1978, to those who were interested in purchasing stock. Within less than ten days he sold all 1,666 shares in three-share lots to approximately 558 individuals at $90 per lot. With those simple steps, he believed he had accomplished his stated objective to transform Belo into a public company with more than 500 shareholders. If that number of shareholders was of record on December 31, SEC rules required the company to report its financial operations for the year.

When the offering sold out so quickly, the representatives of the State Securities Board apologized to Gordon for not accepting his original price per share since it was clear that a market existed for the Belo stock, and that a higher price per share might have been achieved. Gordon's sale of Belo stock resulted in approximately 709 shareholders of Belo stock, with 78 percent of the shareholders owning collectively less than 1 percent of the outstanding shares.

On a roll, Gordon immediately wrote to the SEC requesting authorization to sell another 100,000 shares, which would be most of the rest of what he owned. He notified Joe of his actions, and Joe quickly called a special meeting of the Belo board. At that meeting, the Belo board decided to send Robert as emissary to learn more about what was on Gordon's mind.

Over the next few weeks, Robert and Gordon spoke on the phone and met for coffee at Gordon's favorite hangout, a coffee shop called CoCo's on LBJ Freeway in North Dallas. Robert realized that Gordon was intent on selling his shares, having found how easy it was, but that he seemed completely unaware of the effects of his actions on the company or other shareholders. At the 1979 arbitration hearing, Gordon characterized those conversations with Robert as friendly and enjoyable. He clearly was pleased by the outcome of his actions, and he believed that he had accomplished something good on behalf of the other shareholders. In a way, he had.

When Robert reported his findings to the board, the directors decided that while they sorted out the issues related to SEC reporting, it would be in the company's best interest to buy out Gordon's shares. Once again Robert was dispatched to talk with Gordon. According to Gordon's recollections of the meeting, Robert asked him to submit an offer of sale of his remaining shares to Belo with an asking price that would be acceptable to him. He recalled that Robert had brought along all of the most recent financial reports compiled since the last annual report, which Gordon had already received as a shareholder.

When questioned by the attorneys for both sides in that later hearing, Gordon said that Robert had been open and forthcoming with answers to all of his questions about making such an offer of sale to the company.

In a letter dated July 27, 1978, Gordon offered to sell the company the remainder of his shares for a price of $43 per share, which he had established on his own, with the advice of his personal accountant, John Martin

Davis, Jr. The Belo directors were called together again on August 2, and on the advice of their investment counsel, F. W. Burnett of Rauscher Pierce Securities Corporation, they decided to reject Gordon's offer because, in Burnett's view, the price seemed higher than the public market would support. Once again, Robert was sent to deliver the news, going to Gordon's McEwen Road office to inform him of the negative vote.

The following day Gordon received a phone call from a Dallas financial consultant named Aubrey Good, who said he was calling on behalf of an unnamed buyer who had learned of Gordon's public offering and was interested in buying his stock. However, the buyer wanted to buy a minimum of 300,000 shares, and Gordon had only about 100,000 shares left. Aubrey Good explained to Gordon that the reason the buyer required the large number of shares was because of a complex business tax issue, and his buyer hoped that Gordon could persuade others to join him to put together the required number.

It is very likely that Gordon told Good of his recent dealings with Belo, including his asking price, because one week later Gordon received a written offer on behalf of the unnamed buyer to purchase 300,000 shares at $45 per share, with a 2.5-percent commission to go to Good. That offer would net Gordon and the others he might bring into the deal the sum of $43.87 per share. That was even more than Belo had just refused to pay, which must have been gratifying to Gordon, considering all of his efforts.

Gordon immediately notified Belo of the offer, not as a bargaining effort, according to his later testimony, but rather to be truthful and to let them know of his intent to sell. He then set about to put together the large number of shares required to make the sale. He went to his twin, Gilbert, his nephew Rice R. Jackson III, and Joe Lubben, who by then had retired from the Belo board. But none of them was willing to commit enough shares to arrive at a bundle of 300,000 shares. It is obvious that they could see more clearly than Gordon what his actions were doing to the company. Then, on August 14, Gordon received the word that the SEC had authorized him to sell the rest of his shares, acting again as his own securities dealer, which only increased his eagerness to close the sale, even without knowing who was buying.

Meanwhile, the Belo management team had learned that the unnamed buyer was another media company, Combined Communications, Inc., of Phoenix, Arizona. It was a public company listed on the

New York Stock Exchange, and its holdings included newspapers, radio stations, and billboards. On August 22, 1978, Robert met with Gordon to tell him who the unnamed buyer was and to let him know that the Belo directors believed it would not be in Belo's best interest for him to sell 10 percent of the company's stock to another media company. Robert explained that anyone buying that many shares would rightly expect to have representation on the Belo board.

Gordon was surprised by that explanation, and he responded that he had not understood it that way, because in his own experience it was not a given that an owner of a large percentage of Belo shares would be given a seat on the board. He went on to point out the obvious, that he and his brothers had held a significant percentage of the company's stock for years and that they had never been given any special consideration by the Belo board of directors or by the management of the company.

In that discussion, which surely must have been enlightening for both Robert and Gordon, Robert told him that Joe Dealey, Jimmy Moroney, and he had discussed the matter. He said they had determined that if Gordon was intent on selling all of his shares, the three of them would prefer that he sell to them in three equal portions. He explained that such an arrangement would enable the family members to maintain control of the company while the directors continued to work out the seemingly interminable details of becoming a public company. Robert offered Gordon $44 per share on behalf of his two cousins and himself—a little better than the offer presented by Aubrey Good. Gordon was agreeable to the proposal, but he asked to be allowed to think about it overnight. The next day Robert called back to confirm the offer, and he found Gordon to be enthusiastic about the arrangement. In fact, Gordon was eager enough about the plan that he had persuaded his two children to sell their shares along with his to his three cousins.

The following day, August 24, Joe, Jimmy, and Robert, along with Bob Richardson and Jim Laney, met with Gordon to clarify all of the terms of their agreement to buy him out. After they reviewed the relevant business affairs of the company that would affect Gordon's decision to sell, the agreement was signed by Gordon and his three buyers, Joe, Jimmy, and Robert, and the sale of Gordon's 114,534 shares was closed at $44 per share. After the transaction was complete, Robert explained to Gordon that the Belo directors had voted to make a similar tender offer to the other shareholders, so that everyone who might wish to sell would be treated equitably. The four cousins parted on terms more cordial than in years, and Gordon was pleased with his proceeds of more than $5 million.

Late that night, after Bill Smellage had gone to sleep, his phone rang. Bill kept a daily diary of his long and productive Belo career, and he recorded in that extraordinary log that his boss, Joe Dealey, was on the other end of the phone line that night, and that he was in an agitated state. Joe told Bill that he couldn't sleep for worry over the debt he had incurred in order to have the cash to buy his third of Gordon's stock. Joe said that he wanted to sell the stock immediately, so that he could pay off the bank loan, and that he knew of a few others whom he believed would be interested in having Belo stock. Joe asked for Bill's assistance in carrying out his plan.

Bill was stunned by Joe's decision and told him so, begging him to reconsider. In particular, Bill pointed out to Joe that if he proceeded without first notifying his two allies in the buyout of Gordon's shares, his actions could cause irreparable damage to the stability of the family-owned company. Bill further urged Joe to consider the effect of his losing ground with Jimmy and Robert in the number of shares he would own in the company, and how that would affect him immediately and his grown children going forward. Reluctantly, Joe agreed to talk to his cousins the next day.

Speaking of this many years later, Robert recalled that Joe called him at his desk at the *News* that morning and asked him to drop by the Dealeys' home in Highland Park for a drink after work. Robert recalled being puzzled by the invitation, which was unusual, especially considering the preceding day's transactions. Joe made a similar call to Jimmy, who was equally curious, but he and Robert both knew that such an invitation from the boss was not to be taken lightly, and that "after work" meant promptly at 5:30.

They showed up on time, and Joe fixed drinks for everyone before getting down to business. Then he announced his plan to sell the stock he had just acquired from Gordon, in order to repay the bank loan they had each taken out to participate in the buyout. He said that he just couldn't bear to carry debt and that he had made a mistake in agreeing to the arrangement.

Robert and Jimmy were dumbfounded by Joe's announcement, which they regarded as a betrayal of their agreement. When Joe seemed surprised by their reaction, Robert and Jimmy attempted to dissuade him, explaining the obvious consequences of his actions on the company and on Joe's own position in the ownership of the company. Joe was unmoved. He said that he had already considered all of the consequences and that his mind was made up.

As the discussion wound down, Robert and Jimmy realized that it was incumbent on them to buy out Joe's portion of Gordon's shares, and they agreed to divide them equally. Robert, too, had borrowed the money to buy his third of Gordon's shares. He had been out of college and working for only five years; his personal assets mostly were tied up in his own inherited Belo shares; and this development would mean incurring even more debt. However, before leaving Joe's home, Robert and Jimmy had made the commitment to buy Joe's one-third, whatever they had to do.

Five days later, at their regular monthly meeting on August 29, the Belo directors discussed the company's impending requirement to file reports to the SEC. They had invited representatives of Smith, Barney, Harris, Upham & Co. to the meeting, so that the directors could ask questions about the mechanics of making a public offering. After some discussion, the investment advisors were excused and the directors voted to ask company management to continue to study the matter more thoroughly for the next few weeks before the September meeting.

Joe Dealey appointed an ad hoc committee of himself, Jimmy Moroney, Bill Smellage, Bob Richardson, and Robert Decherd, with Robert acting as chairman of the committee. Robert recalls that he was given such an important role simply as an acknowledgment of his ongoing communications with the Jackson brothers, whom Joe expected him to continue to "handle."

The next regular meeting was held on September 26, and Robert reported to the board that the committee had polled all of the holders of a significant number of shares in the company, and that, except for Gordon's twin brother, Gilbert Jackson, none of them wished to sell any large portion of their holdings, which would make a secondary offering difficult, if not impossible. Of course, Gordon had already sold all of his shares to his cousins, so there was no concern about his position on the matter.

Robert further reported from the committee that since Belo had no immediate cash needs, and no other compelling company reason could be found, a primary offering seemed to the committee members to be inadvisable at the time. After further discussion, the directors passed the following resolution:

> RESOLVED, that the Corporation proceed with preliminary legal, accounting and other work necessary or desirable in order to (1) effect a reduction of the number of shareholders of the Corporation to less than 500 by means of a reverse split of the Corporation's shares and the purchase by the Corporation in cash of resulting fractional share interests; (2) purchase of all shares of the Corporation owned directly or indirectly by Gilbert Jackson; and (3) if successful in purchasing the shares of Gilbert Jackson, the submission by the Corporation to all shareholders of an offer to purchase a limited number of shares of the Corporation; provided no final action is to be taken on behalf of the Corporation with respect to any of the forgoing without approval by the Board of such action, of the number of shares to be purchased and of the price to be paid therefore and the terms of such payments.[8]

At its meeting on November 21, the board approved an amendment to the articles of incorporation to enable the twenty-to-one reverse stock split. The directors authorized a purchase of the shares belonging to those with fewer than twenty shares at the price of $44 per share, the same price Gordon had received for his shares. Notice was given the following day of a special meeting of shareholders to be held on December 14 to approve the amendment to the articles of incorporation and to put into effect the reverse split. The reverse split would eliminate all of the shareholders Gordon had brought into the company with his three-share offering earlier in the year. Since Gordon seemed content to have sold all of his own stock at that price, and to have accomplished his aim, the step seemed routine and uncontroversial.

However, the directors' action set off a cyclone of activity over the next four weeks that left everyone dizzy, including the reporters trying to follow the story. On December 1, Belo directors followed through with their announced plans and passed another resolution, by written consent, to enter into a contract with Gilbert Jackson to purchase all of his shares at $44 per share. However, Gordon's history of suspecting Joe of withholding information from him got the best of Gordon, and on the same day, apparently with Gilbert's cooperation, Gordon commenced an offering of 20,000 shares belonging to Gilbert at $45 per share, to be sold only in twenty-share units.

At once, Belo sought the help of the Texas State Securities Commission to hold off Gordon's actions, and on December 7 the Commission issued an order for Gordon to cease publication and distribution of his prospectus because it contained "misleading information." The following day, Belo obtained a temporary restraining order against Gordon and Gilbert and their transfer agent, First National Bank in Dallas, to stop them from "selling, offering to sell, transferring, or delivering shares" in connection with the documents named in the state cease-publication order.

The December 11, 1978, issue of *Forbes* ran a one-page story headlined "New Year's Surprise in Texas," which began, "every now and then the little guy wins one. So it is with fifty-nine-year-old Gordon Jackson of Dallas." The story was accompanied by a photo of Joe Dealey with the caption "Going public but not talking." Toward the end of the article, for which Joe "steadfastly refused to answer reporters' questions," Gordon is quoted as saying, "It's surprising what you can do if you just try." But the story was already out of date when the magazine reached its readers.

On December 12, determined to get around the restraining order, Gordon announced he would make gifts of Belo stock certificates, each representing twenty shares of Gilbert's Belo stock, to 500 individuals. On December 13, a court hearing on Belo's temporary injunction was convened, and at the end of the day's proceedings the judge adjourned the hearing until December 15, to allow for the special meeting of Belo shareholders that had been called for December 14.

At the special meeting of shareholders on December 14, a quorum of shareholders was present, and they voted in favor of the amendment enabling the twenty-to-one reverse stock split, which became effective with the vote. Gordon had no say, because he had already sold all of his stock. But back at court the following day, Gordon filed a trial amendment, effectively a class action, cross-action appeal for relief from the injunction for all those with less than twenty shares of Belo stock. He further stated that he would not have sold any of his shares had he known the directors could and would approve a reverse stock split. On December 18, the state court ruled in favor of Belo on the temporary injunction.

Finally, on December 28, 1978, the Belo directors convened a special meeting to take action to ensure that Belo could avoid the SEC registration requirements that year. They approved another amendment to the articles of incorporation, this time to effect a second reverse stock split at five-to-one, again with no fractional shares permitted. The holders of more than two-thirds of the shares were present and approved the amendment that day, making it effective immediately.

The two actions of the Belo shareholders and board, in sequence, effected a 100-to-one reverse stock split, reducing the number of shareholders sufficiently for Belo to continue its strategy to go public on its own terms and timetable.

Ultimately Gordon had accomplished something very important for Belo and for G. B. Dealey's other descendants by prying open the doors and windows of G. B. Dealey's beloved company. They had been effectively closed upon G. B.'s death in 1946 by his son Ted and had remained sealed thereafter under Joe's cautious care. Thanks to Gordon's persistence, the Ted Dealey era was finally coming to a close. Unfortunately for him, though, Gordon seemed unable to understand or enjoy his own triumph at the time.

Only a very tight inner circle knew the details of the year's wranglings with Gordon. Throughout the ordeal, Gordon was the only one who openly talked to reporters about the developments. Everyone at Belo was still under Joe's instruction not to discuss the company's financial dealings with outsiders, including their own staff of reporters and editors. So, speculative stories became an amusing game, with business reporters everywhere who were trying to follow the story. In all news accounts on the matter, though, reporters continued to identify Robert as the one to watch.

The January 1978 edition of *D* magazine had run its annual list of who's who in Dallas, and Robert was number sixteen on its list, with the following paragraph under his portrait:

> Robert Decherd, 26, assistant to the executive editor, part owner, *Dallas Morning News*. Decherd and his sister just inherited 16 percent of the Dealey trust: more importantly, Decherd, a former editor of the *Harvard Crimson* in his college days, has urbane editorial sensibilities—something the *News* will need in future years to stem the tide of the onrushing *Times Herald*. Insiders indicate if the *News* has an editorial future, it is with him at the helm.[9]

The September 12, 1978, edition of *Esquire* had a story by Christopher Buckley, the well-known son of the even more well-known, at the time, William F. Buckley, Jr. It was titled "How almost everyone in the media establishment got his job through the *Harvard Crimson*." The story named Robert Decherd among the "media establishment." "Oh, and Bob Dechert," Buckley wrote, getting both names wrong. "He's in the owner's training program at the *Dallas Morning News*," he continued, incorrectly characterizing the management training program as strictly for family shareholders.

As a matter of fact, as with their fathers before them, cousins Robert Decherd and Joe Dealey, Jr., had become friends during their time in the management training program. During all of the intense shareholder and corporate negotiations, Joe Jr. stayed behind the scenes, because he had no official corporate role at the time. Instead, he continued his research and writing duties for the editorial page at the *News*. Editorial page editor Jim Wright praised Joe Jr.'s depth of research and understanding of the issues related to national defense and foreign affairs. For his part, Joe Jr. maintained his personal support of Robert during this turbulent period among the family shareholders.

During 1978, in spite of shareholder turmoil, the *News* made strides, particularly in local coverage, by launching its award-winning section "Fashion!Dallas" and expanding its sports coverage. That year the *News* increased its circulation with a big push in Tarrant, Denton, and Collin counties, as well as in Dallas County, and by September 30, it had regained a narrow lead in Sunday circulation over the *Times Herald*. In his report on the year's revenues, John Rector proudly announced increases in both advertising and circulation of more than 20 percent over 1977.

Over at WFAA-TV in 1978, the station won the nationally prized DuPont/Columbia University Award for the second year in a row, as well as designation as the Best Newscast in Texas from United Press International, with Iola Johnson, Dallas/Fort Worth's first female news anchor, and Tracy Rowlett. The station also launched a local program, *PM Magazine*, following the 6 p.m. newscast, which achieved number-one status forty-five days after its premiere. Its hosts were Bill Ratliff and Candy Hasey. Candy later went on to co-host the ABC network program *Good Morning America* for a short time.

By the end of 1978, Robert had effectively moved out of the *Dallas Morning News* and "up" to A. H. Belo Corporation. He was all of 27½ years old. Although the newsroom staff may have been disappointed that his fresh perspectives were not going to be put into play as executive editor at the *News*, Robert's first important corporate task would be to find someone else with the knowledge and the drive to do what had to be done for the *News* to remain competitive with the *Times Herald*.

It was about that time that Robert sent a note to editors at the *News* that under no circumstances was his name or photograph, or that of his wife or his infant son, William, to be used in the society columns and features in the paper. Robert had become active in community projects and was more and more visible about town, as he and Maureen lent their support to various organizations and moved in Dallas society. However, he felt it was unseemly for him to appear in the columns of a newspaper of which he was a significant owner. And, in addition, he was very protective of his family and his own privacy.

His note was interpreted as a sort of decree and has been upheld ever since, with few exceptions. However, it was a departure from the normal practice at the paper up to that point, and even beyond, as the comings and goings of Joe Dealey's family continued to be chronicled regularly.

Robert had spent a couple of years in the newsroom getting hands-on managerial experience as Tom Simmons's executive assistant and getting to know the staff. When he moved to the corporate ranks, Robert proposed that the *News* seek an outsider to succeed Tom, rather than follow the tradition of automatically promoting the next in line to the top newsroom job.

Eager as they were for new energy in the newsroom, the staff found that approach a bit harsh, especially since many of them had been hoping that Robert would take the job himself. Joe and Jimmy agreed to a national search, so long as in-house candidates were also considered, and they assigned Robert the task of handling the process.

The year 1979 was one in which economic inflation hit every aspect of daily life in America. As Joe detailed in his annual report on the year, inflation rose more than at any time since 1946. He cited energy costs up 37.4 percent, housing up 15.2 percent, mortgage interest rates up 34.7 percent, and food and beverage combined up 10.8 percent over 1978. During 1979, however, Belo continued to flourish. At the annual meeting on March 27, 1979, Jack Kreuger retired after serving as a director for nineteen years. The bylaws required that non-family directors retire at the first meeting after reaching age seventy.

John W. Bassett, Jr., the son-in-law of retired director Joe Lubben, was elected to the board at that meeting. Lubben had remained one of Belo's most significant shareholders.

A native of Roswell, New Mexico, John was a partner in the Roswell law firm Atwood, Malone, Mann and Turner. Before returning to his hometown after law school at the University of Texas at Austin, John had served as a White House Fellow in the Johnson administration in 1966. His inclusion as a member of Belo's board brought a fresh perspective on legal matters, as well as a unique combination of insights with both insider interests and outsider objectivity. John was the first Belo director ever elected who did not live in Dallas.

Companywide during 1979, Belo hired a total of 803 new employees (both replacements and incremental positions), 44.8 percent of whom were minorities. At the *News*, newsroom salaries were increased across the board, and the higher salaries enabled managers to hire more experienced journalists for the openings. During his last full year as executive editor, Tom Simmons was encouraged to improve newsroom management, and he was given the budget to create four new assistant managing editor positions.

The production and circulation departments of the *News* added a 40,000-square-foot warehouse and fuel distribution facility on Greenbriar Street, directly across the Trinity River from the paper's headquarters, and plans were finalized to build a 95,000-square-foot expansion of the Dallas Morning News Building, in the loading docks drive-up area between the main building and the newsprint warehouse.

Meanwhile, Robert had been doing his homework in business strategies, especially in the value of using demographic and marketing data for long-range planning. As the *Times Herald* focused its efforts on the *News*'s strongest markets and its typical readers, Robert supported the hiring of the research firm Belden Associates to study reader demographics, competitive positioning, and sales potential, for immediate use by the advertising staff.

He also initiated a comprehensive market study, to be conducted by Yankelovich, Skelly and White, to take a close look at the past, present, and future of the Dallas/Fort Worth market region, for internal planning, development, and strategy purposes. That study resulted in a recommendation that the company immediately shift its traditional promotional efforts to what the study called "cosmopolites," which it defined as "young, upwardly mobile, better demographic people in the market."

The shift in the *News*'s promotional and marketing strategies began in 1980, even before the new editor arrived that October. And moving into leadership roles were several young people who fit the "cosmopolite" profile perfectly. They were just emerging from the management training program and taking on managerial jobs in promotion, marketing, and advertising.

Another leap for the *News* during 1979 was in the accounting department, which underwent a transformation resulting in the first annual financial statement to be presented to the president in computer-generated form, rather than handwritten on a legal-size, yellow, ruled ledger sheet. The report was prepared by Michael D. Perry, who had been hired earlier that year as assistant controller. Mike had graduated in 1978 with high honors and a Master of Business Administration degree from Michigan State University. He reported to J. William Cox, vice president and controller of the *News*. Perry's arrival in the accounting department had resulted in a 75-percent turnover in the supervisory and managerial positions of the department during the year, which he detailed in his annual report to Cox.

On the other side of the driveway, WFAA-TV won awards for being the best newscast in Texas from both the Associated Press and United Press International; the station acquired its first helicopter; and a heliport was added at the back of the combined *News* and WFAA employee parking lot. Belo Broadcasting Corp., Belo's broadcasting unit, actively pursued the purchase of four different television stations, ultimately signing an agreement to purchase WTVC, the ABC affiliate in Chattanooga, Tennessee, for $19,500,000.

In his report on 1979, which Joe delivered in early 1980 on the twentieth anniversary of his having been elected president, he commented to shareholders, "I will not attempt to minimize or oversimplify the remarkable growth realized by the company during the year just ended." Then he focused on his own twenty-year tenure as president, pointing out that the company's "gross corporate volume" improved by almost 700 percent, growing from $20 million in 1960 to $138 million in 1979. He elaborated further that the broadcast "profits" went from $597,500 in 1960 to $11 million in 1979; that total advertising volume at the *News* went from 35 million lines in 1960 to nearly 91 million lines in 1979; and that circulation went from 220,500 daily and 235,700 Sunday in 1960 to 287,000 daily and 354,200 Sunday in 1979.

Shortly before Joe made his anniversary report, the *News* had published a story on February 15 announcing that "Joe M. Dealey, president and chief executive officer of the *Dallas Morning News* and parent company A. H. Belo Corp. since 1960, has been elected chairman of the board and chief executive officer of Belo Corp." Later in the story a sentence added, "Dealey assumes the title of publisher of the *News*." The same story announced that Jimmy Moroney, Jr., at age fifty-nine, was named president and chief operating officer of Belo Corp., and that he would succeed Joe as president and CEO of the *News*.

The story did not explain that the Belo chairmanship had been vacant since Ben Decherd's death in 1972, or that the "publisher" title had not been used by anyone since 1969, when Ted Dealey died. Nor did the story detail Belo's tradition of maintaining the true operational power under the title of president, nor that for the first time since 1926 the presidency didn't go from one generation to the next, or from one man named Dealey to another named Dealey.

This time the presidency of both Belo Corp. and the *Dallas Morning News*, and along with it the power, went to Joe's first cousin, Jimmy, who had loyally served Joe through the last twenty years. Jimmy's patient and unwavering support of Joe had come even after Ted, in naming Joe to the post in 1960, had "permanently" disqualified Jimmy from holding the presidency on the basis of his being a Catholic.

At the time Jimmy was named president, he was the next most senior executive of Belo and the *News*, as well as chairman and CEO of Belo Broadcasting Corp. Jimmy retained his role as chairman of the broadcasting unit when he became president of Belo and the *News*, but he relinquished the CEO title of the broadcasting unit to Mike Shapiro, who had been president and chief operating officer.

With the changes in leadership, the *News* would operate as a company with its own officers separate from Belo; and on the flip side, Belo Corp. would finally have its own management structure, separate from the *News*. All of the officers of the *News* and Belo Corp. were housed in the executive suite of the Dallas Morning News Building, but the two were separated, with the east side considered the *News*, and the west side, corporate.

Although it was not obvious to most, when all of the subtleties were accounted for, Joe effectively had been promoted out of running the company. The shift in power away from Ted's line in the family had been accomplished by Joe's own decisions and with his full awareness. He had chosen to let his cousins assume command and to allow numerous important changes to occur around him. The shift was essentially complete as soon as Joe sold his one-third of Gordon Jackson's shares to Jimmy and Robert.

The February 1980 story in the *News* reporting the changes said that Joe would "direct corporate policy," and the restructuring was explained in one sentence that read, "A new corporate management group concentrating on planning and development has been formed under Dealey and Moroney." The transition was orderly and friendly, and the Ted Dealey era was over after forty years, with no fanfare and barely any notice paid.

The same story announced that Robert, twenty-eight, would continue his most recent role serving as vice president for administration of Belo Corp., and that he would add a new role as executive vice president of the *News*, with oversight of the news and editorial departments, as well as of the financial and administrative operations.

All of the shuffling resulted in Jimmy and Robert being the only executives of both Belo Corp. and the *Dallas Morning News*. Robert would report to Jimmy, as would John Rector, who was also made an executive vice president of the *News*, with expanded oversight of advertising, marketing, promotion, production, and circulation. John's elevation was another of the steps in the plan to complete the separation of Belo from the operations of the *News*.

To the average reader, and even among employees, the changes in the senior executives' titles and responsibilities were matter-of-fact and routine, hardly noticeable. However, in reality the shifts in power and in the corporate structure were a strategic turning point for the A. H. Belo Corporation. The strategy would become apparent as the plan unfolded during the course of the next two or three years.

The same February 1980 story announcing all of the executive changes and restructuring announced that Joe Jr. would leave his post as editorial staff writer for the *News* to join the corporate management group as vice president and secretary. That move was not Joe Jr.'s idea, but he agreed to it at the insistence of his father, who wanted Joe to be prepared to follow in his footsteps in the corporation. Many years later, Joe Jr. said that he agonized over the opportunity offered him, not wanting to leave the editorial department. Ultimately he felt he owed it to his dad to follow him into the corporate structure, in spite of his own preference for research and writing.

In March 1980, three of Belo's longtime directors retired from the board. Earl Cullum and Sol Katz retired after twenty years on the board.

The third was nineteen-year-veteran Bill Smellage, who had been a close advisor to both Ted and Joe. Joining the board that year was Belo's senior vice president for finance and treasurer, Bob Richardson. Bob was elected to the board after twenty-one years with the company, moving up through the ranks of the financial departments. His thorough knowledge of the company's financial structure was crucial in the planning for taking the company public.

In spite of the 700-percent growth rate touted by Joe, greater change occurred within Belo and its companies during the single year 1980 than had occurred cumulatively over the past twenty years. Beginning with the separation of Belo Corp. from the *News* in operational terms, the new corporate structure enabled greater independence and agility throughout the company.

When Mike Shapiro was made CEO of Belo Broadcasting Corporation, Ward Huey was named chief operating officer, adding to his responsibilities as executive vice president, reporting to Shapiro, and Dave Lane was promoted to general manager of WFAA-TV, expanding his executive responsibilities.

Robert joined the governing board of Belo Broadcasting where Jimmy was chairman, and everyone breathed a sigh of relief on July 28, 1980, when WFAA received its three-year license renewal from the FCC, ending the long-running battle with WADECO. With that battle won, in early 1981, Mike Shapiro moved to Belo Corp. as a senior vice president. The announcement said that he was to "research and develop a program production and syndication division." Ward was named president and CEO of Belo Broadcasting, a position for which he had been groomed for many years.

Also in 1980, an entirely new corporate division was organized to explore the potential of electronic distribution of information, which had only been dreamed of until then. It was called Belo Information Systems Online Network, or BISON. It was led by Gean Holden, who was Belo's director of research and technology, and it launched a partnership with Sammons Communications' Park Cities Cable Television operation, Dow Jones & Co., publisher of the *Wall Street Journal*, and Merrill Lynch & Co.

According to a story in the *News* on May 16, 1980, "The Sammons Park Cities project will be the first anywhere to involve large numbers of cable television subscribers' access to information banks in several cities from private home terminals." The partners in the early project aimed to create an "electronic newspaper and financial encyclopedia," as well as two-way electronic access to classified advertising from the *News*—both revolutionary ideas at the time.

Ultimately, with only 200 cable subscribers who could participate in the project, management proclaimed it a great success and promptly shut it down. The partners had realized that they were too far ahead of the curve in their offerings to make it a profitable business. Belo had to wait years for the proliferation of home computers and ultimately the launch of the World Wide Web for its dreams of an electronic newspaper to become reality.

However, technology did make a big splash in-house during 1980, when the data processing department of the *News* was made a separate division of Belo Corp., and it added a much larger IBM computer so that more of the company's accounting systems could be automated.

At the *News*, John Rector's promotion led to greater roles for two up-and-comers serving under him. New vice presidencies were created for Harry M. Stanley, Jr., in advertising and Jeremy L. Halbreich in marketing. Harry had come to the *News* three years earlier from the *Detroit News*, and Jeremy had been in the *News*'s management training program since 1974, when he graduated from Harvard a year behind Robert.

Across the Belo companies, benefits for all employees were improved during 1980, and two more of the trade unions at the *News* opted to decertify, which left only one union still active. Then, in October, Robert introduced his selection for executive editor of the *News* to replace Tom Simmons. Simmons had retired in June, and managing editor Terry Walsh, a thirty-four-year veteran of the company, took over in the interim while the search was conducted.

Although Walsh was considered a candidate, Robert conducted personal interviews with a large pool of other candidates around the country, traveling to various cities coast to coast. He ultimately narrowed his choice to the one candidate who had never run a large newspaper's newsroom. Burl Osborne was the forty-three-year-old managing editor of the Associated Press, who had worked his way up the AP ladder over twenty years, honing his abilities to serve a diverse clientele of newspaper editors around the world. He was a both a journalist and a savvy business manager.

Burl was born and grew up in eastern Kentucky in coal-mining country, where his father was a miner. He was the first member of his family to graduate from college, which he worked to pay for himself. He set out to study engineering but was sidetracked into journalism by going to work at the *Ashland Independent* newspaper as a "cub reporter,"[10] as his boss called him.

He had found his calling, and after graduating from Marshall College (now Marshall University) he worked briefly as a reporter for a radio and television station across the Ohio River in Huntington, West Virginia. In 1960, Burl began a twenty-year career with the Associated Press that took him all over the country, ending up as managing editor in New York. That was his post when Robert interviewed him for the executive editor's job at the *News*.

Burl was intrigued by the uncertainty of the *News*'s competitive position with the *Times Herald* at that time, and although he had never run a newspaper's newsroom, he found the competitive challenge irresistible. At the *News* he became what Robert later called the perfect field general for such a battle, because of his fierce competitive spirit, street smarts, news judgment, and intelligence.

It is impossible to fully appreciate Burl's steady career of accomplishments, and to understand just how tenacious a person he is, without knowing of his physical challenges over the years. While he was still in elementary school in Kentucky, Burl was diagnosed with nephritis, the incurable kidney disease. As he approached renal failure in early adulthood, the first dialysis programs were being launched, and he was among the first to participate. In 1966 he was among the first people ever to receive a kidney transplant, donated by his mother, and his career never slowed down.

In 1980, when Robert had decided that Burl was the one he wanted at the *News*, Burl was asked to undergo a physical exam, to help gauge his suitability for the job. The doctors in the group practice who conducted the various exams concluded that while Burl was in good health at the time, they were doubtful about his long-term prognosis and recommended against hiring him. Joe, Jimmy, and Robert decided it was worth the risk and ignored the recommendation.

As Burl took over the newsroom, the *News* began same-day delivery to key individuals in Washington, D.C., and he soon hired Carl Leubsdorf away from the *Baltimore Sun* to become Washington Bureau chief, beginning in early 1981.

In the first steps toward a liberalizing of the editorial pages, longtime political writer and editor Carolyn Barta was made editor of the "Viewpoints" opinion page opposite the editorial page, and veteran reporter Rena Pederson moved to the editorial page, specializing in media, politics, and the emerging field of high technology and telecommunications. She was being positioned to take over the page.

Bob Mong was promoted from assistant city editor to editor of the paper's business section. Soon, "Business Tuesday" was launched, on November 11, 1980, to immediate success with greatly expanded business coverage that led to a stand-alone business section on a daily basis.

At the same time, Burl enhanced sports coverage on a daily basis, hiring Dave Smith away from the *Boston Globe* to be sports editor.

When Burl was hired, Robert had laid out his vision for modernizing the newspaper, and he gave Burl the authority to bring it about. Soon after his arrival, Burl encouraged the editors to undertake serious investigative reporting, which many believed had been a deficiency of the paper.

The "most notable" project of the *News* during 1980, in Burl's estimation, was reporter Howard Swindle's project to shine a spotlight on the "illegal alien problem."[11] That coverage took Swindle and George Kuempel, who was at the Austin Bureau at the time, to Mexico, New Mexico, and Washington, D.C., as well as all over Texas, in pursuit of the many angles of the issue. The state desk also focused on the arrival of Cuban refugees that year, sending reporters to Florida and other destinations around the country. Following publication of the immigrant stories, a bound volume of reprints was distributed to government officials in states along the border and in Mexico.

In his report on changes he instituted during the last three months of 1980, Burl said, "The *News* joined a handful of papers, including the *New York Times* and *Los Angeles Times*, that totally prohibit the acceptance of freebies as a method of avoiding even the appearance of conflict."[12] He explained that the new policy "caused some minor dislocations in some areas where many newspapers traditionally have accepted free travel or lodging." He was off to a strong start in demonstrating to top management that many things had to change at the newspaper.

The entire newspaper staff was jolted into action in the spring of 1981, when Burl called for publication of an afternoon extra to report on the attempt on Ronald Reagan's life outside the Washington Hilton Hotel shortly after noon. Never mind that no one at the paper recalled ever putting out an extra; that no production or distribution staff was on duty; that no budgets existed for such an extravagant expense.

Burl recalled years later that sometimes it's good not to know what you don't know or what you can't do. That day, everyone rallied and carried out the impossible, creating a surge of competitive pride and energy throughout every department of the paper, when the *Dallas Morning News* matched the afternoon *Dallas Times Herald* in reporting the breaking news. After about seven months on the job, Burl added the title vice president to executive editor, which made him the number four executive in the newspaper, under Jimmy, Robert, and John Rector.

That was also the year that the rest of the country began to notice what was called in the trade publications "The Great Newspaper War" between the *Times Herald* and the *News*, a battle that had begun ten years earlier. Although several cities had competing morning and afternoon newspapers, the battle in Dallas was considered to be the most intense anywhere, and according to many observers nationally, the real winners were Dallas readers, who were being treated to two of the best newspapers in the country.

While *Times Herald* executives began claiming victory in the war at about that time, the reality was that Belo was investing in its newspaper like never before, while Times Mirror was pulling profits out of the *Times Herald* like never before. In a story published in a regional trade journal, Texas journalist and former *News* reporter Dave McNeely wrote about the state of newspapers in Texas. He ended the piece with "Texas is probably too big for any one newspaper to rule, but keep your eyes on Dallas and the *Dallas Morning News*. That's where the current vigor is."[13]

In June 1981, Burl hired Ralph Langer to become the managing editor with front-line responsibility for the newsroom. Ralph recalls that Burl essentially gave him the mission to "look at everything we were doing, take everything apart, and put it back together in a better way."[14] And he was given the budget to do it, adding nearly 100 staffers to the newsroom in his first year on the job. Ralph was the perfect foil for Burl. Burl had the foresight and imagination to know what needed to be done; Ralph had the equanimity and the insight to accomplish the task, day by day and step by step. The combination was powerful.

On December 26, 1980, Joe, Jimmy, and Robert, along with the directors, had voted to hire investment bankers to start the process of taking Belo public. The prospectus was distributed in the fall of 1981, and the initial public offering of the common stock of A. H. Belo Corporation commenced on December 9, 1981. It was sold out the same day.

The company provided one million of the shares offered, and twenty-six shareholders provided another 957,835. Goldman, Sachs & Co., the principal underwriter of the offering, exercised its right to sell an additional 10 percent of the original offering, bringing the total of shares sold to 2,153,618 at an offering price of $23 per share. Joe sold 133,350 of his own shares and Jimmy sold 111,000 of his, responding to the underwriters' strong suggestion that their participation was essential to a successful offering, as it would alleviate investor concerns about insider control. However, arguing that his age presented a different set of considerations, Robert sold none of his shares.

Chapter 8

THE MODERN BELO EMERGES

1982–1986

Belo's initial public offering, even with its full subscription in less than twenty-four hours, generated little or no immediate attention on Wall Street or in the media circles of the east and west coasts. The intense focus on Dallas's newspaper war during 1981, and the apparent strength of the *Dallas Times Herald* and its high-profile owner, caused most business writers to be looking at the wrong picture on December 9, 1981.

In fact, analysts and writers had made little note of the fundamental changes at Belo more than a year earlier, when Belo announced the separation of the *Dallas Morning News*'s governing structure from that of its parent organization. Everyone had continued to follow the more obvious excitement in the *News*'s newsroom, which was generated by the changes at the executive editor level, focusing on the shift to hiring Burl Osborne, rather than someone from within, as tradition had dictated.

Writers and readers alike noticed the almost weekly launches of new sections, new bureaus, and new columns by both the *News* and the *Times Herald*. As one paper scored a point with readers, the other one responded with something better. Both newspapers shouted their improvements from billboards and by other means all over the region.

Burl continued to improve the match-up between the newspaper's offerings and its readers' interests during 1981. His success was a direct reflection of Jimmy's full support of his efforts and Robert's immediate supervisory encouragement every step of the way. The changes Burl engineered strengthened the paper's ties to the city's most powerful and influential citizens, and he had begun to chip away at the *Times Herald*'s lock on youthful readers. The *News* added a surprisingly popular section called "High Profile," which was devoted to the activities and fund-raising galas of the city's most socially and politically prominent citizens, including not just the affluent white community, but also the African American, Hispanic, and Asian communities. It was launched on September 1, and achieved immediate advertiser acceptance as well as reader approval.

In Belo's 1981 annual report, its first as a public company, on the page after the chairman's letter, a two-page spread shows a photo of Burl in the composing room with assistant managing editor Bill Evans. Bill is the one with a cup of coffee, looking over Burl's shoulder, as Burl, with the marker pen in his left hand, goes over the pages before they are sent to plate-making. The text on that page boasts:

> The *Dallas Morning News* is the dominant newspaper editorially in the state of Texas. The *Morning News* is also the leading newspaper in the Dallas-Fort Worth area, both in circulation and in total advertising linage. In 1981 the *Morning News* successfully continued its strategy to expand its market leadership in every measurement of circulation and advertising.

Apparently by design, Belo Corp. was kept in the background while its leaders quietly and steadily built the company's momentum and prepared it for growth and for diversification. Six years later, Robert commented about the decisions that were made in taking the company public:

> When we made the decision in the late seventies to take the company public, that decision represented more than anything else that we talked about . . . a commitment to the *Dallas Morning News* as an independent, vigorous, distinguished institution. The *Dallas Morning News* represented the linchpin between a family heritage—intensely personal, emotional attachments to the newspaper, the company, and the people who had built it over time—to what the company [Belo] is today, an independent entity which still acknowledges and has great respect for the traditions

> of family ownership and involvement, but which is charting a course as a free-standing, independent (in the financial sense) organization that will provide the base for the *Dallas Morning News* to prosper, for it to flourish as a newspaper. . . .[1]

By the spring of 1982, Jimmy and Robert were not remaining in the background at Belo anymore. They both appeared, along with Joe, in the photograph accompanying the chairman's letter in the annual report. Considering how much thought and planning go into designing any annual report, this photo was surely a message to investors, and anyone else who was paying attention. Even though only Joe's signature appears at the end of the letter, as chairman and CEO, the photograph shows him sitting at one end of a sofa, with Jimmy perched on its arm, making Jimmy's head the top of a pyramid that is completed with Robert's positioning on Jimmy's other side. Robert is seated in a chair slightly apart from his two older cousins and leaning in toward them. The caption names them left-to-right, beginning with Robert. The statement is clear—in spite of the familiar names and faces, a new team spirit is leading Belo.

On January 27, 1982, six weeks after its IPO, Belo announced the hiring of James P. Sheehan as senior vice president and chief financial officer. The story in the *News* described Belo as "a leading Southwestern communications company." Belo was not just a newspaper publisher anymore. Jimmy was at the helm, and he brought along his lifelong experience on the broadcast side of the business, where both he and his father before him had been relegated for fifty years by family dynamics. Robert was by his side, with fresh perspectives on the business model for the company and a youthful enthusiasm for the newly emerging technologies.

Together, Jimmy and Robert, with the support of the board, which met monthly at that time, began to reposition the 140-year-old company. In March 1982, Belo initiated an employee stock purchase plan, which enabled all employees to designate an amount from each paycheck to go toward purchasing Belo stock. Employees reacted enthusiastically, many of them starting with amounts so small that each share of stock was acquired incrementally over several pay periods. Every paycheck stub reflected the employees' ownership stakes, along with the other relevant data.

The old version of the family feel that was described by so many in their oral history interviews about previous eras was reinterpreted with that stock purchase plan, with employees at all levels taking real ownership. Of course that didn't eliminate the skeptics, but it did seem to increase the number of true loyalists and the sense of pride in the company.

A year earlier, in February 1981, Belo had bought its first cable television system, in Clarksville, Tennessee. The purchase was announced with little comment, but it was seen as a regional extension of Belo's interests in the Chattanooga, Tennessee, television market, and it also gave the company entry to the rapidly growing and constantly changing world of cable television. During the full year of 1981, the broadcast unit of pre-public Belo provided 66.4 percent of Belo's earnings from operations on only 32 percent of its operating revenues.[2]

In 1987, Jimmy commented about Belo's transformation from a tightly controlled, family-owned newspaper company to a publicly traded media corporation: "Now, we went public for a number of reasons. One reason, and the primary reason, was to grow." Another reason he cited was to allow family members to have a market for their stock, and a related issue, of special significance to the family, was to instill more management discipline in the corporation by having to "live in a fishbowl."[3]

By that, Jimmy meant that the management of Belo henceforth would be conducted with greater visibility of the decision-making process. He continued, "I think Belo is still essentially family controlled, but nevertheless, we are responsible to many, many shareholders. And though it might be family controlled, the family has to produce in order to stay in position." That was Jimmy's gracious and insightful way of acknowledging that he took nothing for granted, that he intended to work hard to earn shareholders' trust, and that any other family member who was at the company would also have to "produce in order to stay in position."

At the time Belo went public in December 1981, six family members were employed by the company, either on the corporate staff or at one of the operating companies. In addition to Jimmy and Joe, there were four members of the next generation, including Robert and Joe Jr.

Joe Jr.'s younger brother Russell had joined the *News* in 1974 after graduating with a Master of Arts degree from the University of Texas at Austin. Russell had entered as a management trainee, and in 1981 he was serving as assistant to a senior vice president and preparing for a management position in the newspaper's advertising department. The fourth and youngest member of the next generation was Jim Moroney III, who had joined the company in 1978, immediately after graduating from Stanford University, beginning his career as a sales trainee at WFAA-TV. His preparations for a career at Belo would soon take him to graduate school for an MBA from the University of Texas at Austin.

A couple of days following the announcement that Jim Sheehan was joining Belo as CFO, the paper ran the announcement that "Mike Shapiro, a senior vice president of A. H. Belo Corporation, has elected to take early retirement from the company on April 1 to form his own broadcast management consulting firm." He was moving to East Texas and planned to operate his new business from his retirement dream home in the woods. Mike had started as an advertising salesman at WFAA in 1952 and worked his way up to the highest positions in the broadcast unit, before moving into the corporate ranks less than a year earlier. He had also been on the board of Belo since 1968, and he retired from the board at its next meeting, on March 23, 1982.

Mike had spent most of his thirty years at Belo in the thick of operations. He had been the mentor of all of the current management of Belo Broadcasting Corp. and its television stations, so it wasn't surprising that he found life as a corporate officer to be less inspiring. The resolution passed by the directors upon his retirement from the board opened with this paragraph:

> Dedication to duty, loyalty to the public and to his company, foresight and courage; all these things and more describe the career of Mike Shapiro. By this resolution we move to take note of the devotion and service of this unique man on his impending retirement from the Board of Directors of A. H. Belo Corporation.

He was indeed unique, and the positive effect of his many contributions to television was permanent. People in Dallas today, who were around in the 1960s, remember him well, and they still associate him with Belo and with WFAA.

Mike's departure from the board left only ten members. No new directors had been elected to replace the three who retired in 1980, Earl Cullum, Sol Katz, and Bill Smellage, and a fourth member was lost when Pat Haggerty died in October 1980, less than a week after learning he had cancer. At the annual meeting of shareholders on April 20, 1982, three new directors were elected to the board: Thomas B. Walker, Jr.; Ward L. Huey, Jr.; and James P. Sheehan.

Tom Walker had been a Dallas resident for thirty years, and since 1968 he had been a partner with Goldman, Sachs & Co., the investment banking firm that had worked with Belo in taking the company public. A native of Nashville, Tennessee, Tom was a Phi Beta Kappa graduate of Vanderbilt University, and at the time of his election to the board, he was vice chairman of Vanderbilt's board of trust; he later became chairman.

Ward Huey had been one of Mike Shapiro's acolytes, and he had moved up from cameraman through the ranks to become president and chief executive officer of Belo Broadcasting Corp. He had held that post for less than a year, following Shapiro's move into corporate, but he had been at the company for nearly twenty-two years. His energy, enthusiasm, and competitiveness had earned him respect throughout the broadcast industry and had already distinguished him as one of television's real leaders.

Ward grew up in University Park, graduated from Highland Park High School, and went to college a few blocks away at Southern Methodist University. Following his 1960 graduation from Southern Methodist University, he worked briefly for an advertising agency before hiring on as a cameraman at WFAA. He was active in the leadership of several national broadcast organizations throughout his career, and in 1982 he was serving as chairman of the ABC Television Affiliates board of governors.

Rounding out the thirteen-member board was another employee, Jim Sheehan, a newcomer to the company with a forceful personality and an impressive résumé in business. However, he had no background in journalism or media operations. Jim had received a bachelor's degree in accounting from Seton Hall University in 1965. After working for a few years and serving two years in the U.S. Navy, he obtained an MBA in finance from Wayne State University in 1973.

Before coming to Belo in January 1982, Jim had been vice president and controller of the Pratt & Whitney division of United Technologies Corporation, and before that he had been a financial analyst with Ford Motor Company and an accounting manager for Audits and Surveys, Inc. He moved his family to Dallas from New Jersey, his home state.

When Jim Sheehan was hired by Belo three months earlier, the announcement said that his expertise would provide the additional financial leadership necessary to the company's future. Jim was to be the financial strategist who would join Jimmy and Robert in transforming Belo.

The roster of strictly corporate officers was not a long one at that point in Belo's history, and only one of them was not also a director of the company. In addition to Joe, Jimmy, Robert, and Jim Sheehan, Dick Blum was senior corporate vice president, and Bob Richardson was senior vice president for finance and treasurer. Joe Jr. was the only other corporate officer, serving as vice president and secretary. As secretary of the company, he too had a role to play in the monthly board meetings.

After Belo's 1981 annual report was circulated in March 1982, several publications ran routine stories on the newspaper competition in Dallas. A couple of them focused on Robert's emergence as a key Dallas business and community leader. The March 1982 edition of *Texas Business* published a story compiled by Anne Denny, called "The Rising Stars of Texas." The twenty individuals making the list were described as "among today's finest, most promising under-forty upwardly mobile men and women."

In citing Robert's "activities," the list provided a glimpse at what he valued outside of his working life: "past president, trustee, Dallas Symphony [Association]; director, Public Communications Foundation for North Texas; treasurer, the Salvation Army; trustee, St. Mark's School; president, Freedom of Information Foundation of Texas Inc." The listing had a space where subjects described their "philosophy," and Robert had responded, "To be even-handed but decisive."[4]

In the July 1982 issue of *D* magazine, Dallas writer Lee Cullum published a piece called "The Power Brokers: Dallas's top players of the eighties." She first focused on those at the heights of power at the time, then she had her list of "20 Core Comers." She says, "Robert Decherd is heir-apparent to the influence his newspaper and family (the Dealeys) have long exerted in Dallas. He's consumed now with the rebirth and growth of the *Dallas Morning News*, so he won't be out front for a while. But when Decherd does step forward, he'll come on strong."

Even the astute, well-connected Lee Cullum had failed to notice that Robert was distracted not so much by the newspaper as by the newly separate and now public Belo Corp., where his attention was divided between the company's print and broadcast properties.

But the May 10 issue of *Forbes* ran a story by Anne Bagamery called "The best defense . . . ," with the tagline "Dallas's Belo Corp.'s preparations for siege warfare make a better story than its newspaper battle with Times Mirror Co." The writer describes events at Belo over the last eighteen months and concludes: "The result is nothing less than a transformation of the company."

She describes Robert as "an affable former president of the *Harvard Crimson*" and says that he "has been inching Belo into new technologies" and that he "says the company's real future growth will come in the new media." That was 1982—but when she questioned Belo's long-term commitment to newspaper publishing, Robert responded unequivocally: "Broadcasting may be this company's lifeblood, but the *Morning News* is its heart and soul." Soon after that, Belo showed up in the June issue of *Fortune*, making its first appearance on *Fortune*'s "Second 500 Largest Industrials" list. Belo came in at number 822.

The next stage of Belo's unfolding strategic plan was announced three months ahead of its effective date. The advance notice was a milestone in itself, fulfilling Jimmy's pledge of greater openness. On September 29, several executive changes and upcoming retirements were reported, most to become effective on December 31. At the top of the heap was the announcement that Joe Dealey would relinquish the CEO title to Jimmy Moroney. The story in the *News* quoted Joe with the standard "My decision to step down as chief executive officer is part of the continued orderly transition of management responsibility."

However, around that time, Joe gave an interview to Gerald Saxon for the Dallas Public Library's long-term oral history project in which he commented more personally about why he stepped down. He said that he hoped "to occupy an office here [at Belo] which isn't snowed under with paper and people running in and out and shoving stuff under your nose." He further explained that he had told his wife, Doris, a little earlier, "I'm going to see the company through this public offering. After that, then I'm going to think seriously and hard about just withdrawing, just voluntarily step away and let somebody else do it." He said, "This is a young person's world and they are coming along, and they make their own contributions and mistakes."[5]

The announcements in that September 1982 story didn't reveal that the changes were a historical step in the transition away from family management of the *Dallas Morning News*. For the first time in the history of the paper, someone other than a Belo or Dealey family member would hold the title of president. Jimmy would hand over that title to John Rector, one of two executive vice presidents of the *News*. The transition was to be made on January 1, 1983.

Only a few days earlier, on September 24, Belo had lost one of its most valued outside directors when Bob Dennard had died at age fifty-seven. The *News* ran an editorial praising Dennard for his good judgment in all matters, commenting that "his death leaves many corporations and charitable institutions without one of their most dependable and trusted advisors." Another member of Belo's board of directors was also stepping down. Bob Richardson, sixty, had been Belo's senior vice president for finance and treasurer, effectively the CFO, before Jim Sheehan's arrival. He announced he would retire early from Belo at year-end 1982, and from the board at the next annual meeting in March 1983.

Bob had been at Belo since 1959, when he was recruited as a pension and benefits expert. He had been on the Belo board only since March 1980, and in the meantime he had been involved in all of the activities preparing the company for its public offering. It's not hard to imagine, or to understand, that Jim Sheehan, who had been senior vice president and chief financial officer for less than a year, was eager to bring in a younger cast of financial managers with more recent financial training. Bob's departure made that possible.

Belo had completed a policy transformation away from allowing people to remain on the job as long as they wanted. It was apparent by then that in the more high-level executive positions, age sixty was becoming the new sixty-five. However, retirement benefits also had been greatly enhanced by then, which made early retirement possible, even attractive, if one were given no choice in the matter—another phenomenon of the new Belo.

The *New York Times* picked up on the changes at Belo, and on October 1, 1982, it ran a story written by Daniel F. Cuff. The story mainly reported the facts presented in the news release, but apparently the writer also interviewed Jimmy. He quoted him without providing much context or background: "We're in the acquisition field. We're always looking at television stations primarily and newspapers when the opportunity is there." That statement was another example of Jimmy's openly telegraphing to those paying attention what was in the works in the Belo executive suite.

On November 5, the plans were further spelled out when Belo executives made a presentation to the New York Society of Security Analysts in Manhattan. Jimmy told them that "the principal goal of our company is the achievement of long-term growth as an independent media company based primarily in the Southwest."

Robert told the same gathering of analysts that Belo would be improving its production capacity at the *Dallas Morning News*, as well as looking for suitable acquisitions. And Jim Sheehan explained Belo's capacity to fund all of the ambitious plans, pointing out that Belo had no long-term debt and plenty of working capital and available cash.

Only weeks later, on December 2, 1982, a story in the *News* announced plans for a $57 million satellite printing plant in Plano. The building was to have 220,000 square feet, and it would be situated on twenty-nine acres of undeveloped land at the corner of Plano Parkway and Coit Road in Collin County. The "North Plant" was located seventeen miles from the headquarters in downtown Dallas, and content would be transmitted by fiber optic cable from the composing room downtown to plate-making in Plano, a move that heralded the digital age for Belo.

On January 1, 1983, simultaneous to his taking over as president of the *Dallas Morning News*, John Rector was elected to fill the unfinished term of the late Bob Dennard on the board of directors. By then Rector had been with the *News* thirty-six years. His knowledge and understanding of advertising, along with his innate competitiveness and quirky wit, enabled him to rise steadily. He once explained that the reason he kept a stuffed moose head in his office was that it annoyed Joe Dealey, but it got him to laugh. Then there was the time Rector showed up at an important meeting in the *News* boardroom in full disguise as a gorilla. Life was never dull around him, but when it came to results, he was all business. Under his direction, the *News* attained the total advertising linage lead over the *Times Herald* for the first time in its history.

John Rector's promotion to president enabled a series of promotions from within the ranks, especially of those who had been through the management training program. The nearly ten-year-old program had brought in a new generation fully prepared to move up and modernize the newspaper from the inside out.

In addition to the promotion of Burl Osborne, forty-five, to senior vice president and editor, Jeremy Halbreich, thirty, was promoted to senior vice president with responsibility for marketing, promotion, public relations, and circulation; and Harry Stanley, fifty-five, was promoted to senior vice president with responsibility for advertising. Under Jeremy and Harry, several other trainees were moved into more responsible positions, poised to continue to advance.

These strategic promotions gave Robert the freedom to relinquish his direct supervision of operations at the *News* and to move full-time to the corporate ranks. He was ready and eager to focus his attention on the acquisition program. In the January 1987 oral history interview, he commented about that transition time:

> When Joe retired as chief executive officer and Jimmy took on that corporate title, we were both ready to move to a full-time corporate role. We had both had a prominent part to play in taking the company public in 1981, and that was done at the same time we were running the newspaper. So there was a real strain on our ability to do two very different kinds of jobs during that period. We needed to make the leap ourselves away from the newspaper to the corporate management group.

The separation of Belo Corp. from the *Dallas Morning News* was complete.

And while the *News* was training the next management team and promoting from within, the *Times Herald*'s revolving door of managers was continuously turning. Jim Schutze observed in a 1992 dirge following the closing of the *Times Herald*:

> In 1982 the *Times Herald* suffered an outbreak of internecine samurai warfare among the top managers. It started when a new, young managing editor, Jon Katz, went to Los Angeles and told Otis Chandler that the newspaper war had not been won in Dallas [as upper management had been reporting], that the *Morning News* was a very hot paper, and that the *Times Herald* was in a mess.[6]

The effect was a massive "purge" of managers that Schutze observed firsthand from his editorial writer's glass cubicle outside the executive suite. He later concluded that the 1982 episode was the deciding factor in the newspaper's losing battle for survival.

The next few years for Belo were a time of unprecedented growth in all areas of the company. Executives fulfilled the promises made to analysts at the time of going public that Belo would be acquiring properties to diversify both geographically and in the balance between its publishing and broadcasting properties.

The broadcasting industry was astonished in June 1983, when Belo announced its intention to buy the six television stations comprising the Corinthian Broadcasting group of the Dun & Bradstreet Corporation. The deal was worth $606 million, and it was the largest purchase of broadcast properties ever made at once by a single company. Robert and Jim Sheehan had led the charge at Belo, applying Ward Huey's career-long conviction that a properly managed local television station could be highly profitable. They knew that acquiring the Corinthian group would be a transforming event for Belo Corp.

A week before Belo's announcement of the Corinthian deal, the June 20 issue of *Forbes* ran a story reporting that the Dun & Bradstreet stations were on the market, and that some industry analysts were questioning if it were the "demise of commercial television," as a result of the growing audience for cable television. The *Forbes* story further speculated that Dun & Bradstreet was selling at the top of the market on the assumption that prices couldn't continue to escalate.[7]

However, a contrasting point of view quickly emerged. Belo shareholders were told that the board made the decision to purchase the Dun & Bradstreet stations on the basis of three key internal factors that coincided with the availability of Corinthian: 1) Belo had unprecedented financial strength, as well as depth of management talent; 2) profit margins for broadcasting were much greater than those for publishing; and, in contrast to the speculations, 3) "impending liberalization of the Federal Communications Commission's so-called 'Rule of Seven'" would only increase competition for available commercial television properties, and thus their price would likely go up significantly in future years.[8]

Furthermore, shareholders were told that the purchase perfectly matched the long-term strategies of Belo, enabling it to grow in one leap to a size it had expected would take years and multiple deals to accomplish. In fact, it took just one month to make that leap. Dun & Bradstreet had announced on May 9 its intention to sell all of its stations except KHOU-TV in Houston. On June 10, Dun & Bradstreet accepted Belo's offer to purchase all of the stations, including KHOU. The instant doubling of Belo was reported coast to coast, from the *New York Times* and *Wall Street Journal* to the *Los Angeles Times* and *Hollywood Reporter*. It even merited a small notice in the *International Herald Tribune*.

In an interview conducted fifteen years later, Jimmy Moroney chuckled as he recalled the exciting days leading up to the purchase of the Dun & Bradstreet properties, including his own role in making the offer. The company's top three officers made the trip to meet with the sellers:

> Jim Sheehan and Robert and I were in New York, and we were going to meet with Dun & Bradstreet the next day. And so the way the thing was planned, Robert would talk about the company itself just generally, and Sheehan would talk about the financial part of it, and my job was to make the offer. The bid we were going to give them was $600,000,000; and every time it came my turn—this was in our little practice session in the hotel room—I'd say, "And the offer we'd like to make you is six hundred thousand dollars." And Robert and Jim would say, "No! It's six hundred *million*!"

Jimmy was so concerned that he might make the mistake in the real meeting that he used a yellow legal pad from a stack provided in the middle of the conference room table and printed out the offer in words. He kept the pad on his lap so that he could easily glance at it before speaking. No one at Belo was used to such big numbers, and their boldness in deciding to make the offer was a clear sign to Wall Street that a new media company was emerging.

The FCC's Rule of Seven limited a company's ownership to five VHF television stations. To comply with the existing rule in conjunction with the purchase, Belo simultaneously sold two of the six Dun & Bradstreet properties, as well as two of its own stations—KFDM-TV in Beaumont, Texas, and WTVC in Chattanooga. Those sales yielded $153.9 million, and the resulting lineup included the following five television stations: WFAA, the ABC affiliate in Dallas/Fort Worth; KHOU, the CBS affiliate in Houston; KXTV, the CBS affiliate in Sacramento/Stockton/Modesto, California; WVEC, the ABC affiliate in Hampton/Norfolk, Virginia; and KOTV, the CBS affiliate in Tulsa, Oklahoma.

Belo continued to defy conventional wisdom when it soon announced the sale of its Tennessee cable television system. Then, in September 1983, Belo bought two radio stations in Denver, Colorado, for $22 million. The purchase of KOA-AM and KOAQ-FM complemented Belo's two Dallas radio stations, the recently converted WFAA-AM, which was called KRQX-AM with its new rock music top-40 format, and KZEW-FM, the album rock station.

In the September 26, 1983, edition of *Business Week*, the writer commented on the recent activities at Belo:

> When Belo published its offering prospectus in 1981, investors were surprised at the company's profitability. And Moroney and Decherd have continued to impress Wall Street with their success in pitting the *Morning News* against Times Mirror's *Dallas Times Herald*, a battle that Belo is winning handily.

Then the story quoted Jimmy on the recent acquisitions in his characteristic low-key, straightforward way: "We have been the same size for a long time. We could just accumulate earnings and pay dividends or we can grow with the industry. We want to grow."

One of the country's largest media companies, Gannett, had only recently launched its national newspaper, *USA Today*, and their news boxes appeared on the streets in Dallas in October 1983. The cover story of its November 16 edition carried the headline "Doing things in a big way in Dallas." Accompanying the story on page one was a photograph of Robert with the caption "NEW BLOOD: The purchase of six television stations signals an end to A. H. Belo Corp.'s conservative reputation and is a tribute to the leadership of Vice President Robert Decherd."

Toward the end of the *USA Today* story, as writer Gregory Katz praised Robert's "successful effort to moderate what was once a hard-core conservative editorial page" of the *News*, Katz also mentioned "September's surprise resignation of Joe Dealey, Jr., as vice president and secretary . . . ." Joe Jr. had been working in the corporate offices only since 1980, but he had found the work far removed from his personal interests as a writer and as a member of the U.S. Army National Guard.

Although his father, brother, sisters, and he collectively were significant shareholders, it surely was obvious to him that he would not be following in his father's footsteps to the presidency and chairmanship of Belo. Rather than return to the editorial department, where he had thrived, Joe Jr. quietly resigned from Belo and set out to find something more to his liking. He left Belo with the confidence that his Belo shares were in good hands under the watchful eye of his second cousin, Robert.

Like his father before him, Joe Jr. had become actively involved in volunteer community work. At the time, he was a trustee of Children's Medical Center in Dallas, a director of the United Way of Metropolitan Dallas, and a director of the Dallas Zoological Society. He was also involved as a member of the Cotton Bowl Athletic Association and the Salesmanship Club of Dallas. He was a 1981 graduate of Leadership Dallas, a project of the Dallas Chamber of Commerce, and a member of the development committee of the Hockaday School of Dallas. Those varied connections, and his own personal interests, would soon lead to his appointment in 1984 as the spokesman for Dallas/Fort Worth International Airport, where he achieved national recognition during his ensuing fifteen-year career.

However, as Joe Jr. made his exit, another great-grandson entered the business with unbridled enthusiasm and an eagerness to learn from the ground up. In the fall of 1983, Jim Moroney III began working as an advertising salesman for WFAA-TV. That May, Jim completed an MBA at the graduate business school at the University of Texas at Austin, as did his longtime girlfriend, Barbara Joan Bass. Although both were from Dallas, Barbara and Jim first met in California, where they were students at Stanford and by coincidence were registered for the same class on Shakespeare.

Jim and Barbara were from very high-profile Texas families, with Barbara's family being one of the few in the state that was even more well known than Jim's. Her mother, Rita Crocker Bass Clements, and stepfather, Texas Governor William P. Clements, were married in 1975. Her father, Richard D. (Dick) Bass, was a well-known Texas oilman and almost legendary adventurer, whose particular passion was mountain climbing. Jim and Barbara were married in August 1983 on a date that was chosen to accommodate the calendars of their prominent and busy parents, rather than on their preferred date, and Jim went to work at WFAA after their European honeymoon.

In November 1983, Belo successfully completed a common stock offering of 2,200,000 shares, not over the counter like the initial public offering, but this time on the New York Stock Exchange. The company received $75.6 million from the offering, and Robert's earlier goal to grow the broadcast side of the business in order to ensure the long-term stability of the *Dallas Morning News* seemed to be reinforced and extended.

Earlier in 1983, at the annual meeting of shareholders in April, two new directors had been elected to the Belo board. They were Reece A. Overcash, fifty-six, and William T. Solomon, forty. Reese was chairman and chief executive officer of the Associates Corporation of North America, one of the country's largest financial service institutions. When he joined Belo's board, he was a director of several other public companies and considered one of the most talented and insightful businessmen in the country.

Bill Solomon, a Dallas native, was president and chief executive officer of Austin Industries, a general construction company that had evolved from Austin Bridge & Road, the company that built the triple underpass creating Dealey Plaza in the 1930s. Bill's grandfather Charles Moore had bought the company in 1918, after eighteen years as an employee.[9] Bill had joined Austin Industries in 1967 soon after graduating from Harvard, and he had been president since 1970. Bill, like Reece and most other outside directors of Belo, was already active and visible in the civic and philanthropic institutions of Dallas when he was elected to the Belo board.

At the end of 1983, Dick Blum retired from Belo and from the board after twenty-six years with the company. Then, on January 1, 1984, several management changes were put in place that clearly signaled the hierarchy of the succession plan. Robert added chief operating officer to his title of executive vice president. Jim Sheehan was promoted to executive vice president and kept the CFO designation. Mike Perry, whom Jim had brought from the *News* as Belo's director of financial planning, was promoted to vice president and controller. And Robert G. Norvell, who had been hired during 1983 as vice president and treasurer, was given the additional responsibilities of secretary of the company, succeeding Joe Jr.

At the annual meeting in April 1984, Jimmy was elected chairman of the board, replacing Joe, who formally retired from the company. Joe's retirement would not necessarily have precipitated his stepping down as chairman, but he had been asked to do so by the outside directors. In his unalterable conservatism, Joe had continued to express concerns about spending and borrowing money. Even his oldest friends on the board had grown weary of his frequent cautions, and, like the gentleman he had always been, Joe stepped aside without argument. However, Joe continued to be a member of the board for the rest of his life, another eleven years. He moved to an office in North Dallas, which he maintained until his death from lung cancer in 1995 at age seventy-five.

Throughout those eleven years, Joe remained a supporter of Jimmy and Robert in their leadership, always voting with them as a board member and publicly voicing his approval of their leadership, although sometimes in qualified terms. In a 1986 interview conducted in his North Dallas office, Joe said, "The company has changed greatly in the years since 1980. We've got new people in there managing a much bigger operation than what we ever dreamed we might have. Jimmy is overseeing all of those activities, and I think they've done a magnificent job." He acknowledged that things were not being done as he would have done them, and even commented that "[the company] has in my judgment made some errors," but he disengaged himself from the action in a dignified way.

Also at the 1984 meeting, Jim Laney retired from the board upon reaching the board's retirement age, after eleven years as a director. At the time, Jim was president of Locke, Purnell, Boren, Laney & Neely, attorneys for Belo. No directors were added to the board that year.

It was a surprise to no one eight months later, at the end of 1984, when Jimmy announced he was passing along the presidency to Robert, to be effective January 1, 1985. Jimmy maintained the CEO role, and Robert retained the COO position. At the same time, another vice presidency was created to handle the growing volume of work. Walter G. Mullins, an attorney and specialist in labor law who had come into Belo from the *News* as director of administration, was elected vice president of administration. The lineup of officers then was Moroney, Decherd, Sheehan, Norvell, Perry, and Mullins. For a company that had almost no corporate officers only five years earlier, it seemed to the rank and file that vice presidents were popping up everywhere.

At Belo Broadcasting during 1984, Dave Lane, by then an eighteen-year veteran, was named president and general manager of WFAA. And at the *News*, another history-making promotion made John Rector the first non-family publisher of the newspaper. Burl Osborne was elected president, retaining his other role as editor, which made room for Jeremy Halbreich to move up to executive vice president, and for everyone down the line to take another step up in the ranks.

Curiosity about management succession was as much a part of daily life around the Belo companies at that time as the various other developments that were rapidly unfolding. The air was thick with speculations about when and where changes would be announced next, and how that would affect everyone else. A great many things were happening as management sought to accommodate the burgeoning company. A little earlier, the company had negotiated a trade with the city of Dallas for a piece of land that was on the eastern side of Ferris Plaza, directly across the street from WFAA. The land was acquired for future use, and when management found it was impractical to build a multistory building in the loading dock area behind the Dallas Morning News Building, that location seemed ideal.

Using the land as the basis of its investment, Belo became a limited partner with several others to build a seventeen-story building to be called the Belo Building at One Ferris Plaza. The project was announced on August 30, 1983. The other partners included Richard Mullen of the Mullen Company, and Key Kolb and E. G. Hamilton of Omniplan Architects. Omniplan designed the sleek, gray granite building, and as soon as conceptual drawings were complete, the Mullen Company began to market the property.

The plan was that Belo would be the lead tenant in the building, taking up about half the space. The top few floors would become Belo's corporate headquarters, and several floors on the lower levels would be finished out for lease by the Broadcast Division and the *Dallas Morning News*, for accounting, marketing, and circulation customer service departments. Omniplan finished out the ninth and tenth floors for its own headquarters, and the remaining space was to be leased to other users.

Construction began in late 1983 and was nearing completion when the *Dallas Morning News* reached its centennial on October 1, 1985. Preparations for the centennial had been ongoing for more than a year. Plans included a massive special edition of the *News* containing a hundred years in the history of Dallas and Texas, as well as the history of the newspaper and its leadership. The company had sought and been approved for a historical marker, which was dedicated by the Texas State Historical Commission at an outdoor public celebration on October 1, with music and speeches and birthday cake for all the attendees.

An evening gala celebration was held in the lobby of the Dallas Morning News Building, from which glass partition walls had been removed to open the space. Cocktails and wine were served for the first "official" consumption of alcohol on the premises of the newspaper. Guests included Dallas Mayor and Mrs. A. Starke Taylor, Jr., and Texas Governor and Mrs. Mark White. At the event, Lynn Moroney was persuaded to perform an impromptu rendition of "Sentimental Journey," reprising her days as a professional singer on WFAA Radio. Her performance was flawless, and it capped off a joyful celebration of family, employees, and friends. Even Gordon Jackson attended and later wrote warmly of his enjoyment in a thank-you note to Jimmy.

For a year leading up to the big event, many employees of the *News* worked on their routine jobs, as well as some aspect of the centennial plans. Spirits ran high, and October 1, 1985, dawned bright and clear, after a Texas blue norther had blown through the day before with cold rain and gusty winds. The cold and windy day was the occasion of a special groundbreaking ceremony on the vacant lot to the east of the Belo Building. Braving the weather, Belo's officers were joined by officials from the city of Dallas to kick off the creation of a new park designed by Omniplan, to be built by Belo and deeded to the city of Dallas in honor of the longtime employees of the *Dallas Morning News*. The 28,000-square-foot park would be called Lubben Plaza, in recognition of John F. Lubben and his son Joe A. Lubben, who together served the company for 101 years, beginning in Galveston. The ceremony was brief but touching, as company and city officials were joined by members of the Lubben family and by the numerous active employees of the *Dallas Morning News* who had served for twenty-one years or more.

Earlier in 1985, at the annual meeting, two new directors were elected to the Belo board, returning the board to its full complement of fourteen directors. Lester A. Levy, who was chairman of the board of NCH Corporation in Dallas, was elected along with J. McDonald Williams, also of Dallas, who was then managing partner of Trammell Crow Company, the nation's largest real estate developer.

Both of the new directors had extensive management experience and brought knowledge of manufacturing and real estate development to the table as Belo was improving and expanding operations at all of its entities. Some observers of the Belo evolution, with its greater presence in television, were surprised in July 1985 when the board approved a five-year expansion program for the *News*'s North Plant, which had only begun operations in January of that year.

The printing plant expansion would begin in 1986 and add four more presses to the original two Japanese TKS offset presses. If anyone still doubted the company's commitment to the survival and flourishing of the *Dallas Morning News*, they were soon outnumbered.

Even before that announcement, in May 1985 Robert was named Newspaper Executive of the Year by *Adweek*. In the story by Russ Pate,

Robert characteristically diverted attention away from himself to the three executives he and Jimmy had put in place at the *News*: John Rector, publisher; Burl Osborne, president and editor; and Jeremy Halbreich, executive vice president. The story highlighted the many ways the newspaper had grown over the last five years, but then it took a broader view, quoting Wall Street analyst Barry Kaplan saying about Robert, "He's a very thoughtful, calculating and intelligent guy. Belo has a shrewd yet simple strategy: buying media properties in growth markets and adding value to the product. It's a sound investment strategy—get rich slowly."

Two months later, the July 1985 issue of *Texas Monthly* featured a story by staff writer Peter Elkind, titled "The legacy of Citizen Robert," which was a capsule history of Belo Corp., with a special focus on the ins and outs of the family relationships over the years. Robert cooperated fully with the magazine, giving extensive interviews and access to materials. However, Elkind gave the story a conspiratorial spin, which deeply offended Robert because of the way it belittled his cousins' roles.

Elkind had taken advantage of Robert's sincerity and openness, but more than that, he had gotten a lot of things wrong by incorrectly, and perhaps cynically, presuming that no family could have worked things out as amicably and openly as Robert and Jimmy were saying.

On the other hand, Elkind got a lot of things right, and the historical review gave a pretty clear picture of how the company was organized and just what made it so effective, particularly against Times Mirror in the Dallas market. For the first time in more than two generations, the *Texas Monthly* story made it clear that Belo's strategies for the *News* were not based on any response to competition from the *Dallas Times Herald*. They were, instead, part of a 100-year-old natural progression of ideas and philosophies, family traditions, and company goals, all of which had their own vitality and their own inevitabilities, in spite of any outside influences, including "the great newspaper war."

In fact, Elkind unintentionally made the newspaper war seem like a mere distraction for Belo, as it went about its usual business in a well-planned and methodical way.

Robert, like his predecessors in heading Belo, came into the company with an innate appreciation of the significance of the A. H. Belo Corporation as an institution and as part of Texas history. He had never taken for granted the place of the company in history, however. And more importantly, from his earliest days at the company, Robert seems always to have understood his inherited responsibility to record the evolution of the company beyond the formal documents and the views of outsiders. While the cynical might see that as trying to control the company's image, which it does, the historian's view of that impulse would be more generous and appreciative. Robert seemed determined not to perpetuate the company's reputation for being secretive and withholding information from the public. As he had demonstrated in his cooperation with *Texas Monthly*, Robert wanted the whole story known.

In planning for the centennial in 1985, Robert initiated an internal documentary and oral history project, beginning with collecting raw footage of daily life in the newsrooms and production facilities, as well as of every special event, such as the newspaper's centennial. The last time the internal workings had been carefully recorded for posterity was during G. B. Dealey's lifetime, when the Sam Acheson book *35,000 Days in Texas* was written and published in 1938.

For the oral history project in 1985, Robert drew up an initial list of more than thirty retired senior executives and company directors, many of whom had known G. B. Dealey and all of his successors. Robert wanted to record the evolution of the company in the words of those who were there and had made it happen. The oral history project would record the memories of individuals' own careers in the company, as well as their memories of the others with whom they had worked, and most importantly, the human stories behind the changes that occurred over the years.

Over several months, those involved in the project edited the many hours of raw material into a one-hour film about the newspaper's centennial. However, the film was never shown, even to employees. It was placed in the archives for future reference. While Robert wanted to record the history, he was never comfortable with the film's inevitably promotional tone, or with the quality of the production.

His earlier response to the *Texas Monthly* article, the ambivalence about wanting to tell the story of the company but not wanting to draw too much attention to himself, seemed to apply even to his own project. It is impossible to tell the story of Belo without telling the story of the family, including his own role, and he wasn't ready to do that in 1985. However, he did continue the oral history project, and over the years dozens more video interviews have been recorded and transcribed for the archives.

In early 1986, the Belo Building was ready, and all of the Belo corporate officers and their staffs moved into the new headquarters. The offices at the *News* had been very nice, but the new offices were elegant. Jimmy Moroney once voiced his attitude that "they're too nice, really!" On the sixteenth and seventeenth floors, they had spectacular views. Downtown Dallas was to the east. and the Trinity River greenbelt to the west. It was the first high-rise office building to be built in the southwest quadrant of downtown, so the views were unique. The generous allotment of space, compared to the old quarters, allowed for more offices, and Belo was at the point of needing more employees to carry on the business of the company.

During the negotiations with Dun & Bradstreet, Belo was represented and advised by a number of highly skilled and talented lawyers, two of whom continued to work closely with the company afterward and later became significant members of the Belo management team. The first of those was Michael J. McCarthy, who was with the Washington, D.C., firm of Dow, Lohnes & Albertson and who specialized in the intricacies of the FCC rules and regulations. He joined Belo in October 1985 as vice president, secretary, and general counsel, Belo's first in-house counsel. Mike's quick Irish wit and genuine nature perfectly matched Robert's respectful, even-handed style of management. Together, they created a new bonhomie in the corporate offices.

In the annual report published in the spring of 1986, Jimmy and Robert jointly reported that 1985 "was a year of assimilation and stabilization" for Belo. Their muffled enthusiasm reflected that for the first time since going public Belo had reported lower net earnings than the previous year—16.8 percent lower, in fact. However, the first Pulitzer Prize ever awarded to the *Dallas Morning News* was announced a few weeks later, and the newsroom cheered with the first bottle of champagne ever to be poured over the heads of *News* staffers. The 1986 Pulitzer for National Reporting was given to Craig Flournoy, George Rodrigue, and Howard Swindle for "Separate and Unequal," a series examining substandard conditions in public housing.

Two members of the Belo board of directors retired at the spring meeting in 1986, and one very important new director was elected. Lloyd Bowles and John Rector retired, and Dealey Decherd Herndon was elected to join her brother, Robert, on the board. Except for her great-grandmother, Dealey was the only woman to have been elected a director of Belo, and hers was not an honorary election.

Dealey had worked diligently alongside Robert and Jimmy on Belo matters since Ben's death in 1972. In fact, following the announcement of the Dun & Bradstreet purchase in 1983, Dealey commented to Robert that the transaction had been a rather big bet, in her view, and that she would like to have an official voice in such matters going forward. In other words, she wanted a real vote. Robert and Jimmy readily agreed, and together they worked out a logical progression of events so that she could join the board as soon as possible.

Dealey was thirty-nine years old when she joined the board. Like Robert, she had grown up in Dallas, and she attended the Hockaday School, from which she graduated in 1965. She received a Bachelor of Arts degree in government from the University of Texas at Austin in 1969. She married during her senior year of college, and soon she and her husband, David Herndon, were planning for their first child. She recalls that devoting herself to being a mother and wife was not only the "normal" thing for young women at the time, but she relished the opportunity.

However, by the time her two sons were finishing high school, she began to look outside for a new challenge. She commented in a 2006 interview, "There came a time when I thought, 'I have an enormous investment in this company, and I have no voice.'" She began to consider whether to get involved in something else that would distract her and keep her engaged for life, or to find a way to be deeply involved in Belo that wouldn't impose on Robert and his apparent trajectory at the company.

She continued, "I like to understand what is happening and why, and to have a voice in that. I never wanted to be in a position to be going counter to [Robert] because I had so much respect for him and affection, and from the day he was born I treasured him. I knew that if I was informed, I wouldn't be a problem."

She did, however, have no problem challenging him at board meetings, which she said seemed to startle her fellow directors at the time. "When I first came on the board it was an all male board, and it was almost comical. . . . None of the other board members would push Robert like I would. They would graciously ask questions, and I'd go 'Well, wait a minute. I don't understand why in the world we would do that,' and the directors weren't used to that. Women talk more than men." But she was readily accepted as an equal by all the directors, and immediately became an integral part of the decision-making for Belo.

By the time she joined the Belo board, she lived in Austin with her husband, David, and their two sons, and she had been actively involved in historic preservation initiatives in Texas since the early 1970s.

Dealey, a warm, friendly person, was already fairly well known within the higher ranks of the company, because she had often visited Robert at the company when she was in town. After her introduction at the annual meeting, her presence on the Belo "campus" was not so anonymous among the rest of the employees, who were highly interested in this milestone election of another family member to the board. Soon everyone could recognize her smile, although she kept a very low profile.

The new Belo Building included a large, well-appointed corporate boardroom where directors would henceforth meet, after thirty-seven years of meeting in the Dallas Morning News Building. And as the Belo executives settled into their new offices, plans were underway to install the newly restored 175-foot mural by Perry Nichols in the lobby of the Belo Building, as part of Belo's celebration of the Texas Sesquicentennial later in the fall. Installing the mural in the lobby of the new building would be a celebrated return of a much-loved work of art, which had been removed from the Dallas Morning News Building years earlier to accommodate remodeling. The lobby mural had been the thing that all employees and visitors from before 1972 remembered most vividly about the Dallas Morning News Building.

Coinciding with the restoration of the early Texas mural, Robert instituted a program to buy artworks by contemporary Texas artists for use in the new offices, conference rooms, and reception areas. He hired Dallas art consultant Murray Smither to appraise the company's existing collection, much of it acquired during Ted Dealey's tenure, which included the work of many well-known early Texas artists.

Then, on Friday, June 27, 1986, the *New York Times* published a story by Geraldine Fabrikant with this headline: "Newspaper to be sold in Dallas." The first paragraph explained that the Times Mirror Company had agreed to sell the *Dallas Times Herald* for $110 million, "in an apparent acknowledgement that it was unable to win the heated Dallas newspaper war." The story further reported that the buyer, MediaNews Group, headed by William Dean Singleton, paid less for the paper than the newspaper's previous year's revenues, at a time when newspapers often sold for more than twice their revenues.

Over the previous five years, Times Mirror had changed the *Times Herald*'s publisher five times, and each one had pledged his commitment to Dallas and vowed to turn things around at the paper. At the time of the sale, Art Wible had been publisher less than a year, and Shelby Coffey had taken over the newsroom as editor only weeks before. Dean Singleton was reported to have asked them both to stay on, but Coffey soon left to join the *Los Angeles Times*.

The announcement was a good news/bad news sort of shock to the Belo and *News* teams. On the one hand, numerous writers for industry publications and investor reports had declared the *News* the winner of the newspaper war two years before, and the Times Mirror sellout was clear reinforcement of that judgment. However, the *New York Times* also reported that Dean Singleton "has a reputation in the industry for taking unprofitable papers and cutting costs. . . ." That reputation led to speculation that he would cut advertising and circulation rates, as well, which might cause upheavals among the *News*'s advertisers and subscribers.

The *Times Herald* made its own announcement two days later, on June 29, with the headlines "Dallas is a city of winners," a quote from Dean Singleton on his purchase. He was moving his company's headquarters from New Jersey to Dallas, and he was already identifying his new acquisition as a locally owned daily newspaper. Singleton had grown up in Graham, Texas, and he had been working at newspapers since he was a high school student. He had applied for a job at the *Times Herald* when he was about nineteen years old and wasn't hired. However, he had been successful with an application to the *News*, and he worked there for two years while attending the University of Texas at Arlington.

After Singleton bought the *Times Herald*, some of the longtime editors around the *News* referred to him by his old nickname, Dinky—a name newspaper people use for a half-width roll of newsprint. He had been given the name by editors who weren't accustomed to having reporters as young as he was when he got his job at the *News*. But most of his former colleagues remembered him with respect and affection, because he had demonstrated intelligence and ambition as an employee. Everyone at the *News* believed, and even celebrated, that the competition was still alive.

Belo's announcement in October 1986 that it was selling its Dallas radio stations for $20 million may have been puzzling to outsiders, those few who noticed, that is. Belo's radio operations had not been very successful since the advent of television. As radio became more focused on the profitable recorded-music format, Belo attempted to maintain its focus on journalistically sound news-talk radio.

But the company's efforts to expand ownership of radio stations that programmed the news-talk format were thwarted when Belo couldn't find stations available at affordable prices, because of the highly profitable music format most popular at the time. In retrospect, it seems Belo's aims then, as often before, were ahead of the times.

Then, on November 21, the next step in Belo's management succession plan was announced in the *News*. After forty years on the job, Jimmy had reached age sixty-five and would retire from Belo at the end of the year. Robert would become chairman and chief executive officer on January 1, 1987. The announcement explained that Jimmy would remain on the board of directors, serving as chairman of the executive committee, and that he would continue to occupy his office in the Belo Building, where he would continue to advise Robert and the other officers on various matters.

In an oral history recorded at the time of his retirement, Jimmy commented about his career. "It's been a grand time," he said, trying unsuccessfully to hold his emotions in check. "It's been a fascinating forty years."

In addition to the announcement that Robert would become chairman and CEO, the news release said that Jim Sheehan and Ward Huey would be promoted and that Burl Osborne was to become a director. Both Jim and Ward had become directors in 1982, and their dual advancement in the corporate rankings was very likely a strategic move by the new chairman to preserve harmony in the executive suite between two highly competitive and forceful men, one an iconic company veteran and the other a relative newcomer, not only to Belo but to the media business.

Although Burl would remain in his office at the Dallas Morning News Building, his advancement to the board seemed designed to add stability at the upper management level by providing the third side to a triangle of strong executives supporting Robert's leadership. All three were larger than life in personality and equally prepossessing, each in his own way. And each of them was fully aware of the delicate balance of power they juggled under Robert's watchful eye. All three were fiercely competitive businessmen, and their competitiveness, even with each other, set the tone in the corporate offices.

Jim Sheehan was named president and chief operating officer, with oversight for the Newspaper Division as well as the company's financial affairs; Ward, already president and CEO of Belo Broadcasting Corp., added the corporate title vice chairman of the board and continued as president of the renamed Broadcast Division; and Burl, already president and editor of the *News*, reporting to Jim, joined the other two on the Belo board.

Upon joining the *News* in 1980, Burl's immediate success and his unflagging enthusiasm for modernizing the reporting, editing, page design, and institutional voice of the *News* rapidly led to advancement through the ranks of the newspaper, culminating in the spot on the board of directors of Belo. By then Burl also had earned a master's degree in business administration from Long Island University, as well as completed the Harvard Business School Advanced Management Program.

Robert and Burl had developed a strong relationship of mutual respect—warmly friendly, but with a wariness on both sides that came from an emotion something like awe, which each seemed to have of the other.

That development in the power structure of the senior executives seemed to change the tone of the corporate offices as well, where Ward Huey and Jim Sheehan were given offices of equal size and equally favorable locations. Taking the corporate officers out of the Dallas Morning News Building had created a new self-consciousness that wasn't hard to notice. The new executive offices were large, with eighteen-foot ceilings, and at least one wall in each office was lined with rich hardwoods. And the offices were not just quiet, they were virtually silent at all times. The contrast to the old offices couldn't have been more pronounced—no smell of ink or rumble of presses or rowdy reporters or jovial groups pausing for a conversation.

However, the formality of office protocol, which had always existed in the executive offices, seemed more pronounced than ever before. The only rebel of the group was Burl, who found the formality stuffy and appreciated being able to return to his office at the newspaper after meetings with the others. The corporate offices, removed from operation, became an excruciatingly polite society where everyone seemed to be on their best behavior at all times. It was not a particularly comfortable environment.

And the financial news at year-end was not good either. Belo's net earnings for 1986 dropped again from those of 1985, reflecting particularly the Southwest regional recession, and while the picture brightened some in 1987, the downward trend resumed in 1988. In 1986, Belo adopted a differential voting stock (DVS) structure, resulting in two series of common stock. Series A shares had one vote, while Series B shares had ten votes each. Only Series A shares were traded on the NYSE, but Series B shares were transferable at any time to Series A. The plan was designed to preserve the continuity of ownership by concentrating voting power in the hands of individuals and institutions that chose to stay the course with the company. The dual voting stock structure effectively protects the company from takeover by outside investors, so long as the holders of Series B can all agree with one another about what is good for the company.

In setting up its DVS, Belo was following a trend recently begun by the Times Mirror Company, when their shareholders approved a dual voting stock structure in anticipation of an SEC rule change that would have prohibited such structures in public companies. Times Mirror's DVS was patterned after others already in place in the newspaper industry, such as that of the New York Times Company, which that company adopted when it went public in 1969. Belo had considered such a structure in 1981, but it followed the advice of its bankers, who feared it would make the stock less attractive to investors. Ultimately, the SEC did not change the rule, but the DVS was in place.

During 1987, Belo sold its remaining two radio stations in Denver, Colorado. As Robert had been telling shareholders and Wall Street analysts for years, quality journalism was Belo's real business and expertise. The company began to repurchase stock, and in May 1988 it effected a stock split on a one-for-one basis, which doubled the average shares outstanding and cut in half the share price. The high for the second quarter of 1988 after the split was $32 per share.

Paul Crume congratulates Joe Lubben at his retirement party in May 1971. Lubben continued to servc as a director of Belo and as a trustee of the G. B. Dealey Trust after he retired from active participation in the company.

When Ben Decherd died of lung cancer in November 1972, at age fifty-seven, he was chairman of the board of A. H. Belo Corporation. This photo was run with his obituary.

Belo president Joe Dealey poses with his two sons, Joe Jr. and Russell, during the 1970s as they are making their way through the management training program at the *Dallas Morning News*.

Shares of Belo were offered on the New York Stock Exchange for the first time on November 15, 1983. Company executives traveled to New York to mark the milestone: *(from left)* James M. Moroney, Jr.; Robert W. Decherd; Richard D. Blum; Ward L. Huey, Jr.; John A. Rector, Jr.; and James P. Sheehan. The young man behind John Rector and Jim Sheehan is not identified.

On October 1, 1985, Gov. and Mrs. Mark White celebrated the centennial of the *Dallas Morning News* with Robert Decherd, Joe Dealey, and Jimmy Moroney.

Belo and *Dallas Morning News* executives posed for the last time in the old boardroom in the Dallas Morning News Building in early 1986, with the model of the new Belo Building in the background. Robert Decherd stands behind John Rector, Jimmy Moroney, and Burl Osborne.

For the 1995 annual report, Belo chairman and president Robert Decherd posed with the heads of the company's two distinct divisions: Ward L. Huey, Jr., vice chairman of the Belo board and president of the Broadcast Division; and Burl Osborne, publisher of the *Dallas Morning News* and president of the Publishing Division. Photograph by Jim Olvera.

When James M. Moroney III was named publisher and chief executive officer of the *Dallas Morning News* in 2001, he called a meeting of the employees at a downtown hotel ballroom to invite questions about the changes in leadership at the paper.

The board of directors of Belo Corp. posed together in 2004. *Front, left to right*: Judith Craven, Henry Becton, Robert Decherd, Don Williams, Roger Enrico, Dealey Herndon. *Rear, left to right*: Arturo Madrid, France Córdova, Larry Hirsch, Bill Solomon, Lloyd Ward, Wayne Sanders, Louis Caldera, Steve Hamblett. Photograph by Jim Olvera.

Belo's management committee in 2005 included (*standing*) Robert Decherd, Dennis Williamson, Jim Moroney, Dunia Shive, and Jack Sander, and (*seated*) Marian Spitzberg and Guy Kerr. The committee in 2007 includes all of those except Jack Sander, who retired at the end of 2006. Photograph by Jim Olvera.

Robert W. Decherd, chairman and CEO of Belo Corp., and his sister Dealey Decherd Herndon are shown at Belo's 2007 annual meeting, at which she was recognized for reaching her twenty-first anniversary of service on the Belo Corp. board of directors. Photograph by Kristina Bowman.

Chapter 9

THE WORLD TAKES NOTE

1987–2000

January 1987 was a time of change all around for Robert Decherd, as it was for several others in the Belo hierarchy. When Robert promoted Jim Sheehan, Ward Huey, and Burl Osborne, he set up a reporting system such that Sheehan and Huey both reported directly to him, while Osborne reported to Sheehan.

Ward outranked Jim in his role as vice chairman of the board, but not in the operating structure. The earlier promotions of non-family members to the top positions at the *News* had set the stage for a similar transition at Belo, and Sheehan had been groomed for the pioneering role as the first non-family president of Belo.

Robert had been quoted in a 1985 *Advertising Age* story saying, "I would not say I am a 'lifer' at Belo. But there are many different elements to managing a responsible media company . . . and that can challenge me for a considerably long period of time." It appeared that Robert was beginning to move out of day-to-day operations and handing over the reins to Sheehan.

That January, as Robert took over leading Belo, he also had some things to celebrate in his family. Early in the year, Robert and Maureen welcomed a new member of the family, their daughter, Audrey Maureen Decherd, who arrived just two weeks before the Decherds' twelfth wedding anniversary, completing the Decherd household.

Robert's family has always been first in his life. Although he never made an issue of it at Belo, he demonstrated his commitment as he actively participated in his children's upbringing. His son, William, who is now involved in his own career, recalls with some wonder that his father almost always managed to be home for dinner with the family as he and his sister were growing up. That commitment to his own family was reflected in the ethos Robert established immediately with his corporate staff, as well, although few followed his example.

The *Wall Street Journal* took notice of the developments in Robert's life in a front-page feature on Belo, with one of its distinctive stippled portraits of Robert near the top of the story. The story focused on the many changes at Belo in recent times:

> These are heady times for the 35-year-old Mr. Decherd and the Dallas based media company that he is pushing to power in the Southwest. Long a plodding family newspaper concern, Belo has picked up speed since 1981—doubling its size, largely through a huge broadcast acquisition, and prowling for newspapers to buy.[1]

The writer goes on to make note of Sheehan's promotion to president, saying, "For the first time since George Bannerman Dealey bought the company in 1926, Belo's president, James Sheehan, isn't a Dealey descendant."

Even as a young man, Jim Sheehan had the presence of a stern and circumspect four-star general, and except for the other most senior executives, who were spared his usual demeanor, those around him learned to tread lightly. Sheehan soon promoted Mike Perry to senior vice president and chief financial officer, over Bob Norvell, who had been Belo's treasurer for several years. Soon after that he terminated Walt Mullins, the vice president for administration, during the company's first-ever reduction in force, as it was called.

That unprecedented layoff affected company employees across the Dallas region during the depths of the local recession. Next to go in a short time was Bob Norvell, and the treasurer's title also was given to Mike Perry, who seemed to know better than the others how to meet Sheehan's expectations of his staff, which often required Mike to be at the office well before and after normal working hours.

Those seemingly abrupt changes put the rest of the comparatively small corporate staff on edge, but Robert stood by Jim, who had been the company's financial strategist and chief spokesman with the investment community since joining Belo in 1982. Belo's net earnings for 1988 were less than half of those for 1987, as the region's economy hit new lows in real estate, banking, and oil, and Belo was still working off debt from its acquisitions and the expansion of the North Plant.

Another expense had been two years of legal fees fighting lawsuits filed by Dean Singleton soon after he bought the *Times Herald*. He filed an antitrust suit over syndicated features moving to the *News*, and he contested the *News*'s circulation figures and practices. Belo countersued over the circulation charges, and two years later the suits were concluded when the independent Audit Bureau of Circulations failed to find any substantial wrongdoing at either newspaper.

The audit did, however, confirm the *News*'s commanding lead, and Singleton sold the *Times Herald* to one of his former business partners, John Buzzetta, in the summer of 1988. Ultimately, after Singleton had sold out, the antitrust suit was also found in Belo's favor in a Houston court. By then, no one at Belo was surprised by anything that happened across town, as the *Times Herald* seemed to have gone adrift. However, it continued to have strong readership and passionately loyal supporters concerned about losing the city's status as a two-newspaper town.

After exiting the Dallas market, Dean Singleton continued to demonstrate the qualities that his early editors at the *News* had admired about him. He went on to build his MediaNews Group into one of the largest newspaper companies in America.

In 1989, the *News* won another Pulitzer Prize, this time for explanatory journalism. The award was given to reporter David Hanners, graphic designer Karen Blessen, and photographer William Snyder for "Anatomy of an air crash." Also that year, the first African American to be a Belo director was elected at the 1989 annual meeting. Maj. Gen. Hugh G. Robinson (retired) was chairman and CEO of the Tetra Group, a Dallas construction management company. A graduate of West Point and the Massachusetts Institute of Technology, Hugh had retired from the military in 1983, after which he worked at Southland Corporation in Dallas, serving as president of its subsidiary, Cityplace Development Corporation, before forming his own company.

Belo had had an extraordinary board of directors since 1973, when Joe's slate of five prominent Dallas businessmen was elected. With the addition of those talented, community-minded businessmen, the Belo board had operated more like that of a public company than that of a closely held private one. The outside directors had been invited and encouraged to be active in the governance of the company throughout most of the life of the company, beginning with G. B. Dealey. While Ted Dealey was not so open to views from outside the company, all of his successors were wise enough to be good listeners and to learn from the expertise and good judgment of others.

Following Joe's tenure as chairman, Jimmy worked closely with Robert to select new directors. Then, during the first few years of Robert's chairmanship, as he faced an aging board, he began a long-range plan to recruit new directors from outside the company. He launched an ambitious program to build one of the most talented and diverse boards in corporate America. He was interested in diversity of every kind: business expertise, educational background, cultural experience, age, race, gender, and point of view.

Robert openly expressed his aim to have a board that reflected the best of America, and he began the conversion to more and more outsiders on the board. He expected and accepted that such changes would lead to broader discussions and greater challenges to the thinking of those, like himself, who were insiders or who had served for many years. Jimmy Moroney continued to be Robert's partner in selecting board candidates for as long as he continued to be a director.

In 1989, Belo's profitability rebounded, after three years of disappointing results. Belo's stock price rose to a high of $41 per share during that year, which calculated to three and a half times more than the initial offering price eight years earlier. In his letter to shareholders, Robert wrote,

> . . . Belo's purposes extend beyond financial goals. As our society becomes increasingly complex, Belo's operating companies must maintain the will to provide moral leadership and a vision of what our cities and our country can be—as opposed to simply reporting on what others think and do.

Those lofty, even idealistic, goals seemed to be confirmed when WFAA-TV was awarded the 1989 Scripps Howard Foundation National Journalism Award, which Belo's Sacramento station, KXTV, had won the year before.

Also during 1989, Robert had asked his cousin Jim Moroney III to come to corporate from his post at the time of vice president and general manager of KOTV in Tulsa. Robert wanted Jim to become Belo's controller, which Jim later recalled was a great surprise to him. He considered himself to be well qualified for a number of positions around the company, but controller hadn't been on his mind.

Jim's personal style is more like that of a motivational speaker than an accountant. He keeps a small acrylic sign on his desk engraved with "Anyone who doesn't get carried away should be." However, at age thirty-three, Jim took on the challenge with enthusiasm and a sense of humor, and he served for more than a year before moving to another corporate-level assignment to broaden his knowledge and experience. At that point Jim was named assistant to the president of the Broadcast Division, Ward Huey, and in that role his interaction with station managers throughout the division and with national television organizations was a form of high-level training for assignments to come.

Another of G. B. Dealey's great-grandsons left the company in 1989, after fifteen years. Joe Dealey, Jr.'s younger brother Russell had entered the management training program on July 1, 1974, and after the three-year program he began work in the general advertising department as a salesman, after which he was a regional sales manager. He then moved to the advertising services department, where he worked from December 1980 until February 1989.

Russell had not been as successful at the paper as his brother. His quick temper and sometimes abrasive manner were not conducive to a career in sales or in management. When Russell left the company, he began working with his father, assisting in the management of the family's other investments and in their philanthropic efforts.

In January 1990, WFAA was awarded its fourth DuPont-Columbia University Silver Baton in thirteen years. The remaining production operations of the *News* were moved to the North Plant that year, and hiring and salary freezes imposed during the recession in the 1980s were lifted. Profits continued upward throughout the year, and at year-end, the traditional time for announcements of changes in the executive ranks at Belo, promotions included Burl Osborne being named publisher and Jeremy Halbreich becoming president of the *News*.

In his ten years at the *News*, Burl had completely reorganized the news department, bringing in some of the country's best journalists and energizing those who were already on board. He had also revolutionized the production and business operations with his farsighted growth strategies, and he and Robert had groomed Jeremy to take over those duties, freeing Burl to focus on the journalistic product.

On the broadcast side, Dave Lane was given additional responsibility when he was made a Broadcast Division vice president and given additional oversight of KXTV in Sacramento, California. The talented and affable Lane was promoted twice again in rapid succession, moving to Belo Corp. as president of the Television Group before he was diagnosed with brain cancer, which took his life at age fifty-two in August 1993.

The highest journalism awards were once again given to Belo companies during 1991 in both newspaper publishing and broadcasting. The *News* was awarded the Pulitzer for feature photography for a portfolio produced by William Snyder, which he shot inside state-run orphanages in Romania. WFAA received its fifth DuPont-Columbia Award for coverage of the Persian Gulf War, the only local television station in the country to be recognized with a national award for war coverage.

In November 1991, Jim Sheehan's arrogant manner and dictatorial style created a furor in the newsroom at the *News*, leading many reporters and editors to believe that Belo was out to stifle objective reporting. The situation that led to the confrontation between Sheehan and the newsroom occurred very soon after Belo and its insurance carrier had paid out more than $50 million to settle a libel judgment. Another huge libel suit was brought against the company by a South Texas sheriff who disputed claims made by *News* reporters who had relied on the use of confidential sources.

Robert dispatched Jim Sheehan and Burl to talk to the editors and reporters about the situation, in order to press upon them the vulnerability of the company in such cases. It was Robert's aim for Jim to clarify Belo's expectations concerning the accuracy of news sources, and, for the first time in anyone's memory, to provide very specific journalistic guidelines from corporate regarding the future use of confidential sources in investigative reporting.

Until then the words of G. B. Dealey inscribed on the stone façade of the Dallas Morning News Building had sufficed—"Build the news upon the rock of truth . . . ," and so on. However, the early 1990s were the beginning of an era of similar lawsuits against newspapers nationwide that challenged the use of confidential sources and ultimately caused changes in methods of verifying claims made by confidential sources at all newspapers.

After Jim Sheehan outlined the guidelines for them, the reporters pushed back, as they customarily do, reacting to what they considered interference from corporate. And, as was his custom, Jim didn't consider his pronouncements open for discussion. He responded with his considerable force, blasting the editors and reporters for daring to argue with him about what was good for the company. Nothing Burl said to them at that point could erase the image of a corporate attack on the integrity of the news product. The episode jeopardized the trust that Robert had fostered between the newsroom and Belo management for the last eighteen years.

Just as the newsroom was fighting to regain its sense of journalistic independence, the biggest shock of 1991 occurred on December 9, when John Buzzetta, owner of the *Times Herald*, shut down the 112-year-old newspaper and sold most of the assets of the Times Herald Printing Company to Belo for $55 million. That was about the time that Belo was being referred to as the "Evil Empire," even by some of its own reporters, and only half in jest. The conclusion that everyone jumped to automatically was that Belo had bought out and shut down the competition.

The truth was more subtle and complex. John Buzzetta had given up his fight to continue publication after owning the *Times Herald* for less than three years. The *Dallas Business Journal*'s report on the sale, published later that week, outlined the sequence of events as best as they could determine them:

> Only after John Buzzetta appealed for 18 months to his creditors and potential buyers—and made a last-ditch attempt to sell the newspaper to seventeen wealthy Texans hand-picked by the U.S. Justice Department, including Dallas Billionaire H. Ross Perot—did the government approve Belo's $55 million acquisition of the Herald's assets.[2]

According to various reports published at the time, Belo's offer was the best Buzzetta received for the newspaper, for which he had paid a reported $105 million, including $20 million that MediaNews Group had accepted in notes payable in 2000. Ultimately, Buzzetta paid all of his creditors and funded termination packages for employees and the company's retirement plan, which had not been fully endowed by his predecessors. His investors took a reported $45 million loss.

Although the paper employed 900 at the time it closed, by then most of the best writers and editors had already departed for greener pastures; some, like Blackie Sherrod, had earlier moved to the *News*. Others had spread out over the country. Jim Schutze, one of a few *Times Herald* diehards, later said that he was essentially the institutional memory for the newspaper in its last couple of years, and that the newcomers, both management and staff, came to him for background on the paper's better days.

At the time of the *Times Herald*'s closing, the top management at the *News* worked quietly with John Buzzetta in trying to place as many employees as possible, either at the *News* or at other Belo properties. Within hours of the *Times Herald*'s last issue, *News* customer service reps were on the phone notifying all *Times Herald* subscribers that their subscriptions had been acquired by the *News*, and that the following day they would be receiving the *News*, instead of the *Times Herald*, in a seamless continuation of their subscriptions.

No one at the *News* had time for much reflection when the historic cross-town rival shut down, because of the immediate need to accommodate thousands more subscribers and advertisers. All the approved budgets for 1992 went out the window to accommodate the larger circulation, which required more paper, more ink, and more employees in virtually every department, from ad sales and the newsroom to the pressroom and customer service.

A kind of grieving was much more apparent than jubilation around the *News* at the time. It was like losing a lifelong friend with whom one had always competed relentlessly, and then having to preside at his funeral and take over care of his large family.

The mood in the corporate offices was decidedly more upbeat, but even there the celebrations were kept to a respectable minimum. Naturally, the most effusive in his joy was the man who had led the charge for ten years, Burl Osborne.

By March, Belo had hired an assistant general counsel, Marian Spitzberg, to help with the load in the legal department. Marian was hired by Mike McCarthy, with whom she would share the increasing legal responsibilities, after working as an associate in the corporate and securities section of Haynes and Boone in Dallas. A native Texan, she received a bachelor's degree in journalism from the University of California at Berkeley in 1970 and graduated cum laude from the Dedman School of Law at Southern Methodist University.

Around town, the loyalists for the *Times Herald* were angry and bitter about what they saw as an ignoble rout. Many of them were already subscribers of both newspapers, but losing the competing voice was a blow. Soon after the *Times Herald* published its last edition, the alternative Dallas tabloid the *Observer* launched a gossip column it called "Belo Watch," to report whatever rumors it could find about "Dallas's media monolith." More than fifteen years later, many former *Times Herald* readers still begin their critical letters to the editor of the *News* with "Now that you're the only newspaper in town. . . ."

Another event in March 1992 had a profound effect on Belo, although it was little recognized at the time. Jim Sheehan's daughter was in her first year at Holy Cross College in Worcester, Massachusetts, after graduating from Ursuline Academy in Dallas. She and some friends were walking near campus in the early evening and stepped off the curb to cross a street where several streetlights were out. An oncoming car, which was occupied by several Holy Cross students, struck and killed Beth Sheehan.

Jim Sheehan was devastated and took a leave to tend to family matters. He and his wife, Ellen, had two other children. But, returning to Belo, he was not the same. Little more than a year later, at age fifty-one, he announced his retirement from Belo after eleven years on the job, and he soon moved his family back to the East Coast.

Robert took back the presidency of the company, and the experiment featuring a non-family member in that powerful role was concluded. Throughout the corporate ranks, as well as in the newsroom at the *News*, there was relief to have Robert back as the head of operations. His open-minded and equitable style had been missed.

Belo's momentum continued, and on April 7, 1992, the winners of the year's Pulitzer Prizes were announced. For the second year in a row, the *News* had won. The newspaper's fourth Pulitzer was awarded to Dan Malone and Lorraine Adams for investigative reporting on abuses by Texas law enforcement authorities.

Only three days later, the A. H. Belo Corporation celebrated 150 years as a business institution, with another historical marker dedication and an outdoor event staged on the west side of the Belo Building. Texas governor Ann Richards addressed the large crowd of employees, their families, and guests. To celebrate the occasion, the Belo Foundation had earlier commissioned two prominent Texas artists to create monumental works for permanent installation in Lubben Plaza, transforming the landscaped city of Dallas park into a sculpture garden.

The employees and other guests were served lunch on the east side of the Belo Building, where traffic had been rerouted and tables placed in Market Street. Everyone was encouraged to relax with their food and then stroll through the new sculpture garden. A band played jazz, and artists Linnea Glatt of Dallas and George Smith of Houston were on hand to meet everyone and enjoy the spirit of the occasion.

At the annual meeting in 1992, which was held shortly after Belo's sesquicentennial festivities, Robert recognized another important company milestone. It was the fortieth anniversary of his two immediate predecessors' joining the Belo board. Joe Dealey and Jimmy Moroney were on hand to accept specially designed Steuben crystal mementoes and to comment about their years as directors.

Since it became a public company, Belo's annual meetings often had been more like family reunions than corporate business meetings. In addition to the usually good turnout of blood-related family members, many company retirees attended, along with a large proportion of the local employees. Robert had established the practice of recognizing the employee-owners of Belo stock, having them stand as a group at the meeting.

On May 6, 1992, there were few dry eyes in the house as the shareholders heard from their former leaders. Introducing his cousins, Robert said, "I know this much: without their leadership, their understanding of change, and their determined commitment to this institution above personal gain, none of us would be meeting in this room today to declare our confidence in Belo's future." Many in the audience had served under all three men and closely followed the changing of leadership from one to the next. They understood Robert's words as outsiders could not.

Annual-meeting time each year made it obvious that Robert had the support of all descendants of G. B. Dealey, not just those who spent their lives in the company. Both before and after Gordon Jackson's challenges to the status quo, the other Jacksons, as well as Al Dealey and his sons, Patsy Dealey Brooks and her family, Betty Moroney Norsworthy and her family, and Jean Moroney Laney and her family, were solidly behind the company's management. Often several generations of those families attended the annual meetings, arriving in time for socializing in advance. In some cases, the annual meeting was the only time the fourth-generation descendants saw each other; however, Robert communicated with his cousins and fellow trust beneficiaries on a fairly regular basis.

Shortly after the *Times Herald* ceased publication, a former executive under Times Mirror ownership acknowledged the strength and the significance of the family ties that G. B. Dealey's descendants had nurtured and maintained throughout the years. Former executive editor Ken Johnson observed: "One difference in the two companies is that Robert Decherd was sitting there as a young, quiet, self-effacing guy before he took over, knowing it would be his company and his children's company. That causes you to do some long-range planning."[3]

At the 1992 meeting, Robert underscored his long-range approach when he announced a $41 million expansion of the North Plant to begin immediately, so that the presses recently acquired from the Times Herald Printing Company could be moved and printing capacity could be further enlarged to accommodate the increased circulation that came from combining subscribers. A new director was elected to Belo's board, as well, bringing the total number to sixteen. Judith L. Craven, M.D., M.P.H., had recently been named the president of the United Way of the Texas Gulf Coast, a four-county region with its headquarters in Houston. A medical doctor with extensive administrative and leadership experience, she had already become accustomed to being called "the first African American woman to . . ." for her many accomplishments, before that expression applied to her joining the Belo board. Dr. Craven's broad experience as an executive was sought as Belo embarked on a more intensive program of employee-centered administration.

A few weeks later, in the *Dallas Business Journal* published for the week of June 19–25, reporter Len Pierson said of Belo, "The media company's stock has shot up by 74 percent to $43 per share since the *Herald* drew its final breath in December." In September, the board of directors held its meeting in Sacramento, California, the location of its television station KXTV.

By then three new vice presidents had been added to the lineup: Vicky C. Teherani was Belo's first-ever female officer, becoming vice president and treasurer at the end of 1991; subsequently, Brenda C. Maddox had been named vice president for corporate taxes; and Harold F. Gaar, Jr., who had completed management training at the *News* and served there for years, was named vice president for public affairs. Net earnings of Belo Corporation for 1992 were more than three times those of 1991.

In 1993 Belo acquired full ownership of the Belo Building, and a third sculpture was added to those in Lubben Plaza in 1994, when Belo developed the land east of Lubben Plaza as a landscaped employee parking lot. Nationally prominent Dallas native Jesús Bautista Moroles was commissioned to create a sculpture in Fredericksburg granite to serve as an entrance to Lubben Plaza for employees walking from their cars to the Belo Building. Soon thereafter, Belo remodeled the lobby of the Belo Building, adding the same granite to the walls of the elevator bays, to echo the stone of the Moroles sculpture.

Another important event of 1994 was kept under the radar, when Burl Osborne underwent a second kidney transplant, this one donated by his brother, becoming the first person in history to have two transplanted kidneys. He thrived, returning to work in record time, and he dived back into his dual role of executive and corporate director.

In May 1994 Arturo Madrid, PhD, was elected to the board. Dr. Madrid, a native of New Mexico, was the founding president of the Tomás Rivera Center for Policy Studies, the first institution established specifically to study issues relating to the Hispanic populations of the United States, and the Norine R. and T. Frank Murchison Distinguished Professor in the Humanities at Trinity University in San Antonio. His expertise was invaluable as Belo sought ways to serve the nation's expanding Hispanic populations, particularly surrounding its properties in Texas and California.

Another expansion of geographical and cultural diversity for Belo was the purchase of WWL-TV in New Orleans in early 1994. Only three and a half years earlier, the employees of the station had organized a buyout from the station's founder, Loyola University. WWL's vice president and general manager, Mike Early, had served Loyola in that capacity for thirty years before leading the employee acquisition. In fact, when it became apparent that the station needed to join another company, Mike and the station's other leaders had come to Belo with the proposal, and Belo kept Mike on as head of the station until he chose to retire.

Long before Belo came along as owner, WWL, a CBS affiliate, had dominated the New Orleans market with both numbers of viewers and advertising volume. The local newspaper, the *Times-Picayune*, lamented the loss of local ownership of the station and described the reaction of

New Orleanians to the change of owners as shocked. However, the announcement went on to quote Wayne Barnet, the general manager of competing station WDSU, the NBC affiliate, saying "[Belo's] reputation is that of a first-class operator. It can only be something positive for the market."[4]

Meanwhile, the *News* had won two more Pulitzer Prizes, making it four in four years. The 1993 award for Spot News Photography was given to photographers Ken Geiger and William Snyder for their coverage of the Summer Olympics in Barcelona, Spain; and the 1994 award for International Reporting went to the large team of reporters and photographers who produced the series called "Violence Against Women: A Question of Human Rights."

In February 1995, Belo stretched its geographic reach significantly in the other direction by acquiring KIRO-TV, the CBS affiliate in Seattle/Tacoma, Washington. The purchase included the station's state-of-the art facilities and equipment, as well as a separate large production studio. A story in the *Seattle Times* announced the agreement between Bonneville International Corp. and Belo, with a sidebar:

> There are plenty of signs KIRO-TV will be a good fit for A. H. Belo Corp., which is paying $160 million cash for it. Both have a strong commitment to news—especially the local kind—get nervous about risqué network programs and have a conservative management style.[5]

As a matter of fact, like WWL, the KIRO leaders had sought Belo as a buyer of the station rather than put it up for auction. That was a time of great upheaval at local stations all over the country, as they faced changes in their affiliations when the networks swapped, sold, and acquired different stations. When Belo agreed to purchase KIRO, it was a CBS station, but rumors were circulating that CBS was planning to drop the station after thirty-six years. Belo persisted with its purchase, however, and when CBS pulled out, Belo began operation of its first independent station and soon aligned it with a new network, UPN. The mood in-house at Belo was upbeat and enthusiastic, and staffers were eager to learn what might happen next.

At the annual meeting in 1995, Bill Seay retired after twenty-two years on the Belo board, and Reece Overcash retired after twelve years. Joe

Dealey died just weeks before the meeting, after forty-three years as a director. The generational transfer was continued, as Robert added more people of his own generation to the board. That spring the addition was Roger A. Enrico, chairman and chief executive officer of PepsiCo Worldwide Restaurants at the time, who soon became CEO of PepsiCo, Inc. Robert's effort to attract the smartest and broadest-thinking board members in the country was moving forward.

In the middle of 1995, after making annual gifts to the endowment of the Belo Foundation since its founding in 1952, Belo Corp. made a substantial gift enlarging the Foundation's endowment sufficiently to support a much larger giving program every year. The Belo Foundation had over time supported a wide range of charitable giving with small grants, principally in Dallas and elsewhere in Texas.

Following the 1995 gift, the giving program continued its geographical focus, and the foundation began to make larger grants in areas of historical interest to the company's owners, particularly in college-level journalism education and urban parks development.

In 1995 KHOU-TV was the first local station in the country to operate from an all-digital studio, and in 1998, WFAA was the first television station in the United States to broadcast non-experimental High Definition Television (HDTV) on a VHF signal.

Belo television stations were reaching 8 percent of the television households in the United States in 1995, but Belo still considered itself a newspaper publisher. In December the company acquired the *Eagle*, the daily newspaper serving the Bryan-College Station market, home of Texas A&M University, and almost immediately thereafter, in early 1996, it acquired the *Messenger-Inquirer*, a daily paper owned by the Hager family in Owensboro, Kentucky.

Additionally, without doing much market research or even planning ahead beyond the immediate ad sales opportunities, Belo launched the *Arlington Morning News* in April 1996. The *Dallas Morning News*'s fairly modest Tarrant County operations were turned into a completely separate, although short-lived, newspaper. It targeted readers in the so-called Mid-Cities communities in Tarrant County, who had traditionally subscribed to the *Fort Worth Star-Telegram*.

Also in 1996, Belo acquired a 38.5-percent interest in the *Press-Enterprise* in Riverside, California, from Howard H. "Tim" Hays and his family, and by the middle of 1997 it owned the daily paper outright. The

Press-Enterprise had won a Pulitzer in 1968 for Public Service and was the dominant local voice in its region. At the time, the two-county "Inland" region of Southern California was predicted to be one of the fastest-growing areas in the United States, and Belo began investing in the paper to ensure its continued prominence in that market.

Burl Osborne led the newspaper expansions, both in Texas and elsewhere. He had known the Hager family in Kentucky for years. At the time of the acquisition of that paper, he was serving on the board of the Owensboro Publishing Company, owner of the *Messenger-Inquirer*. Belo's publishing philosophy aimed to maintain and enhance the local flavor of its Texas, Kentucky, and California newspapers.

In the realm of new media, the *Dallas Morning News* launched its Web site in 1996, and that year it was the first newspaper in America to break an important newspaper story on the Web before issuing it in print. The *News* received widespread attention, including sharp criticism from other newspaper publishers, for going online with an exclusive story about the Timothy McVeigh trial before it had been published in ink. Ultimately the *News* won an award for pioneering journalism, and the practice was soon commonplace.

Another quiet event in 1996 went largely unnoticed by all but a handful of people dedicated to the preservation of First Amendment rights, open government, and the free flow of information. Robert had helped found the Freedom of Information Foundation of Texas in 1978, and Belo had housed the statewide foundation's headquarters in the Belo Building since 1987, contributing substantially to its operations year after year.

In 1996, the company established an endowment at the Dallas Foundation in the amount of $800,000 for the benefit of the FOIFT. The endowment was set up to be distributed at 5 percent annually for as long as the Freedom of Information Foundation of Texas exists. As the endowment grew under the supervision of the Dallas Foundation, the annual grants increased. Belo's contributions to the Freedom of Information Foundation have added up to more than $1 million over time.

Those years of Robert's tenure were a period of intense focus for Belo Corp., of working to develop what Robert called Belo's "core competencies": the highest-quality journalism with a focus on local coverage and local community leadership in all of its markets. He took every opportunity to address the corporate staff on these matters, taking on a sort of evangelical tone reminding the faithful of their historical mission.

From the beginning of his chairmanship in 1987, Robert had preached about maintaining the integrity of Belo's journalism, because that would be the surest path to market dominance. In turn, he intoned, that dominance was the way to achieve the financial results shareholders would expect.

The highest standards of journalism, in Robert's view, mean always maintaining a tone in news reporting and comment that reflects balance and fairness: no shrill headlines, no snide or harsh editorials. Believing that cynicism and sarcasm do not move issues along in a constructive way, Robert repeatedly proclaimed that positivism is not the same thing as boosterism. In a 1988 speech delivered to the Rotary Club of Houston, Robert had laid out that concept:

> For the press, both television and print media, the best organizations lead their communities as well as report and comment on the events of the day. Criticism can be constructive and provide a framework for advancing ideas that lead to specific actions and political solutions. . . . The media can help us find problems before problems become crises. But the media also must help find answers.[6]

He seemed to be demonstrating that leadership when Belo was the first commercial television station group in the country to provide free airtime for congressional and gubernatorial candidates for the 1996 elections. The practice has been maintained at all Belo stations ever since.

The other basic principle of Robert's business plan for all of Belo's operating companies has been local relevance—not just a focus on local news, but on making news of the rest of the world relevant to the local community. The other part of the local efforts is the involvement of the Belo companies' leaders in the lives of their communities. Robert, like all of his predecessors leading Belo over time, has followed that path.

As soon as he returned to Dallas to join the company, Robert got personally involved in Dallas community projects. He immediately joined the efforts to resuscitate the Dallas Symphony Orchestra, including acquiring a site for what would become the Meyerson Symphony Center; to develop U.T. Southwestern Medical Center; and to build on the strengths of his own school, St. Mark's School of Texas, where he served as a trustee from 1977 to 1992.

Robert served as president of both the Symphony Association, at age twenty-eight, and the St. Mark's board, at age thirty-seven. Later he led a successful $24 million capital campaign for Paul Quinn College, the only historically black college in the Dallas area, and at the same time turned his focus to the company's historical interests in long-range city planning and the development of urban parks and green spaces. In connection to that last effort, in the late eighties he founded the first Dallas Parks Foundation with an endowment at the Dallas Foundation.

In 1996, Belo Corp. participated in a citywide festival of Japanese culture called Sun & Star by hosting Japanese artist Yonekichi Tanaka and Dallas artist Tom Orr, both of whom created monumental works of art in steel for the west terrace of the Belo Building. Later, the Belo Foundation acquired Orr's sculpture for permanent public display on the west terrace.

There is a "Belo way" to run a company, with prescribed values and operating principles, which were carefully worked out at a management retreat in 1993. By then competition in the media business had grown tougher than ever, and the management team realized it had to get tougher and make the hard decisions to keep up. In order to be sure that the decisions were based on shared principles and values, the group spent several days putting into contemporary language the values and principles by which Belo had always operated, and which the leaders believed would be just as relevant moving forward.

Here are the words they listed in describing Belo's values: integrity, excellence, fairness, sense of purpose, and inclusiveness. And these are the operating principles: build common understandings; apply our values; be accountable; practice respect and candor; work as a team. Every employee nationwide was given a small card for their wallets with these words printed on it.

However, while the Belo way is distinct, when it comes to each individual market in which Belo has a company, there is no blueprint for how to connect to the community. That connection has to be discerned and practiced by each individual publisher or general manager in the markets where Belo operates a newspaper or television station, and that requires a certain kind of individual that Belo looks for and grooms for the role. By the mid-1990s, Belo had begun to focus on management development in strategic ways, seeking to build several layers of management potential throughout its properties.

It was Belo's reputation for maintaining the highest standards that opened the door to discussions with the Providence Journal Company about joining forces in the rapidly changing media industry in 1996. On September 26, 1996, Belo announced that it had entered into an agreement to acquire Projo, as it was called by insiders, and the acquisition was completed on February 28, 1997. In its annual report for the year 1996, Belo explained:

> With the passage of the Telecommunications Act of 1996, consolidation accelerated as companies were allowed to own more television stations reaching a greater percentage of the nation's households. Against this backdrop, Belo sought to increase significantly its presence in television, while maintaining our strong historical commitment to newspaper publishing.

In that acquisition, Belo became the owner of Rhode Island's dominant newspaper, the *Providence Journal*, the "oldest major daily newspaper of general circulation in continuous publication in the United States," as it describes itself. The *Providence Journal* had won Pulitzer Prizes in 1945, 1953, 1974, and 1994.[7] The acquisition also included nine network-affiliated television stations and one regional cable television network in the Pacific Northwest.

Once again, Belo had been able to achieve several years' worth of strategic growth with one purchase, this one at $1.5 billion, and to double the size of the company overnight. In his letter to shareholders, Robert said, "The Providence Journal Company's operating philosophy mirrors Belo's commitment to journalistic excellence, local news and community service."

The culture in the Providence Journal Company mirrored Belo's in many ways, as well, in that it had been controlled by one family, the Metcalf family, since the nineteenth century, until its own public offering only three months earlier. Its IPO had been undertaken to avoid unwanted takeover, and it was favored by most of the family members. However, some were not so pleased when Belo came along shortly thereafter. The transition required extensive diplomacy on the part of Belo officers and board members, as well as goodwill gestures both with family members and the heavily unionized employees of the *Providence Journal*.

The coming together of the two companies was a complex arrangement, with the Providence Journal Company becoming a subsidiary of

Belo and maintaining its own local board of directors, albeit with a voting-control representative from Belo in the person of Robert Decherd. Four members of the Providence Journal Company's board joined the Belo board of directors: Metcalf family descendant Fanchon M. "Monty" Burnham, a CPA in private practice in Washington, D.C.; Providence civic leader and investor Peter B. Freeman; the president and general manager of WGBH Educational Foundation in Boston, Henry P. Becton; and the chairman, chief executive officer, and publisher of the *Providence Journal*, Steve Hamblett.

Under the terms of the merger agreement, Peter Freeman served on the Belo board for one year before retiring, and Monty Burnham served for two years. Steve Hamblett served until his retirement from the board in 2005, and Henry Becton continues as a member of the Belo board of directors in 2007.

Also as part of the merger agreement between the two companies, Belo contributed $10 million to create an endowment for the existing Providence Journal Foundation. At that endowment level, the Providence Journal Foundation was able to maintain its annual philanthropic activities the same as before the change in ownership, when the parent company had provided funds to the foundation for distribution on an annual basis. Additionally, the Belo Foundation pledged $1 million to the University of Rhode Island to create an endowed chair in oceanography in the name of the Providence Journal Company's much-beloved former chairman, Michael P. Metcalf, who had been killed at age fifty-four in a bicycle accident near his home in 1987.

That gift reflected Robert's sensitivity to the Metcalf family's concerns about selling to an outside company that might not exhibit the same commitments locally. Belo had become the "foreigners" in the new environment, and it appeared to be mindful not to repeat the tactics of Times Mirror when it purchased the *Dallas Times Herald* nearly thirty years earlier.

To ease the transition for the Projo officers and staff members, Robert asked Belo treasurer Brenda Maddox to go to Providence for an extended period of time as Belo's ambassador and liaison during the changeover. He knew that even beyond her talents as a tax accountant and by then treasurer of the company, she also had the people skills necessary to nurture the new relationships, and to solidify lasting bonds.

Brenda rented an apartment near the downtown offices of the Providence Journal Company and the *Providence Journal* plant, and she stayed there for nearly a year, overseeing every detail that emerged as the Providence Journal Company employees were integrated into the Belo system and as the financial and other reporting systems were integrated.

Many other Belo personnel traveled to Providence periodically over those months, but Brenda was the key connection, and she maintains friendships with many of those she got to know in Providence during that critical time.

That acquisition was beneficial to Belo's geographic diversity and to its mix of network affiliates, from the market-leading NBC affiliate in Seattle/Tacoma, Washington, KING-TV, to the company's first FOX-affiliate station in Tucson, Arizona. The only overlap with Belo's other properties was in Seattle, where Belo traded its recently acquired KIRO for KMOV-TV, the CBS affiliate in St. Louis, Missouri, to comply with FCC regulations.

The Providence Journal Company acquisition also included the managing partnership of the Television Food Network in New York City. Later that year, Belo exchanged its interest in TFN for the E. W. Scripps Company's KENS-TV, the CBS affiliate in San Antonio. The distribution of the entities around the country led to the creation of the "cluster" concept—properties managed in groups in various regions of the country.

To make the most of what media industry professionals were beginning to call synergies, Belo also enlarged its bureau in Washington, D.C., in 1997, making room for newspaper reporters to share space with television reporters, including a well-appointed news set that the stations shared. The Capital Bureau was a quick immersion in the new so-called cross-platform journalism that was emerging then, and the traditional tensions between print and broadcast journalists, who are much more accustomed to competing than cooperating, had to be diffused gradually.

Also that year, Belo's flagship television station, WFAA, got a new, young leader when Kathy Clements was appointed vice president and general manager in February, replacing Cathy Creany, who moved into Belo corporate management. Kathy had begun her Belo career as an account executive at WFAA in 1984, and she had served as vice president and general manager of Belo's KXTV in Sacramento before returning to Dallas in 1997. Two years later, in January 1999, Kathy Clements was promoted to president of WFAA at age forty-one.

Another 1997 acquisition added a group of small newspapers in Henderson, Kentucky. The purchase of the *Gleaner*, which was acquired from Walter and Martha Dear and their family, also included seven weekly newspapers, printing operations, and an AM radio station. And in July 1999, Belo acquired the Denton Publishing Co. from Fred and Patsy Patterson and their son, Bill. The purchase included the *Denton Record Chronicle*, the daily newspaper in Denton, which Bill continued to head as publisher under Belo's ownership. It also included the *Lewisville News*, which is published three times a week, and the *Grapevine Sun*, which publishes twice a week.

During the late 1990s all newspapers, large and small, were faced with a shocking drop in advertising, as the World Wide Web made it easier and easier for employment and automotive advertisers, in particular, to go directly to the marketplace online. Belo faced the difficult task of reevaluating all of its newspaper operations, including those in Providence and Riverside, even as it was getting to know the new markets and employee bases.

Each of the newspapers' management teams was faced with reducing the number of full-time employees when advertising revenue dropped off precipitously in 1998 and thereafter. Those tough decisions are never popular, and morale takes a serious whack, when, characteristically, frontline workers blame the corporate management for what they see as wrongheaded thinking.

In newsrooms, in particular, the cry is always that the corporate officers don't care about journalism, that they are ruining the paper or the television news products. Around 1998, as the Belo management committee was facing some of the toughest decisions since going public, Robert stressed the Belo values and operating principles, which had been formulated to express what was distinct about the culture of Belo companies. As with all companies, Belo's distinct nature is inspiring and invigorating for some, while others find it overly formal, too bureaucratic, or stifling.

At specially organized meetings, Robert urged his management teams to use the values and principles as guidelines in their discussions with employees, and to make their decisions based on each employee's acceptance of them, rather than on personal considerations. Of course, those directives sound reasonable at the time, but they often prove difficult to quantify and carry out with precision when decision time rolls around.

Other tough decisions had to be made regarding whole operating companies. Although Belo's smaller newspapers and its smallest television station, KOTV in Tulsa, remained profitable enterprises during that time,

Belo realized that its ownership of the companies in those small markets was not translating to improving its ratings on Wall Street.

Facing a decision either to invest considerable amounts of money over several years to update with the developing digital technologies at those smaller companies, or to sell them, Belo chose to seek buyers who shared their values. As of 2008, the only papers Belo still owns of those smaller acquisitions are those acquired with the Denton Publishing Company, which are a logical extension of Belo's reach in the Dallas/Fort Worth market, where its chief print rival is the *Fort Worth Star-Telegram.* When it sold the Bryan-College Station *Eagle*, the man Belo had placed there as publisher, longtime *Dallas Morning News* editor Donnis Baggett, chose to remain with that paper. On the broadcast side, Belo sold KOTV to David Griffin of Griffin Communications, the highly respected owner of the CBS affiliate in Oklahoma City.

The explosion in companywide personnel that accompanied the aggressive acquisition program during the mid-to-late 1990s created a need for restructuring the corporate management team. In January 1997, Jim Moroney III, who had been serving in a series of high-level positions gaining experience in all aspects of the business operations, was named president of the Television Group, which gave him responsibility for overseeing the daily operations of all Belo television stations.

Jack Sander, a twenty-five-year broadcast veteran, whom Jim and Ward had gotten to know through industry organizations, was recruited to work with Jim as executive vice president of the greatly enlarged Television Group. Jack came to Belo directly from Atlanta television station WAGA-TV; however, he had extensive experience in television management with several other companies, including serving as president of the Television Division of Taft Broadcasting, with responsibility for twelve stations.

In addition to his depth of talent and experience, Jack Sander's boundless energy, enthusiasm, and positive approach to life were a great match for the spirit that Robert and Jim sought to maintain in the Belo management team. Jack had a gift for bringing people together, which was needed in Belo as the distinction between broadcast and print media continued, while the company's two divisions remained separated by ongoing rivalries.

The Broadcast Division rejoiced that year when WFAA-TV was awarded another DuPont-Columbia Silver Baton, and Belo's recently acquired KREM-TV in Spokane, Washington, won its first DuPont-Columbia Award. Belo's prominence in the broadcasting industry by then, along with Robert's reputation for integrity and commitment to local communities, led to his appointment by President Bill Clinton to the Advisory Committee on Public Interest Obligation of Digital Television Broadcasters in October 1997.

The Advisory Committee, which came to be called the Gore Commission, was asked to define appropriate public interest obligations of television broadcasters as the industry moved into the digital era. The twenty-two-member group included public interest advocates, broadcasters, academicians, and technology experts. It met regularly for nearly a year before presenting its final recommendations to the White House.

In the January 26, 1998, issue of *Forbes*, reporters Robert Lenzner and Carrie Shook published a profile of Robert titled "Texas Darwinist," in which they examined Robert's and Belo's strengths. "Decherd and his crew don't just acquire. They add value, with heavy emphasis on news coverage of their communities."

The writers commented that "Decherd is concerned about the impact of the Internet on traditional newspapers and local television. But he feels strongly that cybernews will never be able to replicate local news coverage." And in addition to his commitment to local audiences, the writers noted, "The second item on Decherd's agenda: to equip his stations to transmit high-definition TV."

In fact, on February 27, 1998, one month after the article ran, WFAA became the first VHF station in the country to transmit a digital signal on a permanent basis, further demonstrating Darwin's theory that survival requires adaptation—constant, ongoing adaptation.

In June 1998, Jim Moroney was promoted to executive vice president of Belo, with responsibility for finance, treasury, and investor relations. He replaced Mike Perry, who resigned after nearly twenty years with the *News* and Belo. Mike's abrupt resignation seemed somehow connected to Belo's not making its predicted revenue for the first quarter. However, the issues were much deeper and longer in coming.

Mike was a gifted financial strategist, and he had been key to the modernizing of accounting systems companywide. However, he had followed in the pattern of his former boss, Jim Sheehan, with an absolutist attitude toward performance. While he was always gracious to his superiors in the company, he had an impulsive temper and no patience with those working under him. Mike's entire tenure with the company had been marked by a revolving door in the finance and accounting areas, and he was often out of step with his management colleagues. Robert's inherent compassion and his loyalty to longtime employees were ultimately tested to their limits, and he asked Mike to resign.

At the same time, Dunia A. Shive was promoted from senior vice president of corporate operations to senior vice president and chief financial officer. She had joined Belo in 1993 and worked under Mike, beginning as corporate controller. Dunia grew up in Killeen, Texas, near Austin, the child of immigrant parents—her father from Syria and her mother from Lebanon.

Dunia graduated from Texas Tech University with a BBA in accounting and went to work at Arthur Young in 1982. While she served as an outside auditor for Arthur Young, Belo was one of her clients for several years, and she got to know the company and its key players as they got to know her. In 1989, she was named assistant controller for Tyler Corporation, another publicly held company with its headquarters in Dallas, where she stayed until coming to Belo.

At Belo, Dunia soon gained the respect and admiration of her colleagues for her intelligence and genial manner. Those personal qualities, along with her business acumen, enabled her to fit well in the Belo culture. She progressed rapidly, being promoted in 1995 to vice president and controller, and a year later to vice president for finance. In 1997 she was named senior vice president of corporate operations, and a year later CFO. Her rapid advancement was accompanied by a busy family life as well, as she and her husband grew their family to three children.

Another executive change in the fall of 1998 took place at the *News*, when Jeremy Halbreich resigned as president after twenty-four years at the company. He soon established his own newspaper holding company, acquiring a group of small and midsize papers. His departure created waves because he was an immensely popular and well-respected leader at the *News*, and in the community at large as a representative of the company.

Jeremy explained his decision to friends at the time by saying that he had faced the reality that his future at the paper was limited, considering that the *News*'s publisher and editor, Burl Osborne, was more likely to favor someone from the news side to succeed him as publisher, rather than someone from the business side of the paper. Jeremy's entire work life had been focused on the business side of newspaper operations, beginning at the *Crimson* at Harvard, and throughout his career at the *News*. As a career newspaper professional, he felt stymied by the prospect that he would not have the chance to rise to the top post at the *News*.

As he had imagined, Jeremy was replaced as president and general manager by a newsroom professional. Bob Mong had recently served as publisher of Belo's Owensboro newspaper, after moving up through the ranks in the news department of the *News* over many years. A graduate of Haverford College, a Quaker institution in Pennsylvania, Bob joined the *News* in 1979 as night assignments editor on the city desk.

His talents and tenacity enabled him to rise quickly, and when he was offered the opportunity to be publisher in Kentucky, he was managing editor of the *News*. Bob was well liked throughout the ranks in the newsroom and respected for his understanding of what makes a newspaper work. Life at the *News* settled down fairly soon with a journalist in the president's office.

The promotion of a newsman to the presidency seemed both to confirm Jeremy's concerns for his own mobility at the *News*, and at the same time reassure others of the sincerity of Belo's insistence on high-quality journalism as the key to business success.

Following the pattern of its successful operations of Northwest Cable News in the Pacific Northwest, Belo launched Texas Cable News (TXCN) on January 1, 1999, in the remodeled newsprint warehouse behind the Dallas Morning News Building. Donald F. (Skip) Cass, Jr., was named vice president and general manager of TXCN in 1998 and launched the station a few months later. Skip had come to Belo in 1996 as manager of finance and administration of the Broadcast Division by way of WWL in New Orleans, where he had worked as a sales account executive while he attended Loyola University School of Law.

When plans for the twenty-four-hour regional cable news operation got underway, it soon became apparent that the best site for it would be on the existing Belo campus in downtown Dallas. The three-story shell of a building had been empty and used only for storage since the printing was moved to Plano years before. Skip was made director of Belo's Cable News Operations and was a key participant in the planning of TXCN, including serving as project manager for design and construction of the converted facility.

Retrofitting the old newsprint warehouse took longer than the time allotted for it, however, and to meet its licensing obligation, TXCN had to go live while work crews were still busy throughout the building. In fact, construction helmets were issued to all of the news editors and sales personnel who had to be in the spaces while work was still underway. But enthusiasm for working in the country's first all-digital television facility was sufficient to make it seem more like play than work for the young workforce that was assembled for the new operation.

In June 1999, to extend its Texas reach even more, Belo traded its station in Sacramento for the Austin ABC affiliate, KVUE-TV. With that addition, TXCN could draw on Belo-generated news and feature stories from the state's most important population centers: the Dallas/Fort Worth region from WFAA; Houston and the upper Texas coastal region from KHOU; San Antonio and south and southwest Texas from KENS; and Austin and central Texas from KVUE. It was a brilliant plan, and the hub of the activities was a futuristic newsroom with remote-controlled cameras, not to mention some of the country's most talented young people clamoring to get jobs there.

Another forward-looking business was formed in 1999, when Belo Online Inc. was created to pursue the development of the online initiatives across the company. An earlier experiment with interactive media had bombed, when Burl and Robert backed a partnership to issue all newspaper subscribers a "Cue Cat" that was to be used to scan printed bar codes to link users to advertisers online. It was an instant failure, and Burl and Robert were vilified by their own employees and industrywide.

As an antidote to that embarrassment, Robert created the new online initiative, and he asked Jim Moroney to head it up. The new initiative was soon renamed Belo Interactive, and everyone at once referred to it by its initials, BI. At a gathering of the corporate staff to announce the launch of BI, Jim joked that he wasn't sure what to make of being named president of a company that had no assets and no employees, but he was willing to give it a go. His humility and humor masked his innate eagerness for Belo to move into the electronic news business.

The Internet and its possibilities had become a constant topic of discussion among management, and Jim was thrilled to be given the time, money, and talent that would be required to start BI and explore the new media.

Jim retained the title of executive vice president of Belo and his responsibility for mergers and acquisitions while he launched the new operation. Soon the fledgling company was upgrading and managing the

Web sites of all of the Belo companies, as well as developing online products to generate new sources of revenue for the company, as Belo faced declining revenues from the print side of the business.

Dunia Shive, as senior vice president and CFO, took over the treasury and investor relations functions so that Jim could divert more of his prodigious energy to BI.

Lester Levy retired from the Belo board of directors after thirteen years in 1998, and in 1999 Tom Walker also retired, after seventeen years. Joining the board in 1999 was Laurence E. Hirsch, the chairman and CEO of Centex Corporation, who had remained active as an advisor to the Wharton School at the University of Pennsylvania and the Villanova University of Law, the schools where he had done his undergraduate and law studies. He was the perfect replacement for Tom Walker, with his extensive knowledge of economics and investment strategies.

In November 1999, the company acquired two more Arizona television stations, KTVK and KASW-TV in Phoenix, and it sold two of the stations it had acquired with the Providence Journal Company, KHNL-TV in Honolulu, Hawaii, and KASA-TV in Albuquerque/Santa Fe, New Mexico. In early March, Belo also acquired two stations it had been operating under local marketing agreements in Seattle/Tacoma and Phoenix.

By the end of 1999, Belo's television properties reached 67 percent of all television households in Texas, and by the end of 2000, 13.7 percent of all television households in the United States.

However, at its flagship television station in Dallas, Belo faced one of the most public rows in the station's history. The recently appointed station manager, Kathy Clements, had entered routine contract discussions with longtime WFAA news anchor Tracy Rowlett, and their negotiations had not gone well.

After a long series of face-offs, Tracy left the station for the number three station in the market, where he wouldn't even be allowed on the air for a year, because of the industry-standard non-compete clause in his contract. Each one felt the other had derailed the relationship, and the other local media outlets jumped at the opportunity to present Belo in a negative light.

Soon after Tracy agreed to join the rival station, which was a CBS network affiliate, and which had lured him by offering him even more than he had demanded of WFAA, CBS announced that it was buying the local station from its owner, Gaylord Communications Group. Losing Tracy was painful for Belo and WFAA in many ways, and his switch affected local ratings for several years.

Another controversial decision that year had the newsrooms at both the *News* and WFAA wondering where Belo was heading next. Following the path already taken by some large media companies, in October 1999, Belo purchased a 12.38-percent interest in the Dallas Mavericks basketball team and a 6.19-percent stake in the new American Airlines Center, the Mavericks' home venue. However, the relationship was never an easy one, and in January 2002 Belo sold both interests to "entities controlled by Mark Cuban" at a small profit.

On the publishing side, in November 1999, the Columbia Journalism Review ranked the *Dallas Morning News* as number five on its list of America's Best Newspapers. The *New York Times* was ranked number one, followed by the *Washington Post*, the *Wall Street Journal*, and the *Los Angeles Times*.

Internally at Belo, Robert was building a new, younger corporate leadership team, drawing on the depth of talent at the many Belo operating companies. The announcements came throughout the year, rather than all at once at year-end, as tradition had dictated, and the excitement of change kept the place humming.

The coming of the new century, or at least the change to numbers starting with 20- rather than with 19-, had raised alarms all over the world among those who understood how computers work. At the time, whole companies were formed to deal with computer problems expected to occur at Y2K, the moment clocks turned from 1999 to the year 2000. Millions of dollars were spent by companies to back up systems, reprogram their computers, and hire staff to handle all of the tasks associated with the anticipated problems.

Media companies had the added pressure of ensuring that no edition of the newspaper was affected and that no downtime occurred on the air at the television stations. At Belo, as at every other company with large computer systems, large crews were scheduled to be on hand all night on New Year's Eve, just in case there was a meltdown of some sort that had to be handled on an emergency basis.

Luckily, there are television sets all over the place in Belo companies, and the crews were entertained with the broadcasts of celebrations all around the world as Y2K emerged at 12:00:01 on 01/01/2000, and nothing happened to the computers.

Belo's net operating revenues and its earnings from operations increased significantly from 1998 to 1999 and from 1999 to 2000, as did the operating cash flow and dividends paid per share. However, the stock price did not keep pace with those increases after its peak in late 1997. All media stocks seemed affected by the uncertainties of the electronic media world.

Even so, Robert remained optimistic, and in his letter to shareholders in the 2000 annual report, he opened with the news that Belo's ten largest operating companies had achieved all-time records in revenue and cash flow. Focusing on the strengths of the Belo companies was his way of urging shareholders to keep the faith, even with growing concerns about media ownership.

He then made reference to the changing media environment, saying, "Belo's business is increasingly an integrated advertising medium that will benefit in any economic circumstance relative to its competitors." And he repeated his career-long conviction that Belo must stay the course in its practice of the highest possible journalistic standards, as well as its commitment to local communities and their readers and viewers. He seemed to be saying that if anyone could succeed in the changing environment, Belo could.

He then addressed another issue that had been more and more obvious with the emergence of electronic media. The generation of senior executives who had managed the turnaround at the *Dallas Morning News* and the Golden Age of broadcast television, and who had willingly embraced change in their separate divisions, had not necessarily been able to accept the rapid overlapping of their two distinct platforms.

For Burl Osborne and Ward Huey, their two divisions were immediate competitors with each other for Belo corporate support. According to many observers, their intransigent partisan views of what was best for Belo created an ethos of uncooperativeness, even disunity, at the highest levels of the company.

In Robert's letter to shareholders, he wrote of "natural changes in leadership," noting that both Jimmy Moroney and Ward Huey had retired from the Belo board of directors at the end of 2000.

Jimmy had relinquished his active management role years before, and his retirement from the board at age seventy-nine was no surprise to anyone. However, Ward's retirement seemed abrupt, as he left both Belo Corp. and, under board policy, the Belo board as well.

He explained his decision to retire at age sixty-two, after a forty-year career at Belo, as difficult but necessary for him. He said that he fully recognized that it was time to hand off some of his executive duties to the next generation of managers in order to prepare them for taking over upon his retirement in a few years. However, he said that facing the prospect of relinquishing some of his authority made him realize that he couldn't operate other than in a full-bore manner.

By then, Ward had been named to the Broadcasting & Cable Hall of Fame, and he had served on the boards of all the important national broadcasting industry organizations. Closer to home, he had been named outstanding alumnus of SMU in 1999, and he was elected to the SMU board of trustees. Rather than moving to the sidelines at Belo, however, he chose to retire immediately. He soon withdrew completely from the company and declined invitations to events to which retired directors were invited.

Burl Osborne, Ward's counterpart on the newspaper side, had chosen differently when faced with the same dilemma at the time. His enthusiasm for the emerging new media was as great as his passion for the more traditional forms. He had taken an active role during the late nineties in the development of new media initiatives at Belo, and as Ward retired, Burl moved into a somewhat different role in the corporate structure, while remaining in the middle of the changing world.

Burl retired as publisher and editor, effective on January 1, 2001, and became publisher emeritus; but he remained on Belo's management committee, and since he was not retiring from Belo, he remained a director. By the time Burl retired from the Belo board at the May 2002 meeting, at age sixty-four, he had been elected chairman of the Associated Press. However, he maintained a fully supported executive suite in the Belo Building, and as part of his agreement to retire before the mandatory age, he negotiated a very generous retirement package, as had Ward Huey.

Burl's staged transition enabled a couple of other significant changes to take place at the *News*. The most significant, even surprising, development was the return of a family member to the publisher's role at the *News*.

Jim Moroney III was named publisher and CEO when Burl relinquished his *News* titles. Jim had spent most of his twenty-three-year career on the television side, then taking on corporate jobs when Robert requested it. And always he had prospered. By 2001, Jim and his wife, Barbara, had a lively family life with five children: Sean Wesley, fifteen; Meagan Lindsay, fourteen; Kyle McQueen, eight; and twins Jennifer Joan and Catherine Lynn, six.

Jim accepted the new challenge with his usual good humor and enthusiasm, and he began a campaign to win over the skeptics within the newspaper ranks, of whom he knew there were many. He immediately created his 60 X 60 X 60 plan, in which he interviewed sixty *News* employees, from all departments and ranks, for sixty minutes each, over his first sixty days on the job. During those interviews, he not only met people he might never have met, he also learned what workers were thinking, and what the employees considered the greatest strengths and challenges the newspaper faced.

He also took on the external challenge facing all newspaper publishers at the time—to reinvent and reorganize the newspaper business model in keeping with the accelerating changes in new media, a process that continues industrywide years later.

The other significant change at the *News* was for Bob Mong to be named editor, in addition to serving as president. Bob had been preparing for that role throughout his entire career, and he had worked closely with Burl since 1980. Coming up through the ranks in the news department, he was a logical and popular successor to head the news side.

The new century opened with Robert Decherd continuing in his role as chairman, president, and chief executive officer, titles which he had held for fourteen years. He was not yet fifty years old. Backing him up was a strong, young team of executives he had brought into the corporate ranks over several years and positioned to help build on Belo's historical strengths.

In July 2000, Guy Kerr, who had represented Belo since 1983 as a member of the firm Locke, Purnell, Boren, Laney & Neely, was hired as senior vice president, general counsel, and secretary. He was hired to succeed Mike McCarthy, who was promoted to senior executive vice president in order to focus his efforts on the changing media technologies and how they affected FCC rulings—and the other way around.

Guy's low-key humor and warm nature were already well known at Belo, and he joined a team whose members already had held several management positions different from those for which they had been hired. Such cross-training was a development tactic that Robert had used strategically throughout his chairmanship, to good advantage. In some cases, it helped cull the ranks of those whose ambitions or talents were too narrow for the challenge. And when it was successful, it supported his efforts to build a team whose members have both broad and deep knowledge of the business, and who can support each other more effectively.

Chapter 10

NEW CENTURY, NEW MEDIA

In February 2001, Robert was the keynote speaker at *Editor & Publisher* magazine's Annual Interactive Newspapers Conference and Trade Show held that year in Dallas. The so-called Internet bubble had burst by then, and many companies formed to do business online were out of business or pulling back and reevaluating such ventures. It had become clear to everyone that the old patterns of generating revenue were not working for most of those startups.

Meanwhile, newspapers had begun to notice that consumers were turning more and more to the Internet for their news and information, and particularly for advertising, but no one had a formula for generating the revenue needed to sustain their online presence in the long run.

Robert told his audience of newspaper publishers and editors, "This is not a time for retrenchment. This is a time for well-managed entrepreneurism, for calculated risk-taking. It's clearly the time to stay the course and find the path to profitability that consumers are telling us is there."[1]

He cited some of the efforts ongoing at Belo at the time, then he reiterated his philosophy: "Our companies have one defensible position, one sustainable advantage: the breadth and depth of local news and information our newspaper franchises provide to our site customers every day." He punctuated that by saying that high journalistic standards continue to be crucial in the new broadband world, and that online consumers were not only growing in number, but also in what they expected from their newspapers online.

Other significant changes occurred that year as Robert continued his quest to have one of the best corporate boards in America, recruiting Louis E. Caldera and Lloyd D. Ward. Louis Caldera was Secretary of the Army in the Clinton Administration, and shortly before joining the Belo board in July 2001, he was named the vice chancellor for university advancement of the California State University System. Lloyd Ward had been chairman and chief executive officer of Maytag Corporation until a few months before election to the Belo board in July 2001, and he soon was named chief executive officer and secretary general of the United States Olympic Committee. Hugh Robinson retired in 2001 after twelve years as a Belo director.

Burl Osborne retired from the board in 2002 after sixteen years, as planned, but Robert was equally affected by the early retirement of Mike McCarthy, on October 1, 2002. Mike had been Robert's closest and most trusted ally among the executive team since joining Belo in 1985.

By the time of his retirement, Mike had become one of the country's experts on the digital television transition, and he had decided to return to the full-time practice of media law in Washington, D.C., where he and his wife, Monica, had enjoyed life for several years before moving to Dallas. By then, Guy Kerr had already been promoted to be Belo's senior vice president, general counsel, and secretary, and although Mike's departure left a void, corporate management continued without pause.

John Bassett retired from the board in 2003, after twenty-four years, and in May, two more directors were elected. France Córdova served as chief scientist of the National Aeronautics and Space Administration (NASA) before becoming vice chancellor for research and a professor of physics at the University of California, Santa Barbara, in 1996. She was named chancellor of the University of California, Riverside, in July 2002. Wayne Sanders was elected to the Belo board shortly after retiring at age fifty-five from Kimberly-Clark Corporation as chairman and chief executive officer, capping off a twenty-eight-year career with that company. The board had completed its generational change, and even more importantly it had completed the shift from mainly company representatives to only one employee serving as a director, the chairman. A broad spectrum of business, academic, and administrative expertise was represented by the new board, demonstrating Robert's goal to have the Belo board represent the best of America.

Also in 2003, following and sometimes even setting industry trends, the *News* launched a Spanish-language daily in North Texas called *Al Dia*; a free weekday paper called *Quick*, targeting the young adult reader; and the first editorial blog in the United States.

In October 2004, M. Anne Szostak was elected to the board, bringing the total number of directors back to thirteen. Until just before her election, Anne was executive vice president of FleetBoston Financial, before which she had been chairman and chief executive officer of Fleet Bank–Rhode Island. Shortly before joining the Belo board, Anne had established her own consultancy business.

In the first half of 2004, Belo Corp. logged a series of record high share prices, after twenty-three years of public trading and twenty-one years on the New York Stock Exchange. After a little more than three years as publisher of the *Dallas Morning News*, Jim Moroney was named Publisher of the Year 2004 by *Editor & Publisher*, the nation's most respected trade journal for newspapers. The April issue of the magazine published a feature story by Mark Fitzgerald about Jim's "effort to change the very culture of the newspaper," which the writer commented had "paid off with several remarkable achievements in 2003."

But in the third quarter of 2004, the flagship of Belo companies, the venerable *Dallas Morning News*, announced that it had discovered its circulation figures had been overstated for some period of time. The discrepancies were uncovered in-house, after announcements of similar problems at two other papers, in New York and Chicago, caused the senior executives to question circulation managers about practices at the *News*.

In particular, Jim Moroney and Robert Decherd questioned why the circulation figures at the *News* weren't diminishing, as they were at most all other major newspapers around the country. Jim instructed Barry Peckham, the executive vice president who supervised the circulation department, to dig deep and find how the numbers were supported, or if anyone was aware of discrepancies.

Immediately the numbers of newspapers bought by the outside contractors for resale dropped precipitously. An internal review was launched, the fraudulent practices were halted, and the problems were made public. Along with the initial announcement, executives of Belo and the *News* made public apologies and announced that a thorough investigation was underway to determine the full extent of the problems.

Jim Moroney stepped to the forefront and accepted responsibility for the overstatements because they had occurred, at least partly, on his watch. The company immediately implemented an advertiser compensation plan, and embarked on one of the most ambitious overhauls of a circulation system ever in the newspaper industry, doing away largely with the outside contractor system, which had been the way most newspapers traditionally operated.

Jim had started his term as publisher by announcing a "revolution" at the *News*, which he believed was crucial for the paper's long-term viability. He had called for everyone to look at things with new eyes, to participate in transforming the paper from the traditions of the pre-Internet age to a new and very different product to meet the challenges posed by competition from all directions.

As pressures on circulation numbers industrywide continued to mount, some of those in charge of meeting circulation goals at the *News* had put in place incentive and compensation programs that led to cheating on the numbers reports that contractors made to *News* management.

Robert, Jim, and the other senior executives made straightforward apologies to employees, readers, advertisers, and the company's stockholders. Robert expressed his "profound personal and professional disappointment" to everyone in several documents and conference calls. In an e-mail to the internal audience of his "Belo Colleagues," Robert used the word "embarrassing," and on at least one occasion he used the word "humiliating" to describe his own reaction.

In making those statements, Robert made reference to the company's historical values, saying, "The Belo values are real. They are our beacon. They apply to all areas of our company, and we won't tolerate questionable practices of any kind." He went on to invite all employees to report "any situation . . . that permits or encourages problematic behavior." He instructed management to redistribute Belo's Code of Business Conduct and Ethics, which had long been part of the employee handbook.

The *News* soon began sending out compensation checks and linage credits to its advertisers in recognition of the circulation overstatement. Within twelve days after the announcement, 19,000 checks had been mailed or hand-delivered, representing $23 million in cash payments to advertisers, and another $4 million was set aside to publish free ads.

The *News* was not the last newspaper to uncover and report circulation irregularities around that time of slowing circulation growth nationwide. Overzealous circulation practices had ratcheted up as the downward trend in sales accelerated. At the *News*, by the end of 2004, all those who had held direct managerial oversight of circulation during the period of the overstatement at the *News* were either reassigned or were no longer employed by the company.

The reporting structure at the top of the newspaper hierarchy was reorganized to have all senior executives report directly to the publisher and CEO, and the title "president" disappeared from the masthead. Barry Peckham resigned. The pall of disappointment, even disillusionment, was widespread and voiced openly for a while. However, circulation irregularities were not the only cause of morale problems in 2004.

Everyone had to face the stark realities of the ever-changing media environment. The loss of newspaper subscribers to electronic news outlets, as well as the ease with which advertisers could create their own Web sites, had led to further loss of ad revenues. On the other hand, both the *Providence Journal* and the Riverside, California, *Press-Enterprise* were "among the fastest growing [newspapers] in the nation," according to media analyst Edward Atorino, who was quoted in a feature on Belo in the *Dallas Business Journal* that November. On the television side, declines in viewers of the traditional networks, with which most of the Belo stations are affiliated, had put pressure on ad revenues there as well. Those economic hits made a dent in the overall profitability of the company, and the stock price reflected it.

Like many media companies in 2004, and based on a study conducted even before the circulation problems were discovered, Belo announced a reduction in force, along with a reevaluation of its operations at Texas Cable News and Belo Interactive, two operating entities that had been created in 1999 at the height of optimism about the possibilities of new media.

At TXCN, the staff was reduced significantly, and the offerings shifted to more news programming created at the individual Belo stations in Texas. The live programming was reduced to weather reports. Those changes maintained TXCN's unique role in statewide reporting in Texas, while acknowledging that the business model was not as promising as it had appeared in 1999. Belo also exited partnerships it had created with Time Warner Cable, freeing up considerable capital to focus on other aspects of the business.

Belo Interactive was reorganized to better accommodate the huge changes that had taken place during the ensuing five years. When the 2004 staff cuts were made, the belt-tightening was felt companywide, including in the corporate staff. However, the majority of cuts were made at the *News*, which had already had one such reduction as a result of the substantial loss of advertisers following the terrorist attacks in New York on September 11, 2001, when the general economy retreated.

Subsequently, almost every large newspaper in America has reduced its employee count, and industry analysts predict that the downsizing and reorganization are not over for newspapers, as they continue to reposition themselves in the electronic world. As fewer employees are needed in the traditional print operations, newsrooms all over the nation are battling serious morale problems.

It's difficult for anyone to accept that adapting the company to a changing world is more important than one's own personal well-being. No matter how carefully the transition is framed, it is much easier, and more common, for journalists to proclaim that their publishers are no longer interested in the integrity of the news product.

Following the elimination of numerous positions in 2004, particularly at the *News*, where a number of prominent bylines disappeared, Charles Layton commented in the April/May 2005 issue of *American Journalism Review*, "Few people expect the *Morning News* to slide into mediocrity as some big metro papers have."[2] But the challenge grew even greater in September 2006, when another 111 news department staff members accepted generous buyout offers.

All of the more than 550 employees in the newsroom were given the opportunity to take the buyout. The announcement stated that the *News* aimed to eliminate eighty-five positions, and that the buyout offer was the first step toward that goal. When more than eighty-five reporters, editors, and other newsroom staffers accepted the buyout offer, the company decided to accommodate the greater number, even though it cost more to do that than to cut it off at the target number.

The objective obviously was not to save money, but rather to be able to spend it differently in the long run—to adapt to the new environment with growth in other areas. In fact, even after the buyouts, the newsroom of the *Dallas Morning News* remained one of the largest in the country, with about 450 professional staff members.

In adapting to the new world, newspapers in general have shifted to a focus on "readership" as the measure of their penetration into any particular market. In fact, the Audit Bureau changed its rules regarding reporting for the same reason. Readership shows how many people *read* the newspaper's content, whether it's hard copy or online, whereas circulation shows the number of copies sold. Readership has long been one of many ways newspapers measured their effectiveness. As Internet traffic increased, publishers adapted and improved methods to count readers, and those who were part of larger media companies began integrating their news operations across all means of dispensing news and information.

Belo Interactive was transformed into Belo Interactive Media (or BIM) to emphasize its important new function, providing a company-wide "architecture" for product development and continuity across all Belo Web sites. Its interactive media content and sales organizations were integrated back into Belo's individual companies across the nation. During less than two years' time, beginning in early 2005, the company spent more than $100 million improving all of those Web sites.

The immediate and growing success of Belo's interactive businesses has continued, in keeping with the predictions of management. Belo's 2005 interactive media advertising revenues grew to $43 million, a sixfold increase since 2000, and they had grown almost 40 percent from 2004 to 2005. During 2006 the company saw an increase in net operating revenue and net earnings, but the pressures on financial performance were relentless.

While everyone seems to agree that the current technological changes and their accompanying societal shifts are far more sweeping and faster in coming than those of the past, not everyone agrees about how to accommodate the changes while maintaining the company's historic strength: quality journalism. However, adaptations to new environments are another of Belo's historically strong qualities.

Its efforts were acknowledged in the November 2006 issue of *SmartMoney*, when Belo was one of five companies recognized for having "strong franchises and smart strategies for growth in the new-media age." The other companies were Comcast, News Corp., Viacom, and the Washington Post Company.

As Belo spread out by acquiring properties across the country since going public on December 9, 1981, the strategy has continued to be to keep a low profile as owners. That approach has been explained internally as an effort to maintain and build upon the loyalty of readers and viewers who already trusted their local news source, such as the 175-year-old *Providence Journal* in Rhode Island, for example, the fifty-seven-year-old KING-TV in Seattle/Tacoma, or the forty-nine-year-old WWL-TV in New Orleans.

The spotlight has been placed instead on the original founders and local histories of individual properties, such as on the Metcalf family in Rhode Island and on Dorothy Bullitt, whose King Broadcasting Co. in the Pacific Northwest had been acquired by the Providence Journal Company. The strategy has sometimes included reinstatement of the property's local history, such as bringing back the founder's portrait to the lobby, as was done with Dorothy Bullitt in Seattle.

While maintaining a low profile may seem counterintuitive as a national corporate marketing strategy, indeed, the underlying basis might be traced to the courtly manners and modest deference found in traditions of the Old South, which were part of the company's origins. However, the benefits of keeping a low profile as owner have been apparent, both in warmer relationships with the employee base at individual properties, and with local advertisers, viewers, and readers.

Belo continued to reinvent itself during 2006, just as it has many times since its beginning in Galveston in 1842. Still, the stock price did not keep pace, reflecting trends across the entire media industry.

During his long career, G. B. Dealey was invited to address the journalism students at the University of Missouri on four different occasions, the first of which was in 1915. In that speech he got everyone's attention by beginning with "Revenue is more necessary and important than policy to a newspaper . . . ." But he quickly added: "for without the practical foundation of financial success there can be no superstructure of general welfare. . . . For a newspaper, to be permanently successful, must live a life of rectitude and must approximate the high ideals, intellectual and moral, set for it by the thinking minds of the public."[3]

Speaking to a reporter for the *Riverside Press-Enterprise* at the time of the acquisition in 1998, Robert had said, "You cannot achieve journalistic excellence and have the kind of influence in communities we feel is so important if you manage companies like ours simply as financial entities."

While that statement confirmed his conviction that the principles of sound, ethical journalism will remain the same in spite of fluctuations in the stock price, he—like his great-grandfather G. B. Dealey—knows that a media company has to stay in business in order to hew to its principles and serve its communities.

In conversations with the management committee in the summer of 2005, as the company's leaders debated why the stock price remained low in spite of the company's strong performance, Robert urged them to maintain a balance between Belo's values and the tenacity with which they pursued financial goals.

According to members of his team, he teased them, saying, "Someday you will all come to see me sitting in my rocking chair and ask, 'Say, Robert, do you still own all of those shares of Belo?' And I'll say, 'I sure do.'" That is the quiet confidence that Robert Decherd has always displayed to those around him. It is a confidence based on First Amendment principles, as well as on financial and management beliefs.

In early 2006, Belo promoted several individuals in its upper ranks, following a succession plan that had been in the works for several years. At the time, Robert maintained the three top titles of chairman, chief executive officer, and president of Belo Corp., and promoted Dunia Shive, forty-five, to be his next in line as president of media operations. That title had most recently been held by Jack Sander, sixty-four, who was promoted to vice chairman, where he continued to provide guidance and oversight of operations until his full retirement at the end of 2006.

Soon after the announcement of Jack's change in the lineup, he was named the 2006 Broadcaster of the Year by *Broadcasting & Cable* magazine, the television industry's highest honor. And by the time of his retirement he had worked across the company to lay the groundwork for the next transition.

The other key promotions announced in January 2006 were also of younger individuals, following behind the top tier of executives, who themselves are relatively young. All of those who were promoted were longtime Belo employees who have served in various capacities in Belo or in the operating companies.

They included Dennis A. Williamson, fifty-eight, who came into Belo as head of one of the Providence Journal Company's television stations in 1997 and moved to the corporate offices as senior vice president of the Television Group in 2000. Dennis was named executive vice president in addition to chief financial officer, a post he had held since 2004.

The bywords in G. B. Dealey's day and now seem to be "change" for the medium, in order to remain a profitable company, and "same" for the message, which must meet the highest journalistic standards and expectations of public service.

In a 2006 column in the business section of the *New York Times*, columnist Joe Nocera made some passing comments about newspaper publishing. He started off saying, "The sale of the *Philadelphia Inquirer* and the *Philadelphia Daily News* to a consortium of local businessmen has me wondering whether the newspaper industry has stumbled on a new business model—or at least a new ownership model."

Nocera goes on to extol the virtues of making local news coverage a priority, in the way that professional sports franchises focus on their local audiences and their own communities. "Sure, the owners want to make money, but they also have other priorities, so 'maximizing profits' is not the only goal." He says that "Local owners [of newspapers] have sacred cows, but they are also far more likely to have real passion for the city the newspaper is charged with covering."[4]

While that might be an innovative approach for much of today's media, it is familiar ground to anyone who ever attended annual meetings of Belo shareholders. After all these years, Belo shareholders could well ask, "What's new about building business on local coverage?"

EPILOGUE

Soon after Jack Sander retired, in the early days of 2007, a retired Belo executive and former company director commented that he was concerned that Robert had not built the depth of leadership that would be needed over time. Looking through the lens of his own era had blinded him to the obvious lineup of young women and men who had slowly moved into positions of more and broader responsibility at Belo. When he was reminded that all of the members of the important management committee, including two women, are fairly young and broadly experienced, and that one of the women was already Robert's second in command, he responded, "A woman will never be president of Belo. It won't happen."

A few days later, Dunia Shive was named president and chief operating officer of Belo Corp. Another promotion announced at the same time moved Skip Cass to a newly created executive vice president role to head up Belo's Internet and business development activities. Both promotions were of people who had been invisible to the retired executive, and probably to others not paying close attention.

Robert had relinquished the title of Belo president once before, when Jim Sheehan had been made president and put in charge of operations. But when that appointment was not successful, Robert took back the title.

Dunia's promotion to president of Belo represented a milestone change at the highest levels of company management. Not only is she the first woman ever to head the company, but she represents a new generation, signaling that Robert is ready to share the load as the new, young team handles the increased pressures of the new media realities. Dunia has the intelligence and the courage required, and she has been at Belo for fourteen years.

She progressed rapidly through the ranks, eventually spending time in virtually all aspects of the company's business. She has a BBA from Texas Tech University and along the way has completed executive courses in strategic marketing management at Harvard Business School and in organizational renewal at Stanford's Graduate School of Business. Over several years she spent time with all the company heads across Belo, getting to know their unique operations and working to coordinate similar efforts company-wide.

In early 2007, a new industry partnership was announced that brings together the massive content resources of 264 newspapers spread across forty-four states to partner with the extensive reach of Yahoo! Inc. According to the publicity, the goal is to combine "the newspapers' unmatched local news and advertising reach with the leading technologies and audience of Yahoo!, the leading global Internet brand and one of the most trafficked Internet destinations worldwide."[1]

In addition to opening up new audiences to local news content, the partners will jointly develop methods to sell advertising online, sharing in the revenues as the business develops. The so-called newspaper consortium was the culmination of the efforts of many newspaper and new media executives across the country, with Dunia Shive leading the way. In a news story announcing the partnership, Robert Decherd was quoted as saying, "It's the way we are going to extend great journalism into an Internet environment."[2]

During the summer of 2007, Dr. France Córdova, Belo director since 2003, resigned from the board in connection with being named president of Purdue University. She explained that her new position would not allow her the time necessary to be an effective director of Belo.

The vacancy created by her resignation from the board was filled immediately by the election of Douglas G. Carlston. Doug Carlston has been a member of the board of Public Radio International for ten years, and its chairman since June 2003. He has spent his working life as a computer software entrepreneur, including co-founding Broderbund Software in 1980, and upon his election to the Belo board he was CEO of Tawala Systems, an Internet technology company that he co-founded in 2005.

Earlier, in February, Belo added another television station to its roster, the first in several years. It purchased WUPL in New Orleans from CBS Corporation. It is affiliated with MyNetwork TV, which will expand Belo's ability to reach the New Orleans market beyond its CBS-affiliate WWL.

Such initiatives are in keeping with Belo's incessant push to expand its audiences, to reach the next generation of news consumers, and to continue to be a trustworthy source of news and information. To do that, the company must find ways to pay for it with new sources of advertising revenue, a challenge that all media companies face.

Acknowledging the challenges and opportunities of this huge transition, the Belo Foundation, Robert and Maureen Decherd, the Moroney family, and the estate of James M. Moroney, Jr., who died in early 2007, pledged a combined $15 million to establish the Belo Center for New Media at the University of Texas at Austin. The new entity, named for Alfred Horatio Belo, will enhance the study and analysis of how emerging technologies affect news consumers and the teaching of communications.

The challenges will only increase along with technological change, and there is rarely time for reflection in the media world. At Belo, in 2007, the six-member management committee, made up of the senior executives of the company, has been in place for several years and continues to lead the company. The roster includes the fourth-generation cousins Robert Decherd and Jim Moroney, and four non-family members: Dunia Shive, Dennis Williamson, Guy Kerr, and Marian Spitzberg. The average tenure with the company of those four non-family committee members is more than ten years.

The formal division of the company in February 2008 acknowledges what has long challenged Belo executives: modern-day broadcasting and cable require distinctly different approaches to building shareholder value from newspaper publishing. While the so-called convergence of all forms of media has occurred in many ways, in many ways it cannot occur so long as the antiquated Federal Communications Commission's regulations are in place prohibiting media cross-ownership.

When the transition is complete, Dunia Shive will be president and CEO of the television company, Belo Corp. Robert Decherd will be chairman, president, and CEO of the newspaper company, A. H. Belo Corporation. Both entities will have boards of directors, which will be created by dividing the original Belo board in half. Robert Decherd and his sister Dealey Decherd Herndon will be directors of both of the new entities, and *Morning News* publisher Jim Moroney will join the board of Belo Corp. Robert will be the non-executive chairman of Belo Corp. as well as the chairman of A. H. Belo Corporation. Both companies will be headquartered in Dallas.

In an October 1, 2007, letter to the more than seven thousand employees, Robert Decherd wrote: "This decision follows an extensive analysis of our businesses, growth strategies, regulatory obstacles, and current market forces. There are profound yet distinct changes occurring in these industries, and each sector appeals to discrete investor groups. . . . By creating two strong companies, we will be more focused and nimble. . . . Both companies will be better positioned to pursue and realize their full potential."

His letter seems to demonstrate that Robert and his management teams carry on very much in the vein established by A. H. Belo, then maintained by G. B. Dealey. Considering the big picture, that vein might best be characterized by the words *optimism* and *persistence*, coupled with good sense and hard work across the board.

Appendix A

G. B. AND OLIVIA ALLEN DEALEY FAMILY TREE

The Children

Annie	Fannie	Walter Allen	Edward Musgrove	Maidie
m.	m.	m.	m.	m.
R. R. Jackson	H. B. Decherd	Willie Gardner	Clara MacDonald	J. M. Moroney

The Grandchildren

Annie's Children	*Fannie's Children*	*Walter's Child*	*Ted's Children*	*Maidie's Children*
Henry Allen Jackson	Ruth Decherd	Walter Allen Dealey, Jr.	E. M. Dealey, Jr.	Jean Moroney
Rice R. Jackson, Jr.	H. Ben Decherd, Jr.		Joe M. Dealey	Betty Moroney
Gordon Dealey Jackson			Clara Patricia Dealey	James M. Moroney, Jr.
Gilbert Stuart Jackson				

Detail is provided on those in significant leadership roles in Belo Corp. and the *Dallas Morning News*:

Ben Decherd, Jr.	Joe M. Dealey	J. M. Moroney, Jr.
m.	m.	m.
Isabelle Lee Thomason	Doris Carolyn Russell	Lynn Wilhoit

The Great-Grandchildren

Ben Decherd's Children
Dealey Decherd m. Harold David Herndon
Ben Herndon
Bryan Herndon
Robert W. Decherd m. Maureen Healy
William B. Decherd
Audrey M. Decherd

Joe M. Dealey's Children
Joe M. Dealey, Jr.
Russell E. Dealey
Pamela C. Dealey
F. Patricia Dealey

James M. Moroney's Children
Molly Moroney
Mindy Moroney
James M. Moroney III m. Barbara Joan Bass
Sean Wesley Moroney
Meagan Lindsay Moroney
Kyle McQueen Moroney
Jennifer and Catherine Moroney
Michael W. Moroney

Appendix B

CHAIRMEN AND DIRECTORS OF BELO CORP., 1926–2007

It has been the custom of Belo Corp. to elect directors in the spring of each year, at the annual meeting of stockholders. The end dates in this list reflect the spring meeting at which the director's term formally ended or, in some cases, the year of the director's death. The chairmen's and chairwoman's names are in boldface, and their tenures as chair are in parentheses.

George Bannerman Dealey	1926–1946	(Chairman, 1926–1946)
Walter A. Dealey	1926–1934	
John F. Lubben	1926–1938	
Tom Finty, Jr.	1926–1929	
E. M. (Ted) Dealey	1926–1969	(1960–1964)
Ennis Cargill	1926–1935	
E. B. Doran	1926–1937	
Dr. James Q. Dealey	1929–1937	
James M. Moroney	1934–1968	(1964–1968)
George Waverley Briggs	1936–1957	
R. M. Buchanan	1937–1964	
Myer M. Donosky	1938–1950	
Jack Estes	1938–1952	
John E. King	1938–1939	
Harry C. Withers	1938–1959	
Leven T. Deputy	1940–1964	
Martin B. Campbell	1946–1954	
Mrs. G. B. Dealey	1946–1960	(1946–1960)
Joe A. Lubben	1948–1976	
Maurice E. Purnell	1950–1972	
Joe M. Dealey	1952–1995	(1980–1984)

H. Ben Decherd, Jr.	1952–1972	(1968–1972)
James M. Moroney, Jr.	1952–2000	(1984–1986)
A. Earl Cullum	1960–1980	
Sol M. Katz	1960–1980	
Jack B. Krueger	1960–1979	
D. Gordon Rupe	1960–1970	
William C. Smellage	1961–1980	
Richard D. Blum	1968–1983	
Myron F. (Mike) Shapiro	1968–1982	
Lloyd S. Bowles, Jr.	1973–1986	
Robert E. Dennard	1973–1982	
Patrick E. Haggerty	1973–1980	
James J. Laney	1973–1984	
William H. Seay	1973–1995	
Robert W. Decherd	1976–present	(1987–present)
John W. Bassett, Jr.	1979–2003	
Robert T. Richardson	1980–1983	
Ward L. Huey, Jr.	1982–2000	
James P. Sheehan	1982–1993	
Thomas B. Walker, Jr.	1982–1999	
Reece A. Overcash, Jr.	1983–1995	
John A. Rector, Jr.	1983–1986	
William T. Solomon	1983–present	
Lester A. Levy	1985–1998	
J. McDonald Williams	1985–present	
Dealey D. Herndon	1986–present	
Burl Osborne	1987–2002	
Hugh G. Robinson	1989–2001	
Judith L. Craven, M.D., M.P.H.	1992–present	
Arturo Madrid, PhD	1994–2004	
Roger A. Enrico	1995–2007	
Henry P. Becton, Jr.	1997–present	
Fanchon M. Burnham	1997–1999	
Peter B. Freeman	1997–1998	
Stephen Hamblett	1997–2005	
Laurence E. Hirsch	1999–present	
Louis E. Caldera	2001–present	
Lloyd D. Ward	2001–present	

France A. Córdova, PhD	2003–2007
Wayne R. Sanders	2003–present
M. Anne Szostak	2004–present
Douglas G. Carlston	2007–present

Appendix C

TIME LINE OF SIGNIFICANT EVENTS IN COMPANY HISTORY

1842 The *Daily News* begins publication in Galveston.

1857 The company begins publication of the *Texas Almanac*.

1865 Alfred Horatio Belo joins the company and soon becomes a partner with publisher Willard Richardson.

1874 George Bannerman Dealey joins the company as a fifteen-year-old.

1885 The *Dallas Morning News* is launched on October 1, with G. B. Dealey as general manager.

1901 A. H. Belo dies at age sixty-two, and his son succeeds him as head of the company.

1906 A. H. Belo, Jr., dies at age thirty-three.

1920 The Belo descendants appoint G. B. Dealey president of the company.

1922 WFAA Radio is launched.

1923 The *Galveston Daily News* is sold.

1926 G. B. Dealey buys the company from the Belo descendants, reorganizing it as A. H. Belo Corporation.

1940 E. M. (Ted) Dealey succeeds his father as president of the company.

1946 G. B. Dealey dies, and Olivia Allen Dealey is elected chairman of the board, an honorary position.

1949 Belo Corp. purchases Dallas's first television station, KBTV, from its founder months after it goes on the air.

1950 Upon approval by the FCC, Belo changes the television call letters to WFAA.

1960 Joe M. Dealey succeeds his father as president of the

	company, and Ted is elected chairman of the board, succeeding his mother.
1964	James M. Moroney, Sr., succeeds Ted Dealey as chairman of the board.
1968	H. Ben Decherd succeeds James Moroney, Sr., as chairman of the board.
1976	The G. B. Dealey Trust is distributed to the descendants of the five children of G. B. and Olivia Allen Dealey.
1980	James M. Moroney, Jr., succeeds Joe Dealey as president of the company, and Joe is elected chairman of the board.
1981	Belo's stock is publicly traded over the counter, and two years later it is listed on the New York Stock Exchange.
1983	Belo doubles its size by purchasing the Corinthian Group of television stations from Dun & Bradstreet in the largest purchase ever by one media company.
1984	Jim Moroney, Jr., succeeds Joe Dealey as chairman of the board.
1985	Robert W. Decherd succeeds Jim Moroney, Jr., as president of the company.
1987	Robert Decherd succeeds Jim Moroney, Jr., as chairman of the board.
1992	Belo celebrates 150 years of continuous operation.
1997	Belo doubles its size again by purchasing the Providence Journal Company.
2001	Jim Moroney III is named publisher and chief executive officer of the *Dallas Morning News*.
2004	The *Providence Journal* celebrates 175 years of publication.
2006	Robert Decherd celebrates thirty years as a director.
2007	Dunia Shive is named president of Belo Corp.
2008	Belo Corp. spins off its newspapers to form A. H. Belo Corporation.

Appendix D

TEXT OF THE BLACK-BORDERED ADVERTISEMENT RUN ON NOVEMBER 22, 1963, IN THE *DALLAS MORNING NEWS*

WELCOME MR. KENNEDY TO DALLAS . . .

. . . A CITY so disgraced by a recent Liberal smear attempt that its citizens have just elected two more Conservative Americans to public office.
. . . A CITY that is an economic "boom town," not because of Federal handouts, but through conservative economic and business practices.
. . . A CITY that will continue to grow and prosper despite efforts by you and your administration to penalize it for its non-conformity to "New Frontierism."
. . . A CITY that rejected your philosophy and policies in 1960 and will do so again in 1964—even more emphatically than before.

MR. KENNEDY, despite contentions on the part of your administration, the State Department, the Mayor of Dallas, the Dallas City Council, and members of your party, we free-thinking and America-thinking citizens of Dallas still have, through a Constitution largely ignored by you, the right to address our grievances, to question you, to disagree with you, and to criticize you.

In asserting this constitutional right, we wish to ask you publicly the following questions—indeed, questions of paramount importance and interest to all free peoples everywhere—which we trust you will answer . . . in public, without sophistry. These questions are:

WHY is Latin America turning either anti-American or Communistic, or both, despite increased U.S. foreign aid, State Department policy, and your own Ivy-Tower pronouncements?

WELCOME MR. KENNEDY

TO DALLAS...

. . . A CITY so disgraced by a recent Liberal smear attempt that its citizens have just elected two more Conservative Americans to public office.

. . . A CITY that is an economic "boom town," not because of Federal handouts, but through conservative economic and business practices.

. . . A CITY that will continue to grow and prosper despite efforts by you and your administration to penalize it for its non-conformity to "New Frontierism."

. . . A CITY that rejected your philosophy and policies in 1960 and will do so again in 1964—even more emphatically than before.

MR. KENNEDY, despite contentions on the part of your administration, the State Department, the Mayor of Dallas, the Dallas City Council, and members of your party, we free-thinking and America-thinking citizens of Dallas still have, through a Constitution largely ignored by you, the right to address our grievances, to question you, to disagree with you, and to criticize you.

In asserting this constitutional right, we wish to ask you publicly the following questions—indeed, questions of paramount importance and interest to all free peoples everywhere—which we trust you will answer . . . in public, without sophistry. These questions are:

WHY is Latin America turning either anti-American or Communistic, or both, despite increased U. S. foreign aid, State Department policy, and your own Ivy-Tower pronouncements?

WHY do you say we have built a "wall of freedom" around Cuba when there is no freedom in Cuba today? Because of your policy, thousands of Cubans have been imprisoned, are starving and being persecuted—with thousands already murdered and thousands more awaiting execution and, in addition, the entire population of almost 7,000,000 Cubans are living in slavery.

WHY have you approved the sale of wheat and corn to our enemies when you know the Communist soldiers "travel on their stomachs" just as ours do? Communist soldiers are daily wounding and/or killing American soldiers in South Viet Nam.

WHY did you host, salute and entertain Tito — Moscow's Trojan Horse — just a short time after our sworn enemy, Khrushchev, embraced the Yugoslav dictator as a great hero and leader of Communism?

WHY have you urged greater aid, comfort, recognition, and understanding for Yugoslavia, Poland, Hungary, and other Communist countries, while turning your back on the pleas of Hungarian, East German, Cuban and other anti-Communist freedom fighters?

WHY did Cambodia kick the U.S. out of its country after we poured nearly 400 Million Dollars of aid into its ultra-leftist government?

WHY has Gus Hall, head of the U.S. Communist Party praised almost every one of your policies and announced that the party will endorse and support your re-election in 1964?

WHY have you banned the showing at U.S. military bases of the film "Operation Abolition"—the movie by the House Committee on Un-American Activities exposing Communism in America?

WHY have you ordered or permitted your brother Bobby, the Attorney General, to go soft on Communists, fellow-travelers, and ultra-leftists in America, while permitting him to persecute loyal Americans who criticize you, your administration, and your leadership?

WHY are you in favor of the U.S. continuing to give economic aid to Argentina, in spite of that fact that Argentina has just seized almost 400 Million Dollars of American private property?

WHY has the Foreign Policy of the United States degenerated to the point that the C.I.A. is arranging coups and having staunch Anti-Communist Allies of the U.S. bloodily exterminated.

WHY have you scrapped the Monroe Doctrine in favor of the "Spirit of Moscow"?

MR. KENNEDY, as citizens of these United States of America, we DEMAND answers to these questions, and we want them NOW.

THE AMERICAN FACT-FINDING COMMITTEE

"An unaffiliated and non-partisan group of citizens who wish truth"

BERNARD WEISSMAN,
Chairman

P.O. Box 1792 — Dallas 21, Texas

WHY do you say we have built a "wall of freedom" around Cuba when there is no freedom in Cuba today? Because of your policy, thousands of Cubans have been imprisoned, are starving and being persecuted—with thousands already murdered and thousands more awaiting execution and, in addition, the entire population of almost 7,000,000 Cubans are living in slavery.

WHY have you approved the sale of wheat and corn to our enemies when you know the Communist soldiers "travel on their stomachs" just as ours do? Communist soldiers are daily wounding and/or killing American soldiers in South Viet Nam.

WHY did you host, salute and entertain Tito—Moscow's Trojan Horse—just a short time after our sworn enemy, Krushchev, embraced the Yugoslav dictator as a great hero and leader of Communism?

WHY have you urged greater aid, comfort, recognition, and understanding for Yugoslavia, Poland, Hungary, and other Communist countries, while turning your back on the pleas of Hungarian, East German, Cuban and other anti-Communist freedom fighters?

WHY did Cambodia kick the U.S. out of its country after we poured nearly 400 Million Dollars of aid into its ultra-leftist government?

WHY has Gus Hall, head of the U.S. Communist Party praised almost every one of your policies and announced that the party will endorse and support your re-election in 1964?

WHY have you banned the showing at U.S. military bases of the film "Operation Abolition"—the movie by the House Committee on Un-American Activities exposing Communism in America?

WHY have you ordered or permitted your brother Bobby, the Attorney General, to go soft on Communists, fellow-travelers, and ultra-leftists in America, while permitting him to persecute loyal Americans who criticize you, your administration, and your leadership?

WHY are you in favor of the U.S. continuing to give economic aid to Argentina, in spite of the fact that Argentina has just seized almost 400 Million Dollars of American private property?

WHY has the Foreign Policy of the United States degenerated to the point that the C.I.A. is arranging coups and having staunch Anti-Communist Allies of the U.S. bloodily exterminated?

WHY have you scrapped the Monroe Doctrine in favor of the "Spirit of Moscow"?

MR. KENNEDY, as citizens of these United States of America, we DEMAND answers to these questions, and we want them NOW.

THE AMERICAN FACT-FINDING COMMITTEE
"An unaffiliated and non-partisan group of citizens who wish truth"
BERNARD WEISSMAN,
Chairman

NOTES

Prologue

The epigraph is taken from Emerson's *Essays: First and Second Series* (New York: Gramercy Books, 1993), 32.

1. www.belo.com.

2. "Tell all the Truth but tell it slant— / Success in Circuit lies / Too bright for our infirm Delight / The Truth's superb surprise / As Lightning to the Children eased / With explanation kind / The Truth must dazzle gradually / Or every man be blind—" From *The Complete Poems of Emily Dickinson*, edited by Thomas H. Johnson (New York: Little, Brown and Company, 1961), 506.

Chapter 1

1. Alfred H. Belo recounted the story of his father's name in his memoirs, which he dictated to his son-in-law, Charles Peabody, who published them in a small, private edition in 1904. A copy is held in the Belo Archives. As for the home, in 1951, following the death of Belo's daughter, Jeannette Belo Peabody, the Belo heirs gave the Salem family home to the Moravian Church, which continues to operate the village of Old Salem as a living history museum. The church converted the home to accommodate twenty-nine apartments for the elderly Single Sisters and Single Brothers of the Church. Although the gilding is dulled, those same letters, B E L O, remain over the door leading to the lobby of the Main Street entrance of the building, which has been maintained on the exterior as it originally appeared. In 2004, when asked about the Belos' son, Alfred, the manager of the converted Belo home in Salem said that he didn't know what had become of him.

2. Many different versions of the earliest history of the *Daily News* in Galveston have been recounted over the years. Two that provide exceptional detail are a book by Marilyn McAdams Sibley, *Lone Stars and State Gazettes: Texas Newspapers Before the Civil War* (College Station: Texas A&M University Press, 1983); and an unpublished master's thesis by Lillian Davis Martin, "The history of the *Galveston News*" (University of Texas at Austin, August 1929).

3. Correspondence between G. B. Dealey and W. L. Moody, Jr., can be found in the G. B. Dealey Collection at the Dallas Historical Society.

4. Records of the Peabody Museum of Archaeology and Ethnology at Harvard University.

5. *Memoirs of Alfred Horatio Belo Dictated by Him to and with a Short Introduction by Charles Peabody, May 1902* (Boston: Alfred Mudge & Son Inc., Printers, 1904), 10.

6. Dallas Historical Society, G. B. Dealey Collection, File 190.

7. *Dallas Morning News*, April 21, 1901.

8. Ibid.

9. *Dallas Morning News*, July 29, 1951 (Jeannette Belo Peabody's obituary).

10. Alfred and Helen's two young daughters, Helen and Jane, moved with their mother to New York, and ultimately Jane Belo became an anthropologist and close friend and collaborator with Margaret Mead. Mead's autobiography, *Blackberry Winter*, has many references to Jane, particularly in regard to their work in Bali. Jane was married three times, but she never had children. Her last husband was a celebrated professor of Latin American history at Columbia. Helen Belo married a man from North Carolina named Allen Turner Morrison, and they had four children. Most of the descendants of A. H. Belo's two children, Jeannette and Alfred, live along the East Coast, and several of Alfred Jr.'s descendants attended Belo Corp.'s sesquicentennial celebration in 1992.

11. Ernest Sharpe, *G. B. Dealey of the* Dallas News (New York: Henry Holt and Company, 1955), 25.

12. Ibid.

13. Ibid., 24.

14. Dallas Historical Society, G. B. Dealey Collection, Box 7:14.

15. Dallas Historical Society, G. B. Dealey Collection, Box 7:8.

16. Dallas Historical Society, G. B. Dealey Collection, Box 7:14.

17. Ibid.

18. Sam Acheson, *35,000 Days in Texas: A History of the* Dallas News *and Its Forbears* (New York: Macmillan, 1938), 257.

19. Sharpe, *G. B. Dealey*, 239.

20. Darwin Payne, *Big D: Triumphs and Troubles of an American Supercity in the 20th Century* (Dallas: Three Forks Press, 1994), 87.

21. Darwin Payne, "The *Dallas Morning News* and the Ku Klux Klan," *Legacies: A History Journal for Dallas and North Central Texas*, Spring 1997, 18.

22. Ibid., 21.

23. Dallas Historical Society, G. B. Dealey Collection, Box 7:8.

24. Ibid.

25. Ibid.

26. Ibid.

27. Ibid.

28. Sharpe, *G. B. Dealey*, 221.

29. The speeches made at the July 26, 1926, reorganization meeting for A. H. Belo Corporation are recorded in the minutes of that meeting, which are in the Belo Archives.

30. Ted Dealey, *Diaper Days of Dallas* (Nashville: Abingdon Press, 1966). (Ted organized a collection of his published and unpublished reminiscences of early Dallas, and it was published by his friend Bliss Albright, who owned Cokesbury Books in Dallas.)

31. Dallas Historical Society, G. B. Dealey Collection, Box 48:432.
32. Dallas Historical Society, G. B. Dealey Collection, Box 28:265.
33. Ibid.
34. Dallas Park Board Minutes, Book 10, 552.
35. Dealey Decherd Herndon Oral History, 2006.
36. Belo Archives, G. B. Dealey Collection, Box 8.

Chapter 2

1. Sharpe, *G. B. Dealey*, 63.
2. *Dallas Morning News*, January 30, 1909.
3. *Dallas Morning News*, October 1, 1935.
4. Richard Schroeder, *Texas Signs On: The Early Days of Radio and Television* (College Station: Texas A&M University Press, 1998), 9.
5. *Dallas Morning News*, October 2, 1960.
6. Selling the company essentially ended the Belo family's active involvement with the events of life in Dallas. However, Helen Ponder Belo seems to have had misgivings about giving up her elegant home, so rather than selling the home along with the company, she and her two daughters kept it and signed a long-term lease with a local Dallas funeral operator, Sparkman Co. Sparkman converted the home to a funeral parlor and continued to use it for nearly fifty years as tenants of the Belo family descendants. The Belo family's reluctance to part with the home almost certainly saved it from the fate of all of the other grand mansions that once lined Ross Avenue. The formally named Belo Mansion is the only one to survive, and it is owned by the Dallas Bar Foundation, which bought it from the Belo heirs in 1978.
7. *Houston Chronicle*, March 12, 1928.
8. Belo Archives, G. B. Dealey Collection, Box 7:9.
9. E. M. Dealey Collection, Box 1:24.
10. Directors' Minutes, September 28, 1934.
11. Directors' Minutes, March 29, 1935.
12. Dealey, *Diaper Days of Dallas*, 7.
13. Ibid., 28.
14. *Dallas Morning News*, November 27, 1969.
15. E. M. Dealey Collection, unpublished memoir.
16. Ibid.
17. E. M. Dealey Collection, Box 7:4.
18. Sharpe, *G. B. Dealey*, 280.
19. Ibid., 192.
20. E. M. Dealey Collection, Box 1:16.
21. Belo Archives, G. B. Dealey Collection, Box 3:7.
22. Felix McKnight Oral History, 1992.
23. Jack Krueger Oral History, 1986.
24. Sol Katz Oral History, 1986.

25. Richard D. Blum Oral History, 1986.

26. Belo History Collection, 1946 Annual Report.

CHAPTER 3

1. Belo History Collection, Archives Box 8:1.

2. Directors' Minutes, July 29, 1926.

3. Ibid.

4. Robert W. Decherd Collection, Box 1:7.

5. Robert W. Decherd Collection, Box 1:8.

6. Dallas Public Library, Joe M. Dealey Oral History, 1983.

7. James M. Moroney, Jr., Oral History, 1986.

8. Tom Simmons, "The Old Building," unpublished manuscript, Ready Reference Files, Belo Archives.

9. Dallas Historical Society, G. B. Dealey Collection, Box 28:256.

10. Ibid.

11. *Dallas Morning News*, May 22, 1949.

12. Tom Simmons, "The Old Building."

13. Belo History Collection, Archives Box 8:4.

14. Sol Katz Oral History, 1986.

15. 1949 Annual Report.

16. 1950 Annual Report.

17. 1954 Annual Report.

18. E. M. Dealey Collection, Box 7:5.

19. Walter A. Dealey, Jr., Oral History, 1986.

20. Dallas Public Library, Joe M. Dealey Oral History, 1983.

21. 1952 Annual Report.

22. 1948 Annual Report.

23. Gay Talese, *The Kingdom and the Power* (New York: Cleveland: New American Library, Inc., Fourth Printing, 1969), 236.

24. 1954 Annual Report.

25. Conversations with Dr. Marsh Terry, Southern Methodist University, 2005.

26. Directors' Minutes, 1955.

27. Directors' Minutes, 1958.

CHAPTER 4

1. Felix McKnight Oral History, 1992.

2. Belo History Collection, Documents Box 9:4.

3. Ibid.

4. Ibid.

5. Ward L. Huey Oral History, 1996.

6. E. M. Dealey Collection, Archives Box 1:14.

7. Joe M. Dealey Collection, Archives Box 1:5.

8. E. M. Dealey Collection, Archives Box 1:14.

9. William Manchester, *The Death of a President* (New York: Harper & Row, 1967), 48.

10. Ibid.

11. E. M. Dealey Collection, Documents Box 7:5.

12. E. M. Dealey Collection, Documents Box 3:2.

13. Ibid.

14. Ibid.

15. Ibid.

16. Ibid.

17. Ibid.

18. Manchester, *The Death of a President.*

19. 1961 Annual Report.

20. 1962 Annual Report.

21. Stanley Marcus Oral History, 1992.

22. Telephone interview with Mildred McLerran, 2003.

23. Dallas Public Library, Joe M. Dealey Oral History, 1983.

24. Joe M. Dealey Oral History, 1986.

25. 1963 Annual Report.

26. Unrecorded interviews with Bill Smellage and Robert Decherd.

27. Directors' Minutes, 1964.

28. Leland Renfro Oral History, 1986.

CHAPTER 5

1. Belo History Collection, Documents Box 9:10.

2. Directors' Minutes, 1966.

3. Carolyn Carney, "Bruce Alger: The voice of Cold War politics in Dallas," *Legacies*, Fall 2003, 60.

4. Charles Inge, "Remembering Mr. J and the GRC," *Legacies*, Fall 1988, 29.

5. Belo History Collection, Archives Box 9:10.

6. Joe M. Dealey Collection, Documents Box 1:1.

7. Interview with Peggy Lubben Gould, 2006.

8. Dick Jeffrey Oral History, 1986.

9. Ibid.

10. Robert W. Decherd Collection, Documents Box 1:8.

11. Dallas Times Herald Collection, Documents Box 6:20.

12. Ibid.

13. Reginald Conway Westmoreland, "The *Dallas Times Herald*, 1879–1961" (unpublished dissertation, University of Missouri, 1961), 335.

14. Interview with Robert Solender, 2005.

15. Dallas Times Herald Collection, Documents Box 15:1.

16. Dallas Times Herald Collection, Documents Box 15:1a.

17. Ibid.
18. Joe M. Dealey Oral History, 1986.
19. Jack Kreuger Oral History, 1986.
20. Tom Simmons Oral History, 1986.
21. Belo History Collection, Documents Box 10:1.
22. *Dallas Times Herald*—100 Years, May 6, 1979, 34.
23. Felix McKnight Oral History, 1992.
24. Darwin Payne, *Big D*, 347.
25. Jim Moroney Oral History, 1987.
26. Directors' Minutes, 1972.

CHAPTER 6

1. Robert Decherd Oral History, 1987.
2. 1972 Annual Report.
3. Biographical files.
4. *Dallas Morning News*, March 27, 1973.
5. Robert Decherd Personal Collection, Archives Box 5:5.
6. Ibid.
7. Robert Decherd Oral History, 1987.
8. Robert Decherd Personal Collection, Archives Box 5:5.
9. Belo History Collection, Archives Box 10:5.
10. *Dallas Morning News*, February 6, 1971.
11. Dick Blum Oral History, 1986.
12. *Dallas Morning News*, May 1, 1974.
13. 1974 Annual Report.
14. Private papers of Joe Lubben, held by Peggy L. Gould
15. Robert Decherd Personal Collection, Archives Box 5:5.
16. Ibid.
17. Ibid.
18. Robert Decherd Personal Collection, Archives Box 5:6.
19. Ibid.
20. Robert Decherd Oral History, 1987.
21. Directors' Minutes, 1976.
22. 1976 Annual Report.

CHAPTER 7

1. *Dallas Times Herald*—100 Years, May 6, 1979, 34.
2. 1976 Annual Report.
3. Bill Smellage Diaries.
4. Laura Miller, "Who killed the *Times Herald*? A tale of villains, idiots, and greed," *Dallas Observer*, December 19, 1991.

5. *Dallas Times Herald*—100 Years.

6. Transcript of the testimony of Gordon Jackson in an arbitration hearing in Dallas on May 19, 1979.

7. Ibid.

8. Directors' Minutes, 1978.

9. *D*, January 1978.

10. 1983 Annual Report.

11. 1980 Annual Report.

12. Ibid.

13. Dave McNeely, *Adweek*: Southwest Edition, April 1981.

14. Ralph Langer Oral History, 1997.

Chapter 8

1. Robert Decherd Oral History, 1987.

2. 1981 Annual Report.

3. James M. Moroney, Jr., Oral History, 1987.

4. Anne Denny, ed., "The rising stars of Texas," *Texas Business*, March 1982.

5. Dallas Public Library, Joe M. Dealey Oral History, 1983.

6. Jim Schutze, "It wasn't murder. Was it suicide? How the *Times Herald* died," *D*, February 1992.

7. Paul B. Brown, "Where else can you go?" *Forbes*, June 20, 1983.

8. 1983 Annual Report.

9. www.austin-ind.com.

Chapter 9

1. Francis C. Brown III, "Fighting spirit: Aggressive strategy helps A. H. Belo Corp. keep its independence," *Wall Street Journal*, February 25, 1987.

2. Tracy Staton, Darrell Preston, and Dave Scott, "Death throes of the *Times Herald*," *Dallas Business Journal*, December 13–19, 1991, cover.

3. Laura Miller, "Who killed the *Times Herald*?"

4. Mark Lorando, "WWL-TV to be sold in $110 million deal," *Times-Picayune*, February 24, 1994.

5. Chuck Taylor, "KIRO-TV sale: What'll change?" *Seattle Times*, September 14, 1994.

6. Robert Decherd Collection, news clippings, 1988.

7. Garrett D. Byrnes and Charles H. Spilman, *The Providence Journal: 150 Years*, Providence Journal Company, 1980.

Chapter 10

1. "Web media's future touted," *Dallas Morning News*, February 24, 2001.

2. Charles Layton, "The Dallas Mourning News," *American Journalism Review*, April/May 2005.

3. Belo Archives, G. B. Dealey Collection.

4. Joseph Nocera, "A column that needs no introduction," *New York Times*, June 3, 2006.

EPILOGUE

1. "Yahoo! and newspaper consortium expand strategic partnership." Press release issued jointly by all partners on April 16, 2007.

2. Elise Ackerman, "Newspapers join Yahoo partnership," contracostatimes.com, April 25, 2007.

BIBLIOGRAPHY

Archival Collections and Primary Sources Consulted

www.belo.com

Belo Corp. Archives, Dallas, Texas

Annual Reports (unpublished), 1926–1980

Annual Reports (published), 1981–2004

Belo History Collection

Biographical Files

Dallas Times Herald Collection

Dealey, E. M., Papers

Dealey, George Bannerman, Papers

Dealey, Joe M., Papers

Decherd, H. Ben, Papers

Decherd, Robert W., Papers

Minutes of the Meetings of the Board of Directors, 1926–1995

Minutes of the Meetings of the Shareholders, 1926–1995

Moroney, James M., Papers

Moroney, James M. Jr., Papers

Texas Almanacs, 1857–2006

Dallas Historical Society, G. B. Dealey Library

Acheson, Sam H., Papers

Belo, Alfred Horatio, Letters

Briggs, George Waverley, Papers

Critic Club of Dallas, Papers

Dealey, G. B., Collection

Smellage, William C., Private Diaries, Dallas

Belo Oral History Project, 1984–2006

Barnes, Carlton, retired executive of the *Dallas Morning News*

Barta, Carolyn, former political reporter and editor of op-ed page of the *Dallas Morning News*

Blum, Dick, retired executive and director of Belo Corp.

Bowles, Lloyd, retired director of Belo Corp.

Boynton, Louise Mackey, retired performer who sang on WFAA Radio and Television

Buckner, Ruth, retired secretary for the *News* who had begun working under G. B. Dealey (GBD) and who cut the cake for the *News*'s centennial celebration in 1985

Campbell, Martin B., retired executive of WFAA Radio and director of Belo, who participated in the transition to television

Dealey, Joe M., GBD grandson and retired chairman of Belo

Dealey, Walter Allen, Jr., Rev., GBD grandson and retired minister

Decherd, Robert W., GBD great-grandson and Belo chairman

Evans, Bill, retired managing editor of the *News*

Grant, Clint, retired photographer of the *News*

Haag, Marty, retired news director of WFAA-TV

Halbreich, Jeremy, former president of the *News*

Herndon, Dealey Decherd, GBD great-granddaughter, sister of Robert Decherd

Huey, Ward, retired executive and director of Belo Corp.

Jeffrey, Dick, retired promotions director of the *News*

Katz, Sol, retired executive and director of the *News*

Krueger, Jack, retired executive editor of the *News* and director of Belo

Laney, James, retired director of Belo and husband of GBD granddaughter Jean Moroney

Langer, Ralph, retired executive editor of the *News*

Lubben, Joe, retired executive of the *News* and director of Belo Corp.

Lyles, Olga Utley, retired former secretary of GBD

Malone, John, retired employee of the *News* who began work at age eighteen and never worked anywhere else

Marcus, Stanley, retired chairman of Neiman Marcus

McCarthy, Mike, retired executive of Belo Corp.

McKnight, Felix, retired executive of the *Dallas Times Herald*

Moroney, James M. Jr., GBD grandson and retired chairman

Moroney, Jim III, GBD great-grandson and publisher of the *News*

Osborne, Burl, retired publisher of the *News* and director of Belo Corp.

Perry, Mike, former CFO of Belo Corp.

Pruitt, Richard, longtime photographer for the *News*

Rector, John, retired publisher of the *News*

Renfro, Leland, retired executive of the *News*

Richardson, Robert T., retired executive of the *News* and Belo, retired Belo director

Salzberger, Lee, retired executive of Belo Corp.

Seay, William H., retired director of Belo Corp.

Simmons, Jean, retired travel writer and editor of the *News*

Simmons, Tom, retired executive editor of the *News*

Smellage, William C., retired executive of the *News* and director of Belo

Stemmons, John, Dallas businessman who had known GBD

Swank, Patsy, Dallas journalist

Walker, Denson, retired executive of WFAA Radio and Television

West, Dick, retired editorial page editor of the *News*

Additional Interviews

Barta, Carolyn, former reporter and editor of op-ed page at the *News*

Dealey, Joe M. Jr., great-grandson of GBD, former employee of the *News* and Belo Corp.

Decherd, Robert W., great-grandson of GBD, chairman of Belo Corp.

Gould, Peggy, daughter of Joe Lubben

Jackson, Rice R. III, great-grandson of GBD

Jackson, Walt, great-grandson of GBD

Langer, Ralph, retired executive editor and vice president of the *News*

McLerran, Mildred, retired employee of several departments of the *News*

Moroney, James M. Jr., grandson of GBD

Pederson, Rena, former reporter and editor of the editorial page of the *News*

Sander, Jack, retired vice chairman of Belo

Simmons, Tom, retired executive editor of the *News*

Smellage, William C., retired executive and director of Belo

Solender, Robert, retired executive and director of the *Dallas Times Herald*

Terry, Marshall, Professor of English, SMU, since 1954; former book reviewer for the *News*

Wilk, Stuart, retired managing editor of the *News*

Secondary Sources Consulted

Books

Acheson, Sam. *35,000 Days in Texas: A History of the* Dallas News *and Its Forbears*. New York: Macmillan, 1938.

———. *Dallas Yesterday*. Lee Milazzo, editor. Dallas: Southern Methodist University Press, 1977.

Auletta, Ken. *Backstory: Inside the Business of News*. New York: Penguin Books, 2003.

Barkley, Roy R., and Mark F. Odintz, editors. *The Portable Handbook of Texas*. Austin: Texas State Historical Association, in conjunction with the Center for Texas Studies at the University of Texas at Austin, 2000.

Belo, Alfred Horatio. *Memoirs Dictated by Him to and with a Short Introduction by Charles Peabody, May 1902*. Boston: Alfred Mudge & Son Inc., Printers, 1904.

Byrnes, Garrett D., and Charles H. Spilman. *The Providence Journal: 150 Years*. Providence Journal Company, 1980.

Cox, Patrick. *The First Texas News Barons*. Austin: University of Texas Press, 2005.

Crews, C. Daniel. *A Storm in the Land: Southern Moravians and the Civil War*. Winston-Salem: Moravian Archives, 1997.

Davis, Ronald L. *John Rosenfield's Dallas*. Dallas: Three Forks Press, 2002.

Dealey, Ted. *Diaper Days of Dallas*. Nashville: Abingdon Press, 1966.

———. *Three Men of Texas and a Texas Institution: The* Dallas Morning News. New York: Newcomen Society in North America, 1957.

Emerson, Ralph Waldo. "Self-Reliance." *Essays: First and Second Series*. New York: Gramercy Books, 1993. 23–48.

Gelsanliter, David. *Fresh Ink: Behind the Scenes at a Major Metropolitan Newspaper*. Denton: University of North Texas Press, 1995.

Graham, Katharine. *Personal History*. New York: Vintage Books, 1998.

Greene, A. C. *Dallas: The Deciding Years—A Historical Portrait*. Austin: Encino Press, 1973.

Hazel, Michael V. *Dallas: A History of Big D.* Austin: Texas State Historical Association, 1997.

———. *The Dallas Historical Society: The Early Years, 1922–1946.* Dallas: Belo Foundation, 2002.

Johnson, Thomas H. *The Complete Poems of Emily Dickinson.* New York: Little, Brown and Company, 1961.

Kelley, Mary L. *The Foundations of Texas Philanthropy.* College Station: Texas A&M University Press, 2004.

Manchester, William. *The Death of a President.* New York: Harper & Row, 1967.

McElhaney, Jacquelyn Masur. *Pauline Periwinkle and Progressive Reform in Dallas.* College Station: Texas A&M University Press, 1998.

Newton, Lewis W., and Herbert P. Gambrell. *Texas Yesterday & Today with the Constitution of the State of Texas.* Dallas: Turner Company, 1949.

Niven, Penelope, and Cornelia Wright. *Old Salem: The Official Guidebook.* Winston-Salem: Old Salem Inc., 2004.

Payne, Darwin. *As Old as Dallas Itself: A History of the Lawyers of Dallas, the Dallas Bar Association, and the City They Helped Build.* Dallas: Three Forks Press, 1999.

———. *Big D: Triumphs and Troubles of an American Supercity in the 20th Century.* Dallas: Three Forks Press, 1994.

———. *Dynamic Dallas: An Illustrated History.* Carlsbad, California: Heritage Media Corporation, 2002.

———, ed. *Sketches of a Growing Town: Episodes and People of Dallas from Early Days to Recent Times.* Dallas: Southern Methodist University, 1991.

Schroeder, Richard. *Texas Signs On: The Early Days of Radio and Television.* College Station: Texas A&M University Press, 1998.

Sharpe, Ernest. *G. B. Dealey of the* Dallas News. New York: Henry Holt and Company, 1955.

Sibley, Marilyn McAdams. *Lone Stars and State Gazettes: Texas Newspapers Before the Civil War.* College Station: Texas A&M University Press, 1983.

Talese, Gay. *The Kingdom and the Power.* Cleveland: New American Library, Inc., Fourth Printing, 1969.

The Handbook of Texas Online. www.tsha.utexas.edu/handbook.

Periodicals and Journals Cited and Consulted

"78 People to Watch in '78." *D*, January 1978.

Abrams, Bill. "A. H. Belo is getting some banner headlines from analysts enthused by its TV purchases." *Wall Street Journal*, December 11, 1984.

Acheson, Sam. "George Bannerman Dealey." *Southwestern Historical Quarterly*, January 1947.

Ackerman, Elise. "Newspapers join Yahoo partnership." contracostatimes.com, April 25, 2007.

"A Dallas dynamo breaks into the big leagues." *Business Week*, September 26, 1983.

"A. H. Belo announces $606 million TV deal." *Editor & Publisher*, June 25, 1983.

Applebome, Peter. "War of the words: Have Dallas's newspapers begun a battle to the death?" *Texas Monthly*, April 1982.

Arnold, J. D. "Wretched excess in Dallas." *Texas Observer*, May 11, 1973.

Auletta, Ken. "Fault line: Can the *Los Angeles Times* survive its owners?" *New Yorker*, October 10, 2005.

———. "The inheritance: Can Arthur Sulzberger, Jr., save the *Times*—and himself?" *New Yorker*, December 19, 2005.

Bagamery, Anne. "The best defense . . ." *Forbes*, May 10, 1982.

Bayer, Tom. "Luck is the residue of A. H. Belo's design." *Advertising Age*, February 4, 1985.

"Belo Corporation (BLC): Company interview." *The Wall Street Transcript—Bear Stearns Media, Entertainment & Information Special*, March 2002.

Bauman, Kit. "Hark the *Herald*." *Downtown Dallas News*, September 12–18, 1983.

Bayer, Tom. "Dallas dailies tussle over Ann Landers." *Advertising Age*, August 31, 1981.

"Belo's record buy." *Broadcasting*, June 27, 1983.

"Belo to buy Corinthian stations." *Advertising Age*, June 27, 1983.

Benenson, Lisa. "Big enough for Texas: Belo stays at home." *NewsInc*, October 1991.

Berger, Loren, and Candace Talmadge. "Winds of war shift in favor of *Morning News*." *Adweek*: Southwest Edition, September 12, 1983.

Bianco, Anthony. "The future of the *New York Times*." *Business Week*, January 17, 2005.

Bloom, John, and William Broyles, Jr. "Behind the lines." *Texas Monthly*, March 1980.

Blow, Steve. "Lesson hounds Osborne." *Dallas Morning News*, September 28, 1980.

Brown, Francis C. III. "Fighting spirit: Aggressive strategy helps A. H. Belo Corp. keep its independence." *Wall Street Journal*, February 25, 1987.

Brown, Paul B. "Where else can you go?" *Forbes*, June 20, 1983.

Buckley, Christopher. "How almost everyone in the media establishment got his job through the *Harvard Crimson*." *Esquire*, September 12, 1978.

Campanella, Frank W. "Battle in Dallas: A. H. Belo keeps its commitment to newspapering." *Barron's Investment News & Views*, March 21, 1983.

"Campuses cool on McGovern." *Boston Herald Traveler & Record American*, October 12, 1972.

Carney, Carolyn. "Bruce Alger: The voice of Cold War politics in Dallas." *Legacies: A History Journal for Dallas and North Central Texas*, Fall 2003.

Carr, David. "Washington Post Company buys *Slate Magazine*." *New York Times*, December 22, 2004.

Castro, Janice, and Anne Constable. "Shootout in the Big D." *Time*, September 7, 1981.

Celeste, Eric. "At the ripping point." *Dallas Observer*, November 18–24, 2004.

Chunovic, Louis. "Deep in the heart of Texas, local roots rule." *Broadcasting & Cable*, March 29, 2004.

Crossley, Dave. "Decherd of Dallas: Sprucing up the *News*." *Texas Monthly*, October 1977.

Cuff, Daniel. "President of Belo Corp. to assume chief's title." *New York Times*, October 1, 1982.

Cullum, Lee. "The power brokers: Dallas's top players of the eighties." *D*, July 1982.

Dahl, Jonathan. "*Dallas Times Herald* is losing its war with *Morning News* for readers, ads." *Wall Street Journal*, May 15, 1985.

"Dallas is a city of winners." *Dallas Times Herald*, June 29, 1986.

"The Dallas Morning Feud." *Texas Monthly*, February 1979.

Dallas Times Herald—100 Years, supplement to the newspaper, May 6, 1979.

"Decherd fine-tunes DSO bond strategy." *D*, September 1979.

Denny, Anne, ed. "The rising stars of Texas." *Texas Business*, March 1982.

Fabrikant, Geraldine. "Newspapers to be sold in Dallas." *New York Times*, June 27, 1986.

Fitzgerald, Mark. "Big ideas in the Big D: Jim Moroney carries on a family tradition in Dallas—as a new breed of publisher." *Editor & Publisher*, April 2004.

Flournoy, Craig. "Red dawn in Dallas." *Columbia Journalism Review*, May/June 2004.

Fox, Steve. "Web site starts from a memo, gains millions of readers: A brief history of washingtonpost.com." washingtonpost.com, June 19, 2006.

"Fresh blood for the old gray lady: A new *News*." *D*, May 1980.

Friendly, Jonathan. "2 papers in Dallas in a 'free-for-all.'" *New York Times*, July 12, 1981.

Graham, Martin. "Of regimental honor." *Civil War Times Illustrated*, January 1988.

Gwynne, S. C. "The Dallas Morning Blues." *Texas Monthly*, January 2005.

Hall, Cheryl. "Belo exec sees opportunity amid industry turmoil." *Dallas Morning News*, February 1, 2006.

Hazel, Mike. "The making of two modern dailies." *Legacies*, Spring 1997.

Heuton, Cheryl. "Leaders of the pack: Four executives whose distinctive visions have made a difference." *Channels*, August 13, 1990.

Hollie, Pamela G. "A. H. Belo president adds chairman's post." *New York Times*, April 19, 1984.

Houston Chronicle, clipping from March 12, 1928.

Hughes, Ted. "Broadcasting takes lead as Belo enters new era." *Dallas/Fort Worth Business*, April 23, 1984.

———. "Editors define battleground in heated Dallas newspaper war." *Dallas/Fort Worth Business*, December 13, 1982.

Inge, Charles. "Remembering Mr. J and the GRC." *Legacies*, Fall 1998.

"Joe Dealey elected chairman of Belo." *Dallas Morning News*, February 15, 1980.

Katz, Gregory. "Doing things in a big way in Dallas: TV deal seen as means to increased profits and cash flow." *USA Today*, November 16, 1983.

King, Wayne. "G.O.P. gives Dallas dailies a prominent battlefield in a long-running war." *New York Times*, August 26, 1984.

Lancaster, Hal. "*Dallas Times Herald* to close, sell assets to A. H. Belo, publisher of rival paper." *Wall Street Journal*, December 9, 1991.

Layton, Charles. "Breaking news: Belo stockholders cry foul." *American Journalism Review*, April/May 2005.

———. "The Dallas Mourning News." *American Journalism Review*, April/May 2005.

Lemann, Nicholas. "The wayward press: Amateur hour, journalism without journalists." *New Yorker*, August 7 and 14, 2006.

Lenzner, Robert, and Carrie Shook. "Texas Darwinist." *Forbes*, January 26, 1998.

Lieberman, David. "Papers take a leap forward." *USA Today*, January 31, 2006.

———. "Pressure grows for Knight Ridder to sell." *USA Today*, November 4, 2005.

"Look out, Belo!" *Adweek*: Southwest Edition, June 27, 1983.

"Look out, Belo." *Texas Monthly*, August 1981.

Lorando, Mark. "WWL-TV to be sold in $110 million deal." *Times-Picayune*, February 24, 1994.

MacMillan, Robert. "US newspapers say going private no answer to woes." today.reuters.com, December 6, 2006.

Malan, Rian. "Paper giant." *California*, October 1982.

McClellan, Steve. "Ward Huey: In the business of doing the right thing." *Broadcasting & Cable*, April 7, 1997.

McConnell, Bill. "Grip slips on LMA squeeze." *Broadcasting & Cable*, January 25, 1999.

McNeely, Dave. *Adweek*: Southwest Edition, April 1981.

Merwin, John. "Is the *Dallas Morning News* up for grabs?" *D*, August 1976.

———. "Investor unloading *Morning News* stock." *D*, July 1978.

Miller, Laura. "Who killed the *Times Herald*? A tale of villains, idiots, and greed." *Dallas Observer*, December 19, 1991.

"Movers & shakers." *Washington Journalism Review*, September 1981.

"*News* cutting back on sales outside area." *Dallas Morning News*, February 10, 2006.

Nocera, Joseph. "A column that needs no introduction." *New York Times*, June 3, 2006.

———. "Hot Coffey." *Texas Monthly*, April 1986.

Pate, Russ. "Robert Decherd of the *Dallas Morning News*." *Adweek*: Southwest Edition, May 1985.

Payne, Darwin. "The *Dallas Morning News* and the Ku Klux Klan." *Legacies*, Spring 1997.

Pearlman, Russell. "Tuning in." *SmartMoney*, November 2006.

Pierson, Len. "Banner year for Belo after *Herald* buyout." *Dallas Business Journal*, June 19–25, 1992.

"Quiet days on campus." *Women's Wear Daily*, March 9, 1972.

Richardson, Tim. "20 who hold the power in Texas." *Texas Business*, February 1986.

Rogers, Tim. "How screwed is Robert Decherd?" *D*, October 2005.

Romano, Allison. "More than a numbers cruncher." *Broadcasting & Cable*, March 6, 2006.

Rosen, Jay. "Web users open the gates." washingtonpost.com, June 19, 2006.

Rosser, John E. "G. B. Dealey of the *News*." *Southwest Review*, Autumn 1946.

Schutze, Jim. "It wasn't murder. Was it suicide? How the *Times Herald* died." *D*, February 1992.

"Second 500 largest industrials." *Forbes*, June 1982.

Seelye, Katherine Q. "McClatchy to resell 12 papers it's buying." *New York Times*, March 14, 2006.

Seelye, Katherine Q., and Andrew Ross Sorkin. "Are papers about to land or take off?" *New York Times*, March 9, 2006.

Shafer, Jack. "Don't bury them yet." *Dallas Morning News*, July 2, 2006.

Shropshire, Mike. "Captain of the *News*." *D*, September 2000.

Siklos, Richard. "How did newspapers land in this mess?" *New York Times*, October 1, 2006.

"Silver tea set christened." *Dallas Times Herald*, October 14, 1895.

Smith, Griffin Jr. "Deadline in Dallas." *Texas Monthly*, June 1974.

Staton, Tracy, Darrell Preston, and Dave Scott. "Death throes of the *Times Herald*." *Dallas Business Journal*, December 13–19, 1991.

Stiteler, Rowland. "Family feud threatens full disclosure for Belo." *D*, January 1979.

Sullivan, Patricia. "As the Internet grows up, the news industry is forever changed." washingtonpost.com, June 19, 2006.

Surowiecki, James. "The financial page: Printing money." *New Yorker*, April 3, 2006.

Talmadge, Candace. "Newspaper reader surveys: Just the facts, ma'am?"

Adweek: Southwest Edition, September 12, 1983.

Taylor, Chuck. "KIRO-TV sale: What'll change?" *Seattle Times*, September 14, 1994.

Tempest, Rone. "Family coalition may continue Belo policies." *Dallas Times Herald*, August 22, 1976.

"Tribune media company sticking to buyback plan." *Dallas Morning News*, June 9, 2006.

Watt, Chad Eric. "Belo's growth slowing." *Dallas Business Journal*, November 5–11, 2004.

"Web media's future touted." *Dallas Morning News*, February 24, 2001.

Whitley, Glenna. "Blindsided." *D*, November 1999.

———. "Should A. H. Belo sell the *Dallas Morning News*?" *Business Dallas*, January/February 1999.

"Why Dun & Bradstreet is going off the air." *Business Week*, July 4, 1983.

"Winds of war shift in favor of *Morning News*." *Adweek*: Southwest Edition, September 12, 1983.

Wyeth, John A. "Col. Alfred H. Belo." *Harper's Weekly*, May 4, 1901.

Theses and Dissertations Cited

Bagby, Nathe Parks. "Editorial policies of the *Dallas News*." MJ thesis, University of Texas at Austin, June 1930.

Martin, Lillian Davis. "The history of the *Galveston News*." MA thesis, University of Texas at Austin, August 1929.

Stokes, George M. "A public service program history of radio station WFAA." PhD dissertation, Northwestern University, 1954.

Westmoreland, Reginald Conway. "The *Dallas Times Herald*, 1879–1961." PhD dissertation, University of Missouri, 1961.

Legal Transcripts Cited

"An excerpt: Testimony of Gordon D. Jackson." May 19, 1979. Unpublished news release.

"Yahoo! and newspaper consortium expand strategic partnership." Issued jointly by all partners, April 16, 2007.

INDEX

Acheson, Sam, 4, 9, 54, 107, 109
Adams, Lorraine, 239
Advertising Age, 231
Adweek, 215
A. Earl Cullum & Associates, 106, 190
A. H. Belo & Co.: creation of, 22; and KKK, opposition to and defeat of, 10, 11, 33; move to Dallas of, 24; sale of, 34, 42
A. H. Belo Corporation: board of directors of, 279–281; and Corinthian Broadcasting, purchase of, 208; Fair Labor Standards Act, sued under, 61; founding of, 34, 35, 36; historical timeline of, 282; initial public offering of, 195; and newspaper spin-off, 275; and Providence Journal Company, purchase of, 248; and radio stations, sale of, 221–224, 234; and spin-off in 2008, 2
Albright, Bliss, 289n30
Al Dia, 265
Alger, Bruce, 126
Allen, George L., 133
Allen, Olivia. *See* Dealey, Olivia Allen
American Airlines Center, 258
American Broadcasting Company (ABC), 98
American Journalism Review, 268
American Nazi Party, 126
American Newspaper Guild, 160
American Newspaper Publishers Association, 128
American Red Cross, 155
Andover-Newton Theological School, 92
Area Television Educational Foundation, 99
Arlington Morning News, 244
Armstrong, J. S., 49
Arthur Young, 254
Ashland Independent, 193
Associated Press, 12, 105, 111, 116
Associates Corporation of North America, 212
Atlas Match Corporation, 169
Atorino, Edward, 267
Austin American-Statesman, 167
Austin Industries, 212
Automobile Building, 89

Bagamery, Anne, 203
Baggett, Donnie, 252
Baker, Botts, Parker & Garwood, 34
Baker, George, 111
Baltimore Sun, 74, 193
Bangs, Samuel, 9, 10
Barta, Carolyn, 174, 193, 194
Baskin, Bob, 112
Bass, Barbara Joan. *See* Moroney, Barbara Joan Bass
Bass, Richard D. (Dick), 211
Bassett, John W., Jr., 186, 264, 280
Bennett, Reveau, 45, 63, 117
Becton, Henry P., Jr., 229, 249, 280
Beers, Jack, 115
Belden Associates, 187
Belo, Alfred Horatio (A. H.), 2, 7; Civil War memoirs of, 11–14; joins company, 15–17; legacy of, recalled, 52; memorialized, 86, 113, 119; move of, to Dallas, 24; new media center, named for, 275, 282
Belo, Alfred Horatio, Jr., 17–19, 105, 173, 282, 289n10; death of, 27
Belo, Helen Ponder, 17–20, 31–34, 52
Belo, Jane, 289n10
Belo, Nettie Ennis, 17, 19, 28
Belo Archives, 3, 8
Belo Broadcasting Corporation, 159, 169, 202
Belo Building, 214, 220, 239, 240, 242
Belo Center for New Media, 275
Belo Corp., 2, 3, 12; and formal division, 275
Belo Foundation, 240, 244, 249, 275
Belo Information Systems Online

(BISON), 191
Belo Interactive (BI), 256, 268, 269
Belo Interactive Media (BIM), 269
Belo Mansion, 18, 173, 290n6
Belo Plan, 61, 147, 161
"Belo Watch," 239
Big D Productions, 132
Blackberry Winter, 289n10
Black-bordered Advertisement, 284–287
Blessen, Karen, 233
Blum, Richard D. (Dick), 65, 135, 161, 212, 227, 280
Boehlo, Edward, 7, 8
Borger (Texas) *News-Herald*, 110
Boston Globe, 194
Boston Herald-Traveler, 168
Bowles, Lloyd S., Jr., 153, 154, 218, 280
Briggs, George Waverley, 33, 34, 71, 279
Broadcaster of the Year, 271
Broadcasting & Cable, 271
Broderbund Software, 274
Brooks, Clara Patricia (Patsy) Dealey, 144–146, 277
Brown University, 22, 35, 45
Bryan-College Station, Texas *Eagle*, 244
Buchanan, R. M., 106, 279
Buckley, Christopher, 184
Buckley, William F., 184
Bullitt, Dorothy, 270
Burnett, F. W., 178
Burnham, Fanchon M. (Monty), 249, 280
Buzzetta, John, 233, 237, 238
bylaws, 25, 70, 71, 136, 145; repeal of, 147

Cabell, Earle, 126
Caldera, Louis E., 229, 264, 280
Campbell, Martin B., 66, 279
Capital Bureau, 250
Cargill, Ennis, 31, 34, 35, 279
Carlston, Douglas G., 274, 281
Carney, Carolyn, 292n3
Carter, Amon, 89
Carter, Amon, Jr., 123
Casey, Albert V., 141
Cass, Donald F., Jr. (Skip), 255, 273
CBS, 136
Centex Corporation, 257
Chambers, James F., 111, 137, 139, 141
Chandler, Otis, 137, 141, 207
Chandor, Douglas, 47
Chase Manhattan Bank, 155
Cherry, Wilbur, 9, 11
Children's Medical Center, 38
Christie, Bertram G., 58
Churchill Way Presbyterian Church, 92
Civil Rights Act of 1964, 126
Civil War, 12, 13
Clarke, Frank, 133
Clements, Kathy, 250, 257
Clements, Rita Crocker Bass, 211
Clements, William P., 211
Cleveland, President Grover, 18
Clinton, Bill, 253; administration of, 264
Cockrell, Mary Alice (Mackie), 76, 77
Coffey, Shelby, 221
Cokesbury Books, 289n30
Cold War, 94
Columbia Journalism Review, 258
Combined Communications, Inc., 178
Communism, 94
Conrad, Emmett J., 132
Córdova, France, 229, 264, 274, 281
Corinthian Broadcasting Group, 208, 283
Cox, J. William, 188
Craven, Judith, 229, 241, 280
Creany, Cathy, 250
Crockett, Davy, 40
Cronican, Michael, 9
Crume, Paul, 130, 225
Cuban, Mark, 258
Cue Cat, 256
Cuff, Daniel, 205
Cullum, A. Earl, Jr., 105, 158, 190, 201, 280
Cullum, Lee, 203
Cumberland Hill School, 57

D, 184
Dahl, George, 83, 84
Daily News (Galveston), 4, 24, 282; earliest edition of, 8–9, 11; history of, 19–23
Dallas Art Association, 46
Dallas Bar Foundation, 173, 290n6
Dallas Business Journal, 237, 241, 267
Dallas City Council, 133
Dallas Convention Center, 159
Dallas Country Club, 92
Dallas County Medical Society Auxiliary, 46
Dallas Cowboys, 130
Dallas Dispatch, 30
Dallas Federal Savings and Loan, 154
Dallas/Fort Worth International Airport, 159
Dallas Foundation, 38, 247
Dallas Garden Club, 50
Dallas Historical Society, 41; founding of, 38

Dallas Independent School District, 132
Dallas Journal, 30, 74, 78, 134, 142
Dallas Legal Education Center, 173
Dallas Mavericks, 258
Dallas Morning News, 1, 3, 5, 282; and African American columnist, first at, 132; "Angels Among Us" column in, 130; building housing, first, 23; "Business Tuesday" section in, 194; centennial celebration of, 214–215; Centennial Edition of, 11; and circulation overstatement, 265–267; and community development editorials, 38–41; and computers, introduction of, 125; and conservatism, editorials voicing, 94–95; established, 17; "Fashion!Dallas" section in, 185; female writer at, first at, 37; "High Profile" section in, 198; and KKK, opposition to, 29–33; management training program at, 160; and Pressmen's Union, strike by, 161; and production capacity, increase of, 206; and Web site, launch of, 245
Dallas Morning News Building, 99, 125, 132, 187, 189, 214; façade of, 86; moving into, 87; planning for, 81–85
Dallas Museum of Art, 20
Dallas Museum of Natural History, 117, 132
Dallas Observer, 172, 239
Dallas Park and Recreation Department, 38, 39
Dallas Parks Foundation, 247
Dallas Rupe & Son, 106, 154
Dallas Society for the Prevention of Cruelty to Animals, 117
Dallas Symphony Orchestra, 106, 203, 246
Dallas Times Herald, 64, 84, 97–99, 115, 127, 137–143, 155, 160, 161, 168, 171–196, 220, 221, 233, 237
Dallas Women's Club, 50
Dallas Zoo, 116
Davis, John Martin, Jr., 177
Dealey, Amanda Mayhew, 148
Dealey, Annie. *See* Jackson, Annie Dealey
Dealey, Clara McDonald, 59, 77, 277
Dealey, Clara Patricia. *See* Brooks, Clara Patricia (Patsy) Dealey
Dealey, Doris Russell, 79, 124, 277
Dealey, Edward Musgrove (Ted), 34–36, 39, 63–66, 79, 93, 107, 120–122, 124, 126, 135, 277, 279, 282, 283, 289n30; death of, 145; early life of, 56–58; and JFK White House, visit to, 110; joins company, 29; and KKK, reporting on, 58–60; and LBJ ranch, visit to, 117; as president, 61; steps aside, at board request, 134; succession of, to presidency (memo on), 101–104
Dealey, Edward Musgrove, Jr., 59, 277
Dealey, Fannie. *See* Decherd, Fannie Dealey
Dealey, George Bannerman (G. B.), 2, 113, 120, 122, 127, 143, 144, 277, 279, 282, 283; acquires company, 33–36; Dealey Plaza named for, 38–41; early life of, 20–24; last words of, 81; named president, 29; tribute to, 85; twenty-first anniversary, congratulated on, 25–26; and University of Missouri address to students, 270
Dealey, James Quayle, 21, 22, 35, 36, 45, 122, 279
Dealey, John, 91
Dealey, Joseph McDonald (Joe), 101, 114, 122–125, 131, 143–149, 152, 158, 167, 169, 199, 277, 279, 282–283; birth of, 59–60; community involvement of, 127; death of, 244; early career of, 72, 78–79, 90; elected to board, 93; elected chairman and relinquished presidency, 189; and LBJ White House, visit to, 133; named president, 103–105; retires as CEO, 204; retires from company and as chairman, 212–213; shareholders challenge, 175–185; and *Time* comments on, 108; and WWII, return from, 68
Dealey, Joseph McDonald, Jr. (Scoop), 79, 148, 160, 185, 190, 151, 200, 162, 164, 203, 210, 226, 278
Dealey, Maidie. *See* Moroney, Maidie Dealey
Dealey, Olivia Allen (wife of G. B.), 22, 36, 71, 83, 105, 120, 121, 277, 279, 282, 283
Dealey, Patsy. *See* Brooks, Clara Patricia (Patsy) Dealey
Dealey, Russell E., 160, 162, 200, 226, 235, 278
Dealey, Thomas W., 21–24, 27
Dealey, Trudie Lewellen Kelley, 93, 124
Dealey, Walter Allen, 29–36, 43, 50, 52–54, 120–122, 144, 277, 279
Dealey, Walter Allen, Jr. (Al), 51–56, 68–92, 144–146, 277
Dealey Plaza, 39, 113, 160
Dear, Martha, 251
Dear, Walter, 251
Death of a President, 107
Decherd, Dealey. *See* Herndon, Dealey Decherd
Decherd, Fannie Dealey, 36, 44–48, 71, 120,

121, 135, 277
Decherd, Henry Benjamin, 44, 277
Decherd, Henry Benjamin, Jr., 96, 100–103, 122–124, 128, 129, 144–146, 150, 165, 225, 277, 280, 283; as assistant to the president, 90; birth of, 48; death of, 147; early life and career of, 73–76; elected vice president, 104; and executive committee, creation of, 117; and G. B. Dealey Trust, made trustee of, 133; and Gordon Jackson, liaison with, 143; and WWII, return from, 68
Decherd, Isabelle. *See* Thomason, Isabelle Lee
Decherd, Maureen Healy, 162, 275, 278
Decherd, Robert William, 1, 105, 150, 151, 162, 164–166, 169, 173, 198–212, 216–220, 223, 224, 227–230, 231, 232, 234, 236, 240, 241, 244, 245, 251–253, 256, 258–266, 270, 271, 273–276, 278, 280, 283; Annual Stockholders Meeting, first attendance at, 152; birth of, 75; community involvement of, 246–247, 249; elected to board, 163; elected chairman and CEO, 222; and management training, 160; named president, 213; as Newspaper Executive of the Year, 215; and notes on meeting, 155–158
Decherd, Ruth, 48, 122, 277
Dennard, Paula, 154
Dennard, Robert E., 153, 154, 167, 205, 280
Denton Publishing Company, 251
Denton Record Chronicle, 251
Deputy, Leven T., 69, 86, 102, 106, 122, 279
Detroit Free Press, 171
Detroit News, 192
de Weldon, Felix, 40
Diaper Days of Dallas, 56, 289n30
Dobie, J. Frank, 59
Donosky, Myer M., 69, 90, 279
Doran, E. B., 34, 35, 122, 279
Dougherty, Dudley, 111
Doughty, Dorothy, 117
Dow, Lohnes & Albertson, 218
Dow Jones & Co., 191
Dun & Bradstreet, 208, 218, 283
Dupont-Columbia University Awards, 3, 185, 235, 236, 252
DVS (differential voting stock), 223

Early, Mike, 242
Editor & Publisher, 264, 265
Edward R. Murrow Awards, 3
Eisenlohr, E. G., 45
Elkind, Peter, 216
Ennis, Cornelius, 12, 22
Ennis, Nettie. *See* Belo, Nettie Ennis
Enrico, Roger A., 229, 244, 280
Eppler, Guerin & Turner, Inc., 166
Esquire, 184
Estes, Jack, 279
Evans, Bill, 198

"facsimile radio," 88
Fair Labor Standards Act, 61
Fair Park, 38, 83, 89
Federal Bureau of Investigation, 115
Federal Communications Commission (FCC), 143, 156, 159, 168, 170, 171, 191, 208, 275
Federal Reserve, 38
Ferguson, Hugh W., Jr., 73
Ferguson, James E., 33, 59
Ferguson, Miriam (Ma), 33, 59
Ferris, Royal A., 49
Ferris Plaza, 82, 126, 214
Fields, Thomas, 49
Finty, Tom, Jr., 34, 35, 279
First National Bank of Dallas, 84, 183
Fitzgerald, Mark, 265
FleetBoston Financial, 265
Flippen, Adoue & Lobit, 49
Flournoy, Craig, 218
Forbes, 183, 203
Ford Foundation, 142
Foree, Kenneth, 84
Forsythe Riflemen, 13
Fort Worth Star-Telegram, 244
Freedom of Information Foundation of Texas (FOIFT), 203, 245
Freedoms Foundation at Valley Forge, 134, 141
Freeman, Peter B., 249, 280
French, George H., 9, 10
French, Henry R., 9
Frisco Railway System, 82

Gaar, Harold F., Jr., 241
Galveston, 8, 20–33
Galveston County Daily News, 10
Galveston Daily News. See *Daily News*
Gannett Company, 210
Gano Brothers, 49
Gardner, B. H., 55, 56
Gardner, Willie Pearl, 51, 55, 277
Gaston, W. H., 49
Gaylord Communications Group, 257

G. B. Dealey Foundation, 96
G. B. Dealey Retirement Pension Plan, 66, 76, 90, 96
G. B. Dealey Trust, 47, 50, 102, 103, 133–135, 144, 146, 150–151, 156, 158, 163, 166, 283; expiration of, 168, 169, 174, 176; terms of, 70–71
Geiger, Ken, 243
Geophysical Service, Inc., 155
Glatt, Linnea, 240
Gleaner, 251
Glenn Advertising, 151
Goals for Dallas program, 126
Goldman, Sachs & Co., 196, 202
Goldwater, Barry, 117
Gooch, Tom C., 138
Good, Aubrey, 178, 179
Good Morning America, 185
Gore Commission, 253
Grapevine Sun, 251
"Great Newspaper War, The" 195
Green, Cecil H., 155
Greene, A. C., 138
Greenwell, Dennis A., 138
Griffin, David, 252
Griffin Communications, 252
Guittar, Lee J., 171, 172

Haag, Marty, 152
Haggerty, Patrick E., 153, 155, 157, 167, 201, 280
Halbreich, Jeremy L., [illegible], 254
Hamblett, Steve, 229, 249, 280
Hamilton, E. G., 214
Hanners, David, 233
Harper's Weekly, 11
Harry Hines Boulevard, 99
Harte, Houston H., Jr., 111
Harvard University, 12, 19, 57, 150, 160, 165, 192; Business School, 223, 274; *Crimson*, 150, 160, 166, 184, 185; Medical School, 48; Peabody Museum of Archaeology and Ethnology, 289n4; Radio Research Laboratory, 106
Hasey, Candy, 185
Haverford College, 255
Haynes and Boone, 238
Hays, Howard H. (Tim), 244
HDTV, 244
Headliner Club's Publisher of the Year Award, 127
Healy, Maureen. *See* Decherd, Maureen Healy
Herbert, 20
Herndon, David, 150, 219, 278
Herndon, Dealey Decherd, 40, 75, 150, 162–165, 218–220, 229, 230, 275, 278, 280
Highland Park High School, 78, 202
Hirsch, Laurence E. (Larry), 229, 257, 280
Hockaday School, 219
Hogue, Alexandre, 45
Holden, Gean, 191
Holy Trinity Catholic Church, 49, 93
Horne, B. J., 112
House Un-American Activities Committee, 95
Houston Chronicle, 52, 112, 290n7
Houston Post, 23
Hoyt, Lynn. *See* Moroney, Lynn Wilhoit
Huey, Ward L., Jr., 100, 151, 191, 202, 227, 228, 231–259, 280
Hurricane Katrina, 3

Inside Television, 100
Institute of Texan Cultures, 143

Jackson, Annie Dealey, 36, 43–48, 71, 120, 121, 277
Jackson, Gilbert Stuart, 47, 122, 144–146, 152, 154, 158, 166, 178, 181, 182, 183, 277
Jackson, Gordon Dealey, 47, 122, 143, 147, 152, 154, 157, 158, 166, 167, 181–184, 215, 277; challenges management, 174–178, sells shares to cousins, 179
Jackson, Henry Allen, 47, 73, 122, 144, 158, 166, 277
Jackson, Rice R., Jr., 47, 48, 73, 122, 144, 166, 277
Jackson, Rice R., III, 178
Jackson, Rice Robinson, 44, 46, 277
Jackson, Robert H., 115
Jackson, Walt, 46
Jefferson, B. C., 138
Jeffrey, Dick, 128, 129
JJAB Room, 69, 79
John Birch Society, 94, 114
Johns Hopkins University, 77
Johnson, Iola, 133, 152, 185
Johnson, Ken, 172
Johnson, Lyndon Baines, 117, 133, 134
Johnson, Philip, 160
Johnson, W. Thomas, Jr. (Tom), 140, 160, 171
Jones, Jesse H., 52

Jonsson, J. Erik, 126, 140, 155
Jonsson, Philip R., 140
Junior League of Dallas, 50

Kahn, E. M., 49
KASW-TV, 257
Katz, Gregory, 210
Katz, Jon, 207
Katz, Sol M., 65, 87, 105, 112, 190, 201, 280
KBTV, 88, 282
KDFW-TV, 140
Kelley, Trudie Lewellen. *See* Dealey, Trudie Lewellen Kelley
Kennedy, John F., 107, 110–113, 126, 160
KENS-TV, 250, 256
KERA-FM Radio, 66, 88
KERA-TV, 99, 125, 142
Kerr, Guy, 230, 261, 275
Kessler, George E., 37, 82
Kessler Plan, 38, 82
KFDM-TV, 136, 152, 169, 209
KHOU-TV, 208, 244, 256
Kiest, Edwin J., 30, 131, 138
Kimberly-Clark Corporation, 264
King, Frank H., 56
King, John E., 122, 279
King Broadcasting Co., 270
KING-TV, 250, 270
KIRO-TV, 243, 250
Klein, Herb, 132
KMOV-TV, 250
KOA-AM, 209
KOAQ-FM, 209
Kolb, Key, 214
KOTV, 209, 235, 252
KREM-TV, 253
KRLD-AM Radio, 140
KRLD-FM Radio, 140
KRLD-TV, 88, 137, 140
KRQX-AM Radio, 210
Krueger, Jack B., 64, 80, 98, 105, 127, 133, 134, 136, 139, 186, 280
Krueger, Walter B., 74
KTBC-TV, 140
KTVK, 257
Kuempel, George, 194
Ku Klux Klan, 10, 29–33, 43, 58, 60
KVUE-TV, 256
KXTV, 209, 236, 241, 250
KZEW-FM Radio, 159, 169, 210

Landrum, Lynn W., 107, 113
Lane, David T. (Dave), 152, 191, 213, 236
Laney, James J. (Jim), 153, 158, 213, 280
Laney, Jean Moroney, 49, 144, 277
Langer, Ralph, 195
LaRoche and Dahl, 83
Lasell College, 44, 49, 59
Layton, Charles, 268
LBJ Library, 140
Lehrer, Jim, 142
Lenzner, Robert, 253
Let Me Speak to the Manager, 100
Leubsdorf, Carl, 193
Levy, Lester A., 215, 257, 280
Lewisville News, 251
Linz Award, 127
Locke, Eugene P., 33–35, 64, 94, 106
Locke, Purnell, Boren, Laney & Neeley, 153, 213, 261
Locke & Locke, 33
Lombardi, Cesar, 19, 28, 29, 58
Long Island University, 223
Los Angeles Times, 137, 171, 221
Louisville Courier Journal, 171
Lowe, R. G., 27
Loyola University, 242
Lubben, Joe A., 72, 73, 101–106, 124, 128–169, 178, 215, 225, 279
Lubben, John F., 34–36, 52, 72, 122, 215, 279
Lubben, Rene, 73
Lubben Plaza, 215, 240, 242

Maddox, Brenda, 241, 249
Madrid, Arturo, 229, 242, 280
Malone, Dan, 239
Manchester, England, 20
Manchester, William, 107
Marble Collegiate Church, 92
Marcus, Stanley, 60, 64, 114, 118
Marquette University, 155
Marsalis, T. L., 49
Marsalis Park Zoo, 39. *See also* Dallas Zoo
Marshall College, 193
Martinez, Anita, 133
Massachusetts Institute of Technology, 106, 233
Maxon, Terry, 1
Maxwell Communications, 143, 168
Mayfield, Earl B., 59
Mayhew, Charles, 148
Maytag, 264
McCarthy, Joseph, 95
McCarthy, Michael J., 218, 238, 261, 264

McCartin, Tom, 171, 172
McClung, Florence, 45
McDermott, Eugene, 155
McDonald, Clara. *See* Dealey, Clara McDonald
McKnight, Felix, 64, 79, 95, 97, 98, 105, 139, 141
McLerran, Mildred, 114
McNeely, Dave, 195
McVeigh, Timothy, trial of, 245
M. D. Anderson Hospital, 150
Mead, E. K., 138
Mead, Margaret, 289n10
MediaNews Group, 220
Merriam, Allen, 138
Merrill Lynch & Co., 191
Meyerson Symphony Center, 246
Miami Herald, 171
Michigan State University, 188
Milford, Dale, 132
Miller, Laura, 172
Miner, Isadora, 37
Mong, Robert W., Jr. (Bob), 194, 255, 261
Moody, W. L., Jr., 10, 32, 52
Moravian Church, 288n1 (chap. 1)
Morgan Stanley, 106
Moroles, Jesús Bautista, 242
Moroney, Barbara Joan Bass, 211, 278
Moroney, Betty. *See* Norsworthy, Betty Moroney
Moroney, James, 49
Moroney, James M., 44, 49, [illegible], [illegible], [illegible], [illegible], 105, 122, 134, 277, 279, 283; death of, 135; elected to board, 54; elected chairman, 117; elected vice chairman, 104; G. B. Dealey Trust, named trustee of, 70
Moroney, James M., Jr. (Jimmy), 47, 90, 106, 122, 123, 124, 144–145, 150–151, 158, 163, 179–181, 190, 193, 195–197, 199–200, 203–204, 207, 209–210, 215, 218, 240, 277, 280, 283; birth of, 49; early career of, 79–81; elected to board, 93; elected chairman, 212; estate of, 275; named president, 189; named secretary, 104; retirement of, from board, 259; retirement of, from company, 222
Moroney, James M., III (Jim), 164, 211, 229, 230, 235, 261, 278, 283; birth of, 93; and circulation announcements, 266; joins company, 201; named publisher, 260; as Publisher of the Year, 265
Moroney, Jean. *See* Laney, Jean Moroney
Moroney, Lynn Wilhoit, 92, 93, 177, 214
Moroney, Maidie Dealey, 36, 44–48, 71, 120, 121, 135, 277; death of, 145
Moroney Hardware Company, 49, 54
Morrison, Allen Turner, 289n10
Mullen, Richard, 214
Mullen Company, 214
Mullins, Walter G. (Walt), 213, 232
Murchison, William (Bill), 141
Murphy, Franklin, 137
Murphy & Bolanz, 49

National Broadcasting Company (NBC), 98
National Typographical Union, 15, 161
NCH Corporation, 215
Neiman Marcus, 83, 93
New Orleans, 3, 14, 242
Newspaper Executive of the Year, 215
Newsroom, 142
News Texas, Inc., 116
New York Stock Exchange (NYSE), 2, 179, 211, 224, 283
New York Times, 1, 18, 53, 94, 139, 205
Nichols, Perry, 85, 142, 220
Nocera, Joe, 272
Norsworthy, Betty Moroney, 49, 144–146, 277
North Plant, 206, 215, 233, 241
Northwest Cable News, 255
Northwestern University, 92
Norvell, Robert G., 212, 232

Oakland Cemetery, 19
Ochs, Adolph S., 18, 52
Old Red Museum of Dallas County History and Culture, 38
Old Salem, North Carolina, 12, 288n1 (chap. 1)
Omniplan Architects, 214
Optigraphics Corporation, 169
Orr, Tom, 247
Osborne, Burl, 192–196, 198–224, 228, 231–260, 264, 280
Oswald, Lee Harvey, 115
Overcash, Reese A., Jr., 212, 243, 280
Owensboro, Kentucky *Messenger-Inquirer*, 244
Owensboro Publishing Company, 245

Padgitt Brothers, 49
Park Cities Cable Television, 191
Pate, Russ, 215
Patterson, Bill, 251

Patterson, Fred and Patsy, 251
Paul Quinn College, 247
Peabody, Charles, 12, 13, 19, 288n1 (chap. 1)
Peabody, Jeannette Belo, 19, 28, 31–34, 57, 288n1 (chap. 1)
Peacock, H. B., 155
Peale, Dr. Norman Vincent, 92
Peckham, Barry, 265, 267
Pederson, Rena, 173, 194
Pei, I. M., 159
PepsiCo, Inc., 244
Periwinkle, Pauline. *See* Miner, Isadora
Perry, Michael D., 188, 212, 232, 253
Phi Beta Kappa, 74, 202
Philadelphia Daily News, 272
Philadelphia Inquirer, 171, 272
PM Magazine, 185
Ponder, Helen. *See* Belo, Helen Ponder
Pool, Joe, 95
Potter, Tom, 88, 89
Prather, W. H., 49
Pressman's Union, 161
Preston Hollow Presbyterian Church, 92
Projo. *See* Providence Journal Company
Providence, Rhode Island, 22, 249
Providence Journal, 267, 270, 283
Providence Journal Company, 248, 270, 283
Providence Journal Foundation, 249
Public Radio International, 274
Publisher of the Year, 127, 265
Pulitzer Prize, 2, 115, 218, 233, 236, 239, 243, 245, 248
Purnell, Maurice E., 94, 106, 146, 147, 153, 279

Quantico, Virginia, 76
Quick, 265
Quincy, 80

Rather, Dan, 115
Ratliff, Bill, 185
Rauscher Pierce Securities Corporation, 166, 178
Reagan, President Ronald, 194
Reaugh, Frank, 44
Rector, John A., Jr., 131, 185, 190, 192, 195, 204, 206, 213, 218, 227, 228, 280
Reid, Julia Scott, 132
Rembert, Clyde, 137
Republic National Bank of Dallas, 84
Republic of Texas, 8
Richards, Ann, 239
Richardson, Robert T. (Bob), 100, 168, 191, 205, 280
Richardson, Willard, 11, 14, 17, 21, 86, 282
Riverside, California *Press-Enterprise*, 244, 267, 270
Robertson, Felix, 33, 59
Robinson, Hugh G., 233, 264, 280
Rockefeller University, 155
Rodrick, Dorrance D., 111
Rodrigue, George, 218
Roosevelt, Franklin D., 80
Roter, Helen, 68
Rowlett, Tracy, 185, 257
Ruby, Jack, 115
Ruggles, William B., 107
"Rule of Seven," 208–210
Runyon, John W., 138
Rupe, D. Gordon, 105, 106, 154, 280
Rupe Investment, 154
Russell, Doris Carolyn. *See* Dealey, Doris Russell

Salem, North Carolina, 8, 12, 13, 18
Salinger, Pierre, 111
Salvation Army, 203
Sammons Communications, 191
San Angelo Standard Times, 112
San Antonio Light, 112
Sander, Jack, 230, 252, 271, 273
Sanders, Wayne R., 229, 264, 281
Sanger Brothers, 49
Santa Fe Building, 80
Saxon, Gerald, 204
Schoffelmayor, Victor, 52
Schutze, Jim, 207, 238
Seattle Times, 243
Seay, C. M., 153
Seay, Elizabeth Dealey, 153
Seay, William H. (Bill), 153, 157, 158, 167, 243, 280
Securities Exchange Commission (SEC), 176, 181
Seton Hall University, 202
Shapiro, Myron F. (Mike), 99, 100, 135, 136, 189, 191, 201, 280
Sharpe, Ernest, 5, 44
S. H. Cockrell & Co., 49
Sheehan, James P. (Jim), 199–224, 227, 232–239, 280
Sherrod, Blackie, 238
Shive, Dunia A., 230, 254, 257, 271, 273–276, 283

Shook, Carrie, 253
Simmons, Tom, 64, 87, 134, 165, 171, 173, 192
Simmons, Tom and Jean, 63
Singleton, William Dean, 220, 221, 233
SmartMoney, 269
Smellage, William C. (Bill), 47, 62, 92, 106, 146, 152, 168, 172, 180, 191, 201, 280
Smith, Barney, Harris, Upham & Co., 181
Smith, Dave, 194
Smith, George, 240
Smither, Murray, 220
Snyder, William, 233, 236, 243
Solender, Robert, 138, 139
Soloman, William T. (Bill), 212, 229, 280
Southern Methodist University, 38, 95, 154, 202; Dedman School of Law, 239
Southland Corporation, 233
Southland Paper Company, 116
Southwestern Life Insurance, 84, 153, 154
Sparkman Funeral Home, 173, 290n6
Spitzberg, Marian, 230, 238, 275
Stanford, 211, 274
Stanley, Harry M., Jr., 192, 206
State Fair of Texas, 49, 88
Stemmons, John, 60
St. John's Military Academy, 80
St. Mark's School of Texas, 165, 246
Sunset High School, 134
Swindle, Howard, 194, 218
Swinsky, Albert, 138
Szostak, M. Anne, 265, 281

Taber, Clyde, 138
Taggert, Pat, 111
Tanaka, Yonekichi, 247
Tate, Willis, 95
Tawala Systems, 275
Taylor, A. Starke, Jr., 214
Teddy Phillips Orchestra, 92
Teherani, Vicky C., 241
Telecommunications Act of 1996, 248
Terrill, M. B., 57
Terrill Prep School, 57
Texas Almanac, 14, 169, 282
Texas Business Corporation Act, 98
Texas Cable News (TXCN), 255, 267
Texas Centennial Exposition, 38, 83
Texas Daily Newspaper Association, 172
Texas Instruments, 155
Texas Monthly, 173, 216
Texas School Book Depository Building, 160
Texas Sesquicentennial, 220
Texas State Historical Commission, 214
Texas State Securities Board, 176, 177
Texas State Securities Commission, 183
Texas Tech University, 254
Texas Woman's University, 77
35,000 Days in Texas, 9, 54, 107, 109
Thomason, Isabelle Lee, 74, 157, 277
Thomason, Robert Ewing, 74, 75
Time, 108
Times Herald Printing Co., 137–143, 237, 241
Times Mirror Company, 137–143, 168, 171–196, 204, 220
Times-Picayune, 242
Time Warner Cable, 267
Titche-Goettinger Building, 83
Tolbert, Frank, 130
Tomás Rivera Center for Policy Studies, 242
Trammell Crow Company, 215
Trinity University, 148, 242
Truman, President Harry, 111
Tyler Corporation, 254

Union Station, 82. *See also* Union Terminal
Union Terminal, 38
United Fund Campaign, 127
United Press International, 185
United States Department of Labor, 61
United States Olympic Committee, 264
United States Supreme Court, 61, 147
United Way of the Texas Gulf Coast, 241
University of California at Berkeley, 239
University of Dallas, 111
University of Missouri, 270
University of Pennsylvania, 257
University of Rhode Island, 249
University of Texas at Austin, 5, 48, 49, 51, 57, 72, 76, 77, 140, 154, 187, 200, 219, 275
University of Texas Medical School at Galveston, 48
University of Texas Southwestern Medical Center, 246
University of Texas System, 142
U.S. Army, 154
U.S. Army Air Corps, 78
U.S. Army National Guard, 160
USA Today, 210
U.S. Marine Corps Reserve, 76
U.S. Navy, 80, 155, 202
U.S. Postal Service, 155

Villanova University of Law, 257
Visual Panographics, Inc., 169

Wade, Henry, 143
Wade, Jim, 143
WADECO, 143, 159, 168, 191
Walker, Thomas B., Jr., 202, 257, 280
Wall Street Journal, 84, 135, 139, 176, 191, 232
Walsh, Terry, 192
Ward, Lloyd D., 229, 264, 280
Washington Post, 171
Wayne State University, 202
WBAP-TV, 89
Weather Warnings, Inc., 132
Webb, Walter Prescott, 59
Welch, Robert, 94
West, C. Richard (Dick), 107, 108, 113, 116, 134, 141
Westmoreland, Reginald A., 138
West Point, 233
WFAA-AM Radio, 32, 43, 51, 66, 68, 80, 92, 93, 105, 169, 209, 282
WFAA-FM Radio, 88, 159
WFAA-TV, 98–100, 125, 130, 132–133, 135–136, 148, 151–152, 185, 188, 191, 201, 209, 213, 236, 244, 250, 252, 256–257, 282; signs on, 89
WGBH Educational Foundation, 249
Wharton School, 257
White, Mark, 214, 227
White House, 110, 112
Wilhoit, Lynn Claire. *See* Moroney, Lynn Wilhoit
Williams, J. McDonald, 215, 229, 280
Williamson, Dennis A., 230, 271, 275
Winslow, Arkansas, 80
Withers, Harry C., 279
Wolf, John, 131
Woodrow Wilson High School, 154
Wright, Jim, 134, 185
WRR Radio, 51
WTVC-TV, 188, 209
WUPL-TV, 275
WWL-TV, 3, 242, 243
Wyeth, John C., 11

Yahoo! Inc., 277
Yalta Conference, 81
Yankelovich, Skelly and White, 187
Y2K, 258
Y.W.C.A., 45